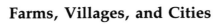

Farms, Villages, and Cities

Also by Peter S. Wells

*Culture Contact and Culture Change: Early Iron Age
Central Europe and the Mediterranean World*

*The Emergence of an Iron Age Economy: The Mecklenburg
Grave Groups from Hallstatt and Stična*

*Rural Economy in the Early Iron Age: Excavations at
Hascherkeller, 1978–1981*

FARMS,
VILLAGES,
AND CITIES

*Commerce and Urban Origins
in Late Prehistoric Europe*

Peter S. Wells

Cornell University Press

ITHACA AND LONDON

First published 1984 by Cornell University Press.
Published in the United Kingdom by
Cornell University Press Ltd., London.

International Standard Book Number (cloth) 0-8014-1554-3
International Standard Book Number (paper) 0-8014-9298-x
Library of Congress Catalog Card Number 84-45142
Printed in the United States of America
Librarians: Library of Congress cataloging information
appears on the last page of the book.

The paper in this book is acid-free and meets the guidelines
for permanence and durability of the Committee on Production
Guidelines for Book Longevity of the Council on Library Resources.

Contents

[5]

Preface

This book interprets the changes that took place in cultural life in Europe during the thousand years preceding the birth of Christ. The first communities that might be recognized as towns and cities came into being during this period, and many of the social, industrial, and commercial patterns that were to characterize European culture until the Renaissance, and in many nonurbanized regions until the Industrial Revolution, were established. The final years of European prehistory were a time of great change, and the nature and results of the changes are critical to understanding the development of medieval and modern Europe.

I have made no attempt here to synthesize even a small portion of the data from the period. The literature on later European prehistory is voluminous, and no work short of a multivolume encyclopedia could hope to do justice to even the most important of the material. Rather, I have limited myself to a general discussion of the principal features of the different periods of that millennium and suggest one interpretation of the changes that occurred. Reference is made to many of the important archaeological sites, but many others are not discussed. In the Bibliographic Essay I have cited the most important literature to steer the reader to major studies of each topic, in which more complete bibliographies can be found.

My focus is on the formation of communities larger and more complex than the agricultural hamlets and villages that constituted the predominant settlement pattern from early Neolithic times to the Industrial Revolution. In Europe north of the Alps it was not until the eighth century B.C. that larger communities began to develop and not until the final one hundred fifty years before Christ that any grew to more than one thousand inhabitants. In my opinion, similar processes of change were involved in the formation of all larger communities of later European prehistory, and these processes were like those that led to the development of the first towns of medieval Europe during the latter half of the first millennium after the birth of Christ.

Most surveys of prehistoric Europe end, and most syntheses of the medieval period begin, with the Romans. I believe that the cultural patterns that developed in late prehistoric times were similar to those of the medieval period, and so I have extended my discussion into the Middle Ages to illustrate this point.

I considered two ways of presenting the material in this book. One was to employ a multicausal perspective, such as Colin Renfrew (1972) so successfully utilized in his classic study of the Aegean world in the third millennium B.C. In such an approach, the complex variety of interacting factors is outlined, their interactions are described, and the effects of interactions in cultural change explained. An alternative approach was to examine cultural changes in terms of one particular factor and to study other factors in relation to it. I selected the latter course because a multicausal perspective would have created too complex a discussion for my purpose. The factors that came into play in the development of the early towns and cities of Europe were numerous, and the combinations of factors varied in different regions at different times. The multicausal approach could work well in a focus on a single site or series of sites in a region, but not in a study of the many major centers in Europe during the last millennium B.C. Singling out one major factor, advances in commercial activity, enabled me to offer a coherent account of the processes involved in the formation of these centers.

Under the heading of commercial activity, I include mining, manufacturing, and trade. The development of the first towns of the early Iron Age, such as Hallstatt, Stična, the Heuneburg, and Mont Lassois, can be understood best in terms of growing commercial activity, as many scholars have argued from many points of view. There is less agreement on the reasons for the formation of the centers of the late Iron Age—the oppida of the last two centuries B.C.—but commercial changes best account for the patterns observed. In concentrating on economic, specifically commercial, changes as the motivating force in the development of the first towns and cities of Europe, I offer here a great simplification of a very complex situation. But my aim is to help the reader see some

[8]

coherent patterns in the multiplicity of changes that occurred during the last thousand years of prehistory.

I have concentrated my discussion on central Europe, the lands encompassed by eastern France, southern and central Germany, Czechoslovakia, eastern Hungary, northwest Yugoslavia, Austria, and Switzerland. It was in this central region of Europe that the formation of larger communities first and most clearly took place in non-Mediterranean lands, and these regions provide the best archaeological documentation. I do, however, discuss important sites and developments in other parts of Europe when appropriate. For example, the urban societies of Greece, Etruria, and Rome— although their course of development was very different from that of communities north of the Alps—did at times influence changes in central Europe.

Many past discussions of the Iron Age peoples of central Europe rely heavily on statements by classical authors such as Polybius, Diodorus of Sicily, Livy, and Caesar. The resulting picture is of aristocratic societies made up of bellicose individuals interested mainly in warfare and riches. These are the aspects of central European societies that the Greek and Roman observers saw because they dealt with the elites of these societies, in war and in trade, and these are the aspects that the classical narrators recorded. They emphasized what to them were the strange, and hence interesting, aspects of these barbarian societies. What literate Greek or Roman citizen would have wished to read an account of central European peasants tilling their fields or forging iron plowshares? Those modern historians who call late Iron Age societies "heroic" and portray their members as swashbuckling adventurers have not discerned that what the ancient authors chose to describe was not typical. There were surely some characters who fitted those descriptions, but they were only a tiny proportion of Iron Age Europeans.

The archaeological evidence often shows with relative clarity what happened in prehistoric Europe, but rarely why and how it happened. The only way the questions why and how can be approached is through analogy. Most analogical thinking in archaeology is commonsensical. Because it will never be possible to look into the minds of the prehistoric inhabitants of Europe, the best we can do to try to understand why people behaved as they did is work with models that derive from similar circumstances. Documentary evidence from the early Middle Ages is a valuable resource here, since the peoples of those times were directly de-

[9]

scended, both ethnically and culturally, from the Iron Age populations—with, of course, new ethnic and cultural elements added
during the intervening Roman period. Patterns of economic and
social organization were similar in later prehistory and in the early
medieval period. Where evidence from the medieval context fails
or is scanty, information from other traditional societies is useful
not for constructing specific models of behavior but for suggesting
the range of behaviors that can come into play in certain kinds of
situations. Documentary evidence from later periods in Europe
and from other societies in comparable levels of economic development can inform us about probable motivations and mechanisms
of human behavior and so can be brought to bear on the material
evidence of archaeology.

Modern industrial societies change rapidly in various ways, but
in traditional peasant societies changes usually occur slowly. Most
aspects of village life in 1000 B.C. were very similar to those of A.D.
1600. During the last thousand years before Christ the principal
change was the replacement of bronze by iron in tools and weapons, with the related proliferation, during the last two hundred
years B.C., of metal tools for farming and other productive work.

Once the economy had developed beyond subsistence level and
could adequately support relatively large numbers of non–food
producers, a change that happened during the Bronze Age in Europe, more human energy could be devoted to such occupations as
mining and trading metals and transporting luxury goods. Increase
in total population may also have played a part. With the development of large-scale mining and metallurgy, the efficiency of agricultural production could be further increased through manufacture and use of bronze sickles and later of iron plowshares and
scythes. Development of trade in metals such as bronze and in
luxury goods such as salt, wine, amber, and glass provided merchants with profit opportunities and stimulated farmers to increase
their production in order to generate surpluses for exchange. The
changes that occurred in the final millennium before Christ can be
understood in terms of the interplay between the basic subsistence
economy and the much smaller but more dynamic economy of
manufacturing and trade. The entrepreneurs who took advantage
of new possibilities of commerce and industry played a major role
in the cultural changes.

PETER S. WELLS

Cambridge, Massachusetts

Acknowledgments

Many individuals and institutions provided helpful information for the preparation of this book. Bernard Wailes of the University of Pennsylvania made many important suggestions on an earlier draft of the manuscript, and I thank him for his time and thoughtfulness. Arthur Bankoff of Brooklyn College also contributed valuable advice on the earlier draft. Others who lent their expertise were Peter I. Bogucki (Princeton), Richard Bradley (Reading), John Coles (Cambridge), Geoffrey W. Conrad (Indiana), Carole Crumley (North Carolina), Stephen L. Dyson (Wesleyan), Antonio Gilman (California State University at Northridge), David Herlihy (Harvard), P. J. R. Modderman (Leiden), Radomir Pleiner (Prague), Margarita Primas (Zurich), Sian E. Rees (Cardiff), Zeph Stewart (Harvard), Caroline Q. Stubbs (Harvard), Kathryn M. Trinkaus (New Mexico), and Geoffrey Wainwright (London). Photographs were kindly provided by Wilhelm Angeli (Naturhistorisches Museum, Vienna), René Joffroy (Musée des Antiquités Nationales, St.-Germain-en-Laye), Wolfgang Kimmig (University of Tübingen), and Hilmar Schickler (Württembergisches Landesmuseum, Stuttgart).

Walter H. Lippincott, Jr., director of Cornell University Press, gave helpful encouragement and guidance throughout the preparation of the book. Editors Carol Betsch and Allison Dodge aided greatly in the organization and final preparation of the manuscript.

The extensive quotations from the classical authors in Chapter 5 are reprinted by permission of the publishers and the Loeb Classical Library from Diodorus of Sicily, translated by C. H. Oldfather, Dionysius of Halicarnassus, *The Roman Antiquities*, translated by E.

ACKNOWLEDGEMENTS

Cary, and Livy, translated by B. O. Foster, Cambridge, Mass.: Harvard University Press, 1954, 1939, and 1967. Individuals and institutions that provided illustrations are listed at the end of the book.

P. S. W.

Farms, Villages, and Cities

1 The First Towns in Prehistoric Europe

The concepts of town and city have been much discussed in anthropological, historical, and sociological literature. Archaeologists have relied for the most part on the definition of urbanism offered by V. Gordon Childe (1950), which consists of ten criteria, all of which must be fulfilled for a community to be designated a city. These criteria are (1) large size in area and population, (2) presence of full-time specialists such as crafts workers, transport workers, merchants, and priests, (3) taxation of food producers for the support of specialists, (4) monumental public buildings, (5) ruling groups of religious, civil, and military character, (6) systems of recording, (7) elaboration of sciences such as mathematics and astronomy, (8) sophisticated art styles, (9) long-distance trade, and (10) organized groups of crafts workers. As Childe made clear, these ten criteria were selected on the basis of comparison of Near Eastern with Mesoamerican centers and distinguished these centers from smaller communities. His definition was tailored for these particular parts of the ancient world and is not applicable to all contexts.

Most dictionary definitions of the words *town* and *city* emphasize population. According to archaeologists, anthropologists, and historians, the two primary aspects of towns are populations larger than those of other settlements and larger numbers of producers of goods, rather than food. Some investigators have suggested the use of some absolute limit—often five thousand inhabitants—for drawing the line between a town and a city, while others favor a more relativistic approach, emphasizing the contrasts between larger and smaller settlements. This latter approach is the one taken by many scholars working in Europe, including Karl Christ, Vilém Hrubý, John Alexander, Daphne Nash, and Richard Hodges.

Three principal kinds of settlement can be distinguished in prehistoric Europe based on size and economic complexity. Agricultural settlements consisting of single households can be called farmsteads. Agglomerated agricultural communities can be termed hamlets and villages. These are occupied by more than a single family unit, sometimes by tens of households, but their economic base is still thoroughly agrarian. In prehistoric Europe it is unlikely that villages were ever inhabited by more than two hundred people. The largest communities that emerged in prehistoric Europe can be designated towns and cities. These had many more inhabitants than agricultural villages, but they were distinguished particularly by substantial proportions of their populations being engaged in commerce. A distinction between towns and cities is arbitrary; both exemplify the phenomenon of "urbanism." For prehistoric Europe, I suggest an arbitrary dividing line between towns and cities at about one thousand inhabitants. In the early Iron Age the first towns developed (chapters 3 and 4), in the late Iron Age the first cities came into being (chapter 6). It must be emphasized that these terms are relative and difficult to define with precision, particularly given the present state of the evidence. A community that would be considered a city in late prehistoric Europe might not be so designated in other parts of the world.

The towns and cities of temperate Europe during late prehistoric times were different in character from those of the Near East and the Aegean region, partly because of environmental differences and partly because commercial and industrial patterns developed differently, as Childe (1950, 1958) and others have argued. Many small, scattered centers developed throughout Europe in the Bronze and Iron ages, while in parts of the Near East and the Aegean and in Mesoamerica and Peru only a few large centers developed. As Fernand Braudel (1981) has shown, not until modern times have any cities in temperate Europe approached the ancient Eastern and Mediterranean urban centers in size.

In the early Iron Age (800–400 B.C.) some communities for the first time grew much larger and more active commercially than most others in temperate Europe. As far as we know, before 800 B.C. no communities were larger than very small villages, with populations probably under one hundred. During the eighth century B.C. larger communities developed in the east Alpine region, some of whose members carried on substantial manufacturing and trading activities. Similar commercial centers emerged in other parts of Europe during the sixth and fifth centuries B.C. From about 200 B.C. until the Roman conquest in the latter half of the last century before Christ many larger communities with populations in the several thousands were established throughout central Europe and engaged in a wide range of specialized industries.

European economy and society remained relatively diffuse throughout prehistoric times. Even after 800 B.C. until the Roman conquest the vast majority of Europeans lived in tiny settlements, and the economy of the continent as a whole reflected this dispersed settlement pattern. During the final century before Christ, when intensive manufacturing and trade were being carried out at the oppida (major commercial centers, so named by Julius Caesar), the same kinds of crafts and commerce were practiced at the smaller settlements, though on a much smaller scale.

The natural environment of continental Europe was an important factor in the formation of these cultural patterns. Almost all of Europe, with the exception of the high, mountainous regions, can produce enough food to sustain comfortably populations the size of those of prehistoric times. Most of the soil is of good or excellent quality for agriculture. The climate is temperate, and precipitation

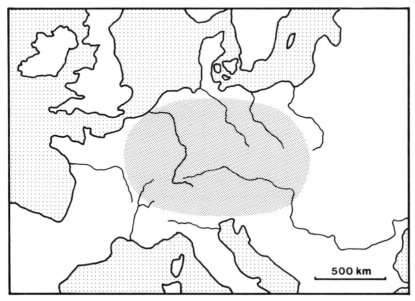

1. Central European area of main concern in this book.

[17]

is moderate in most parts. Europe has no deserts or jungles. Almost all of the land is easily traversed; paths through the mountain passes penetrated even the high Alps. Since regions were more or less equally suitable for farming, the early agricultural populations spread relatively evenly over the landscape. There were no oases to fight over, no irrigation canals to be built, and no essential resources lacking. In such a uniformly productive landscape, neither palace economies such as those of the Near East nor ceremonial centers like those in Mesoamerica developed. In such a homogeneous and propitious environment, why did larger communities that thrived on commerce ever emerge?

PAST APPROACHES TO URBANIZATION IN PREHISTORIC EUROPE

The study of prehistoric Europe has not generally been conducted within an anthropological framework, in which the processes of change and social and economic questions are chief concerns. Past research has concentrated on typology and chronology. Since the beginnings of systematic study of later European prehistory around the middle of the last century, researchers in the field, such as Oscar Montelius, Paul Reinecke, and Joseph Déchelette, to name only the most prominent, concerned themselves primarily with establishing chronological sequences for the archaeological material recovered both accidently and through systematic excavations. One topic that was taken up in much of their work was the connection between the Mediterranean world and societies of temperate Europe in the Bronze and Iron ages. The central Europeans were most often viewed as the Greek and Roman authors had described them, as barbarous tribal peoples whose societies first became organized and complex around the birth of Christ as a result of the Roman conquest. There was little appreciation by modern researchers that much of the archaeological material in temperate Europe reflected complex economic and social developments within that region. Many Iron Age sites that provide important documentation about the formation of early commercial centers such as Hallstatt in Upper Austria, Magdalenska gora in Slovenia, Bibracte in eastern France, and Stradonice in Bohemia were familiar to archaeologists at the turn of the century, but there was little interest in understanding European prehistory in terms

[18]

of intensified production and trade and the formation of larger and more complex communities.

During the second quarter of the twentieth century much large-scale, systematic fieldwork was carried out in Europe. The results of excavations at several important settlements extended the limited information available from burials and provided a new basis for examining patterns of economic and social behavior. Hans Reinerth's excavations at Buchau in Germany (1928, 1936) were a model of research, and Gerhard Bersu's settlement investigations at the Goldberg in southwest Germany and Little Woodbury in southern England (1940) provided new insight into Iron Age settlement structure and economy. Some important interpretive work was also done, such as Joachim Werner's 1939 essay on urbanism and the late Iron Age oppida, but there was little scholarly interest generally in broad synthesis of the data accumulating through excavation.

After the Second World War a new phase of settlement research began in many parts of Europe. Particularly important have been extensive excavations in Germany at the Heuneburg in southern Württemberg and at Manching in Bavaria. Other important, large-scale settlement excavations include those in Czechoslovakia at Třísov, Závist, and Hrazany in Bohemia and Staré Hradisko in Moravia; in East Germany at the Steinsburg in Thuringia; and in southern Britain at Danebury.

Despite this rapid growth in data available on settlement organization, manufacturing, and trade, relatively little interpretive work has been carried out on the development of complex communities during the Iron Age. Only a few individuals working on the continent, for example, Herbert Jankuhn and Ernst Wahle in Germany, Carl-Axel Moberg and Berta Stjernquist in Sweden, Klaus Randsborg in Denmark, Jiří Neustupný in Czechoslovakia, and Karl-Heinz Otto and Joachim Herrmann in East Germany, have concerned themselves with anthropological issues, but these scholars have had few followers in their own countries. Anthropological approaches to later European prehistory, and particularly interest in explanations of the apparent changes, have been pursued mainly by English and American investigators.

V. Gordon Childe was the first person to attempt systematically to account for the changes that occurred during the Bronze and Iron ages and to connect them with more recent developments in European economy and society. His principal works on the subject were published between 1930 and 1958. Like Oscar Montelius and others before him, Childe viewed the critical developments in European prehistory as having been stimulated by contact with the Mediterranean world. Childe argued that the great changes in the organization of European societies that began during the Bronze Age came about in response to demands for metals from markets in the Aegean area. The Mycenaean and Minoan societies had become wealthy and urbanized, and they needed large quantities of raw materials, including bronze. This demand, and the attractive luxury trade goods offered in return for the raw materials, stimulated European societies to increase production and trade.

Of special importance to Childe's thesis is the social character he attributed to European metalsmiths. Childe asserted, on the basis of evidence from burials, hoards, and settlements, that bronzesmiths in Bronze Age Europe lived outside the usual community systems. They were, according to him, itinerant, lived as foreigners in the communities in which they worked, and never became tied to any particular community. Childe even suggested that some form of "intertribal union" of bronzesmiths may have existed. He hypothesized that these itinerant smiths often met and shared ideas, and to such regular interchange he attributed the exceptional inventiveness of the European bronze industries relative to those of the Near East. He believed the political independence of the European bronzesmiths to have been unique in the ancient world and to have enabled crafts workers to act as entrepreneurs in manufacturing and trade—the first businessmen of Europe. This special situation, Childe theorized, gave European metalsmiths a considerably higher status than their counterparts in the Near East, and it was this difference, he thought, that led to the emergence of Europe as the major commercial power of the Middle Ages.

In Childe's thesis it was the professionalization and lack of community affiliation of Bronze Age smiths in Europe that gave them such an advantageous position and enabled them to control the production and distribution of metal objects. They were thus the entrepreneurs behind the intensification of trade and industry that led to the formation of more complex and larger communities. Childe did not directly address the question of the development of towns and cities in prehistoric Europe (such sites as the Heuneburg, Manching, and Staré Hradisko had only begun to be excavated systematically at the time of his death), but his central concern with the growth of economic and social complexity bears directly on that issue.

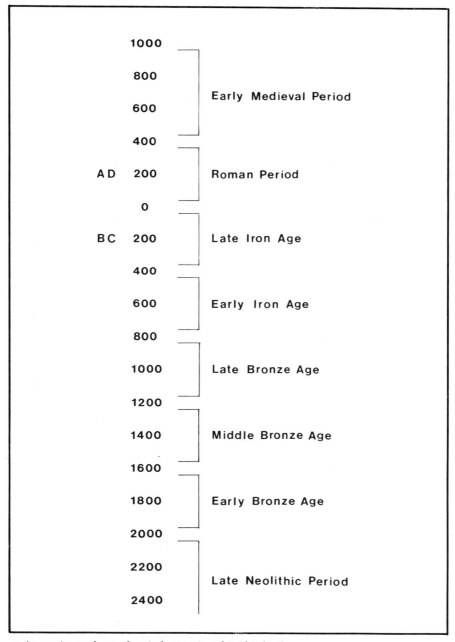

	1000	Early Medieval Period
	800	
	600	
	400	
AD	200	Roman Period
	0	
BC	200	Late Iron Age
	400	
	600	Early Iron Age
	800	
	1000	Late Bronze Age
	1200	
	1400	Middle Bronze Age
	1600	
	1800	Early Bronze Age
	2000	
	2200	Late Neolithic Period
	2400	

2. Approximate dates of periods mentioned in this book.

No other individual has attempted such broad syntheses and interpretations of later European prehistory as Childe did, though some prehistorians have dealt with interpretive problems in shorter works. Like Childe, Christopher Hawkes (1940) portrays metalsmiths as privileged specialists in possession of the technical secrets upon which the wealth and power of elite members of society depended. Grahame Clark and Stuart Piggott (1965) also emphasize the high status of crafts workers and artisans, which derived, in their view, largely from the elite groups whose desires they served. David Clarke (1979:319) notes especially the changes in the status and power of metalworkers that came about with the development of iron metallurgy. Since iron ore was abundant in Europe, once the working of the new metal was widely learned, the wealth and power of the Bronze Age elites who had controlled access to bronze metal waned, and economic systems became democratized. Ludwig Pauli (1978) emphasizes the special independence and entrepreneurial potential of those involved in production for commerce, particularly miners. Pauli's evidence derives from the exceptionally fine archaeological documentation at the Dürrnberg and from medieval textual sources.

Recent discussions of Childe's view of metalworkers in early Europe have challenged his model of independent, itinerant smiths. On the basis of a wide range of ethnographic examples, Michael Rowlands (1972) suggests that metalsmiths tended most often to be part-time specialists in premodern societies and that they were chiefly food producers like the majority of the population. Rowlands implies that for Bronze and Iron Age Europe metalsmiths were, rather than Childe's full-time professionals, more likely full members of their communities and that they did their metalwork primarily during slow periods in the agricultural cycle. Sarunas Milisauskas (1978) agrees in essence with Rowlands's view. Pauli's research on the Dürrnberg (1978) also supports this perspective, showing the skilled salt miners as members of communities that exhibit the same burial patterns and material culture as others throughout central Europe.

Whereas Childe and some of his followers have stressed the importance of metalworkers and of crafts workers in general in the intensification of economic activity in later prehistoric Europe, other investigators have emphasized social competition for limited luxuries and the development of market trade as the critical factors. Jan Filip (1962) suggests that the fortified communities of the sixth and fifth centuries B.C., such as the Heuneburg, Mont Lassois, and

Závist, developed as means for elite groups to protect themselves and their possessions from other members of their societies. He views the high degree of differentiation in burial wealth as evidence of a stratified social system and thus interprets the new fortified settlements in terms of class struggle. Susan Frankenstein and Michael Rowlands (1978) portray the behavior at these new settlements more in terms of social competition for luxury goods.

In considering the emergence of the oppida—the only communities of prehistoric Europe that can arguably be called cities—during the last 150 years B.C., many investigators, including Filip (1962), Piggott (1965), and John Collis (1979, 1982), emphasize defense as the essential motivating factor. Carole Crumley and Daphne Nash, however, both of whom have studied the westernmost oppida, see social behavior as the influential factor. Crumley (1974a and b) argues that during the final centuries before Christ a middle class of artisans, merchants, and bureaucrats emerged in Gaul, where previously only an aristocratic and a lower class had existed—a change stimulated by the influx of luxury goods from the Mediterranean world. Competition for these status goods contributed to increasing social stratification. Nash (1976) emphasizes competition within the elite groups for such luxury materials and views the formation of the larger and more complex communities as a reflection of greater political centralization brought about by social changes.

John Alexander (1972) suggests that local and long-distance trade was the essential factor in the development of the first urban centers of Iron Age Europe, and he notes the importance of specialized manufacturing, especially in metals, that was carried on in these centers. In Alexander's view, political and social factors played no significant part in the development of the oppida. In some of his writings Collis (1976) also stresses trade, though he points in addition to defense as a determining influence. He suggests too that a market economy may have developed at some of the main sites at the end of the prehistoric period.

Many of the authors who have dealt with these questions distinguish between two kinds of trade in late prehistoric Europe. One involved luxury and prestige goods and probably operated along traditional lines of social obligation and gift giving. The other involved items of more everyday use the value of which was dependent on availability and demand rather than on socially determined criteria. The question which kind of trade was more important is part of the substantivist-functionalist debate in economic anthropology. Most circulation of materials probably occurred as traditional, socially determined exchanges, both within the community and between individuals in different communities. Yet although "commercial" behavior accounted for a smaller proportion of circulating material, it was in this commercial sphere that expansion could and did occur rapidly.

The model that I put forward here is based on the concept of entrepreneurial behavior in commerce. Individuals who are willing and able to invest material wealth, energy, and time can amass personal wealth and gain increased material security as well as the status and prestige that usually accompany wealth. These individuals frequently affect the behavior of others in and even beyond their communities. The critical factor in the process of change that began in the late Bronze Age was the great increase in the quantities of metal produced and processed into finished objects. Because there was more bronze available, more wealth could be accumulated. New tools could be manufactured for more efficient production of food and other material goods. Unlike Childe, I do not argue that the metalsmiths were the only entrepreneurs. Merchants trading in bronze and other substances acted as entrepreneurs too. Individuals who accumulated bronze for trade could also have acted as entrepreneurs, as could others making use of the metal-based technology to increase productivity of various goods. On the basis of widespread evidence for local bronze casting at excavated settlements, I disagree with Childe's model of the detribalized, free-thinking, itinerant smith. Most metalsmiths were probably part-time farmers and full-fledged members of the communities in which they worked. I think it likely that a small group of highly specialized smiths introduced new techniques and styles into regions served by resident village smiths. These probably itinerant smiths need not have been entrepreneurs in the sense of amassing wealth. On the contrary, their mobility would have made it difficult for them to control much wealth.

Amid the general intensification of commerce and manufacturing, the traditional, noncommercial circulation of foodstuffs, luxury items, and ritual materials continued unabated. In no way did one system of exchange work to the detriment of the other. The two were different systems, probably involving for the most part different goods and operating in different social contexts. The traditional exchange system based on social obligation and gift giving was probably a stabilizing and conservative influence on economic systems, whereas the commercial one could expand and play a part in major economic and other changes.

The approach advanced here does not deny or affirm the existence of the "warrior aristocracy" so often cited in discussions of later European prehistory and often compared with societies described by Homer and the medieval epics. The existence of such aristocracies and of chieftains was not an important factor in the rise of towns and cities. It was not the traditional sociopolitical hierarchy that lay behind the formation of commercial centers at Hallstatt, Stična, the Heuneburg, and Manching, but rather enterprising individuals who perceived opportunities and took chances on gaining profits in the expanding commercial networks. Their efforts resulted in the introduction of a variety of attractive new trade goods, and in the stimulation of desires for those goods. In order to acquire them, communities had to generate exchangeable products. The first towns of temperate Europe came into being as centers for the production of materials to be traded for sought-after imports.

My approach here is closest to that taken by Alexander (1972) in emphasizing trade and industry. Unlike Filip (1962), I do not feel that class conflict played any major role in the formation of the prehistoric towns. The defensive aspect of the early and late Iron Age towns and cities can best be understood in terms of the need to protect the new wealth being generated and transported from place to place. My approach differs from that of Crumley (1974a and b) and of Nash (1976) largely in emphasis. They focus on the social changes reflected in the archaeological and textual evidence from the end of the Iron Age. Viewing all of the evidence from the late Bronze Age to the Roman period, I feel that the commercial changes were primary and that other changes resulted from them.

ACCUMULATION OF WEALTH IN LATER PREHISTORY

There is little evidence that in the earliest periods of European prehistory, the Paleolithic, Mesolithic, and Neolithic, wealth was available and accumulated or that communities developed to sizes larger than a few families. Ornaments of shell, bone, teeth, amber, and stone have been found in graves, indicating that there was some acquisition of items not directly related to survival. Evidence indicates, though, that it was not until the start of the Bronze Age

[25]

that quantities of disposable wealth were accumulated and special objects manufactured whose possession was restricted to a few individuals. Gold ornaments were found in a small proportion of Bell Beaker graves, and the cemetery at Varna in Bulgaria, with its extraordinary richness in gold, indicates that larger quantities of wealth were being accumulated by some persons in the early Bronze Age, about 2000 B.C. At that time, greater disposable wealth was becoming available, especially in the form of bronze, but also in gold and other special substances. Bronze objects were common in graves of this period, for example, at the large cemeteries of Straubing in Bavaria and Branč in Slovakia. Distribution maps of hoards of ring- and bar-shaped copper and bronze ingots show strong concentrations in lands just north of the copper mines of Tirol and Salzburg, suggesting that individuals in these regions were amassing wealth in this form.

A few rich graves contained ornate bronze objects, such as daggers and gold ornaments. The grave at Leubingen in East Germany was situated under a large burial mound, inside a chamber of oak covered by a dome of stones. It contained the skeletal remains of a man and a child, accompanied by three bronze daggers, a bronze halberd, two bronze axes, three bronze chisels, a serpentine axe, a gold bracelet, two gold pins, two small gold rings, and a gold wire ring. In this grave and a few others like it we first see a pattern that persists throughout the rest of European prehistory and into historical times: the occurrence of a few graves much more richly outfitted than the majority and sharing certain features, including the presence of weapons. Most early Bronze Age cemeteries show patterns of wealth distribution similar to those of the late Neolithic period without great differences in the levels of wealth in individual graves (though a general increase in wealth is apparent).

In the middle part of the second millennium B.C., the middle Bronze Age of the central European chronology, this trend of greater accumulation of wealth, especially in bronze objects, is further reflected in the burials. Hoards of bronze objects, often intentionally cut into pieces, are common in central Europe. Some investigators have interpreted these pieces having standard value for exchange. Swords, much larger than any previous weapons, incorporating more bronze metal and thus permitting increased effectiveness in combat, have also been found in cemeteries of this era. Dress pins worn by both men and women were often exceptionally large, incorporating much more metal than the short, thin pins of the preceding centuries. Bronze daggers and axes and gold ornaments were also well represented in the rich graves. In Britain the rich Wessex burials of this time contained fine bronze daggers and a variety of ornaments of sheet gold. This trend toward amassing increased wealth peaked at the end of the second millennium B.C., the period with which this book begins.

THE ECONOMIC BASE

The societies of later prehistoric Europe were agrarian. The vast majority of the people were farmers and livestock raisers. Their daily lives were spent tending their crops and animals and carrying out the other essential tasks of traditional peasants: building and repairing houses, barns, and sheds; making and maintaining clothing; manufacturing tools and household equipment from wood and bone; and caring for children. Many people did other crafts in their spare time, such as weaving, pottery manufacture, and simple bronze casting. The only communities that differed greatly from this pattern were the few small groups of miners, especially copper and tin miners, who extracted metal for the production of bronze, and salt miners at sites such as Hallstatt.

Long-term agricultural experiments are being carried out at Butser Farm in southern Britain employing plant and animal species similar to those of late prehistoric times and tools and techniques that were available at that time. Results of such experiments suggest that agricultural yields may have been quite high, potentially much higher than the yields recorded in documents from the early medieval period. Written records from medieval times may indicate smaller yields than were actually being produced (to minimize taxes), but such documents form the basis of modern understanding of medieval farming. Productivity certainly varied from region to region in Iron Age Europe, depending on soils, weather conditions, available plant and animal species, and technology, as well as cultural traditions. Iron Age agricultural planning was probably directed toward minimizing the danger of malnutrition, famine, and starvation during years of storms, drought, or disease. There was likely a surplus in most years, sometimes a large one. As agricultural technology became more elaborate—with the introduction of large numbers of bronze sickles in the late Bronze Age and later, in the Iron Age, of iron plowshares, coulters, and scythes—ever larger surpluses could be generated. Modern ethnographic research shows that unless specifically motivated to do so, most peasant communities do not attempt to produce large surpluses. In late prehistoric Europe some communities were apparently so motivated to produce surplus food and goods that could be traded for various desired luxury products.

Trade and specialized manufacture depended on the solid subsistence base. Although trade and manufacture represented a much smaller portion of the prehistoric European economy, it was in this area that there was considerable experimentation and enterprise. Changes in subsistence strategies were slower and resulted largely from intensification of manufacturing: new agricultural tools were produced in the expanded industries which further contributed to the ability of farmers to support increasing numbers of specialist manufacturers. But peasants generally did not experiment with new techniques of food production; they were primarily concerned with minimizing losses in order to stay alive, rather than maximizing gains for profit.

EXCHANGE

In recent decades debate has raged among archaeologists, anthropologists, and ancient and medieval historians about exchange in nonindustrial societies. Karl Polanyi (1944), Johannes Hasebroek (1933), and Moses Finley (1973), in particular, have argued that traditional economies cannot be analyzed on the basis of market principles, but must be understood in terms of social obligations and kinship interactions. Early European epics such as Homer's *Odyssey* and *Beowulf* portray the exchange of goods as motivated by social behavior such as gift exchange, and many scholars feel that value, as a concept independent of social relations, did not come into play.

In fact, a variety of mechanisms of circulation were operating simultaneously as Philip Grierson (1959), Marc Bloch (1961), and David Herlihy (1971) have illustrated for the early medieval period. The early epics cited by Marcel Mauss (1967) and others who argue that market principles were nonexistent in early medieval European societies deal almost exclusively with the behavior of elite individuals such as chieftains, kings, and nobles. In these epics, such individuals were motivated by political and military alliances to exchange gifts with friends and guests. Such subjects as where the peasants got the iron for their knives, though they may tell much about how economies work, are not the stuff of epics. Although the literary sources do not mention them, archaeological evidence demonstrates the development of large-scale industries producing goods primarily for export trade during the eighth ninth, and tenth centuries—for example pottery at Badorf and Pingsdorf in the Rhineland and crafts in stone, bone, amber, and metals at commercial centers such as Dorestad, Haithabu, Helgö, Birka, and Southampton (see chapter 7).

As in the textually documented Middle Ages, so too in prehistoric Europe most exchange took place within communities according to traditional social principles. With the growth of trade in later prehistory, particularly as quantities of materials from outside the immediate territory of a community became more important to its life and economy, factors other than social relations became increasingly important. Imported materials, though often present, were usually not abundant on settlements and in graves of the Neolithic period; almost everything people used was available within the territory of their own settlements. Imports, such as Mediterranean shells, special flint, and stone for polished axes, may have circulated through social exchanges. But it seems that only certain individuals in special social positions had access to these items and maintained relationships with others in distant communities in order to obtain such items through exchange. This pattern is well documented in ethnographic contexts.

The situation changed at the beginning of the Bronze Age, as bronze became increasingly available to all Europeans. By the late Bronze Age (1200–800 B.C.) communities throughout the continent were relying on massive imports of bronze. The graves show that the metal was not restricted to a small group of people but was possessed by a substantial proportion of the population. In the production and distribution of the metal, including mining, alloying, trading, casting, and hoarding, it is unlikely that all transactions, including final confirmation of ownership, were carried out according to social obligations, but rather that the metal was being traded according to principles of value determined by distance from sources. Too many people were involved, over too great distances, for coherent social relationships to have existed. From the late Bronze Age on, the sheer mass of goods being traded argues against circulation being primarily socially based.

The great new quantities of materials—particularly bronze, but also amber, glass, and gold—being traded from about 1200 B.C. on, and the consequent growth in the scale of exchange that was based on value, opened up greater possibilities for individuals involved

[29]

in commerce to generate profits. This new motivating factor played an essential part in the formation of the first towns north of the Alps.

ENTREPRENEURS

An entrepreneur, an individual who undertakes a venture to make a profit, must be in a position to manipulate resources of value and to secure other peoples' confidence in his dealings. People who are successful entrepreneurs must be able to perceive opportunities for gain, elicit the cooperation of others (often producers of particular resources), organize transportation of goods, and engage in commerce to everyone's satisfaction. Thus the individual must have economic skill, ability to get along with other people and inspire trust in them, and personal energy. This combination of traits is rare, and only a few individuals in any society are successful entrepreneurs, although some societies produce more than others. An entrepreneur can come from elite or humble origins. Kings and chieftains can be entrepreneurs, as can even the lowest members of a society, as in ancient Rome, where even former slaves sometimes amassed vast fortunes through shrewd dealings. The ability of entrepreneurs to emerge and operate successfully depends on a range of complex factors of economic organization and social patterns. The subsistence base of a society must be amply secure to allow some people to engage in nonsubsistence activities. Social organization must be sufficiently flexible to permit individuals to move beyond their home communities to engage in commerce. Desirable materials must be available but not readily accessible to all. A sufficient number of people or communities must have the surplus wealth needed to exchange for the desired items. Those individuals who are successful at generating profits (and often those cooperating with them) play a major role in effecting changes in economic patterns and in other aspects of cultural life. "In many ways . . . the entrepreneurs are the movers and shakers of any society" (Schwartz 1979:vii).

In this book I define *entrepreneur* broadly to mean any person who ventures to gain profits, whether through commercial exchanges, raids on communities' treasures, or something in between. During the final millennium of European prehistory and in the early medieval times, raiding other communities for booty— gold, silver, cattle, and slaves—was a normal activity and one of

[30]

the principal sources of income for the nobility (the Viking raids on northwest Europe were only one of the more spectacular cases). This kind of entrepreneurial activity was an important adjunct to the less violent form of circulation of goods known as trade.

In their efforts to gain profits, entrepreneurs change the economic status quo. An entrepreneur might encourage a community to produce more wool for export by promising imported luxury goods, and that surplus wool could then be used for trade at profit. The economic organization of the community would thereby be altered. An entrepreneur who leads a raid on another village would clearly have an effect on the economy of that unfortunate community.

In the dispersed, noncentralized cultural environment of prehistoric Europe no military or political personages emerged to gain control of large regions. Economic and social organization remained dispersed and small-scale. Hence individuals could operate in the milieu of their local communities and regions without coming into conflict with larger, more organized commercial systems. Small-scale raiding and warfare were rampant because of the lack of any regional political or military controls.

DISTRIBUTION OF WEALTH

Archaeological findings do not reveal as much about social organization as that concept is defined by ethnologists and sociologists as they do about settlement structure, subsistence, and trade. Many archaeologists have attempted to interpret their data according to schemes of social organization worked out by ethnologists (e.g., Service 1962), but such schemes have not convincingly contributed to the understanding of prehistoric social organization. An especially clear and well-documented example of this lack of correspondence between ethnographic study and archaeological realities was the attempt by medieval archaeologists to identify in burial patterns the various social levels of persons described in early medieval documents. We have reasonably abundant and consistent written descriptions of the grades of society and of the hierarchical relations between them in the early Middle Ages. Yet the outfitting of the graves does not correspond in any demonstrable way to the textual descriptions. The social categories as perceived by ethnologists, sociologists, and historians simply are not

[31]

parallel to the categories of burial wealth observed by archaeologists.

In this book I work with material criteria, particularly wealth represented in graves, and avoid the social concepts introduced from ethnography and history. Most literature that deals with social patterns of prehistoric Europe uses such terms as "chiefs," "headmen," and "princes" to designate the individuals interred in the richest burials. Use of these terms implies parallels between social organization of prehistoric communities and structures identified in living societies by ethnologists and historians. In considering status relations here, my emphasis is on the distribution of material wealth in society, as reflected most clearly in the burials.

Since the inclusion of grave goods in burials depends on a range of factors, some apparently religious in nature, comparing cemeteries from various times and places according to respective wealth is difficult. But within a single cemetery information about wealth distribution among individuals can be derived from the burial evidence. Although ethnographic examples can be found to show that the material wealth placed in graves does not always correlate directly with wealth and status in living communities, in fact it usually does, and that correlation is particularly clear in the European tradition of burial.

To compare graves with one another within a cemetery, we need a standard measure of wealth. Ideally, we would compute the value of materials in each grave based on the value to the community of the raw materials used and the amount of time and energy devoted to the production of the objects. Very little information about such value is available for later European prehistory, though; John Coles's work (1973, 1979) in manufacturing replicas of bronze objects is an important step, but not enough information is yet available to make this criterion applicable.

Lacking such data, our most useful measure is a simple count of objects in each grave. (The weight of an object is a useful criterion except where objects of various substances were buried because we lack information about relative values of different substances.) There are, however, problems with a simple count method. For example, a sword was surely more difficult to produce than a pin and consumed more material. An ornate gold bowl was probably more valuable than a small, undecorated ceramic cup. On the other hand, graves that are well equipped with such exceptional objects as swords, bronze vessels, and gold ornaments also usually contain a much larger number of grave goods than other burials. Thus

[32]

the simple count in fact provides a reasonably satisfactory means of comparing a wide range of graves in a cemetery.

Two additional qualifications must be mentioned. Some objects such as wagons and harnesses comprise numerous metal parts; rather than counting all the parts as individual objects, I have counted the entire assemblage as one and have made special mention of such objects in individual graves. A set of objects such as buttons or beads that together constitute a whole are also counted as one object; similar dress pins, however, are counted separately, since such objects occur individually as well as in sets.

Excavations at the cemetery of Nebringen, where the well-preserved skeletal remains have been analyzed, have made clear that there are often great differences in grave wealth in men's and women's graves. At Nebringen all of the graves with large numbers of objects were women's graves, mostly because women's graves often contained many pieces of jewelry. In men's graves, many of which contained swords and in one case a helmet, there was little jewelry, and the total number of objects was much lower. In preindustrial societies of Europe members of the same nuclear family (the basic unit of economic activity) were of similar status. Material wealth belonged to the family as a whole; however, it was divided among the individuals for use and distributed among their graves at death. Thus relative distribution of wealth in the living community should be reflected in the burials, whether men or women received the larger number of objects in any given community.

The social categories delineated by the ethnologist and the historian most often describe official positions in society, but they do not tell anything about the effectiveness of the individuals in those positions or about the status accorded them by their fellows. An individual might hold an honored title, but his incompetence might keep him from accumulating wealth or exercising his status and authority. The amount of wealth that accompanies an individual in his grave may provide a more accurate picture of what that person commanded in terms of resources, status, and power.

I am assuming here that most individuals wanted to accumulate wealth. For the period under consideration the evidence suggests that they did. In historical contexts in Europe, from earliest medieval times to the modern world, there is a clear association between an individual's possession of material wealth and that person's status and power in society. There is no reason to think that the pattern was different in the final millennium B.C.

Most cemeteries from that millennium show a common pattern in the distribution of wealth in the graves. The majority of burials contain few grave goods, a few have many, but there is a gradual scale from poorest to richest without major breaks in the continuum of wealth. This evidence suggests that material goods were not evenly distributed, even in the small, family-based communities. Throughout the millennium there were always a few graves that were larger, had more elaborate structures such as chambers and coffins, and were considerably more richly outfitted than most. These often contained not only exceptionally large quantities of grave goods but exceptional kinds as well. They were distinguished by items such as swords, bronze vessels, gold ornaments, wheeled vehicles, and horse-riding equipment. Such graves imply the existence of individuals of substantially greater wealth than their fellows.

Capital in the form of portable wealth accumulated by these people enabled them to invest in such enterprises as trade (apparent in the foreign luxury goods in their graves); employment of specialist crafts workers to produce fine weapons, bronze vessels, and vehicles; and raiding expeditions. If these individuals resembled the ancient and early medieval leaders described by the authors and historians of their time, their principal motivation in life was to gain wealth, prestige, and status, all of which could be acquired through manipulation of capital that they could accumulate from the surplus production of the agricultural communities. Like their later counterparts, these persons who acted in the economic, political, and religious spheres probably lived off the primary producers and did not produce food themselves. Their activities were thus not tied to the agricultural schedule. Their chief interactions with the members of the farming communities may have been the collection and redistribution of surplus produce and the sponsoring of such community events as feasts, fairs, and building projects, as well as of specialized crafts production and trade. Individuals active in this role probably encouraged a community to increase production, especially for trade for foreign luxuries.

POLITICAL INTEGRATION

The forms of political integration often attributed to prehistoric societies, such as bands, tribes, chiefdoms, and states, while useful constructs in some contexts, tend to obscure the social and political situation in late prehistoric Europe rather than illuminate it. The best way to understand the economic and social changes in late prehistoric Europe is to view the cultural landscape as dispersed and decentralized and any divergences from that pattern as the result of specific efforts on the part of individuals to gain wealth through one or another form of entrepreneurial behavior, either commerce in the usual sense or warfare or perhaps clientship. Most of the larger and wealthier communities that emerged were organized principally around commerce and production for commerce, although the centralization of economic activities may have resulted in the centralization of governing functions as well. Yet there is very little evidence that communities such as the Heuneburg and Manching were political centers in anything like the sense that Near Eastern cities and Mesoamerican ceremonial sites were. Since the Heuneburg, Manching, and most of the other larger communities lasted only a century or slightly longer, any kind of political centralization that might have begun to develop would have been very short-lived.

We know of political centers in the early medieval period that were separate from the commercial towns, including Tara in Ireland, Winchester in Britain, and Uppsala in Sweden. Each of these had strong associations with ritual and tradition and served as royal residences. Such political centers may have existed in Iron Age Europe as well, but they have not yet been identified in the archaeological record.

CHANGE

Some societies change faster than others, and the pace of change within a society varies over time, but change is always taking place in every society, no matter how stable it may appear. Aside from the continual, usually gradual change perceptible to archaeologists but often probably not to the people living at the time, there are always minor random variations. Some individuals behave differently from the cultural norm. A metalsmith might, consciously or not, make a mold in a new way or try a different alloy of metals. Most such idiosyncratic variation, however, comes to nothing (the experiment proves a failure or, even if successful, is soon forgotten). In terms of the study of cultural change, it can be regarded as "noise," variation that has no substantial results as far as long-term development is concerned. If, however, the results of such variant behavior are perceived as advantageous, they might be intentionally repeated. When this happens, we are no longer dealing with "noise," but rather with change initiated by one or more individuals with a particular goal in mind.

Change can also be brought about intentionally by individuals who wish to gain particular advantages. A metalsmith might devise a new way of casting axes that uses less metal for an equally effective tool. A merchant might carry his wares to a new area in search of greater profits from trade. An individual might encourage others in the community to produce a larger surplus so that more goods will be available to exchange for products from outside. When an individual makes a change to gain some kind of advantage, his success depends on two sets of conditions: first, the qualities of that individual—his ambition, intelligence, perseverance, and adaptability—and, second, the circumstances of the individual and the context in which he operates. These circumstances in the broadest terms include the general economic conditions of the society and of the individual's community, his relative wealth and prestige in his group, prevailing political and military situations, and a wide range of more specific circumstances such as available raw materials and competition among individuals with similar interests. A person cannot bring about change if the cultural and environmental conditions are not right. Yet an individual can affect economic and social conditions around him and adapt his own behavior to the circumstances. The key interaction is between the innovator and his cultural context.

The reader must keep in mind throughout this book the dichotomy between the lives of the great majority of people who were full-time peasant farmers and those of the small number of persons who were not. For the peasants, life changed very little over the centuries. Those who were not tied primarily to the agrarian life and who could acquire wealth through their own efforts or though inheritance had access to disposable capital in the form of bronze objects, precious metals, and other desired materials, including the subsistence goods they could use to support families larger and healthier than those of their peers. Free of the constraints of the agrarian schedule and possessing usable capital, these individuals could invest in ventures that could generate additional riches. Their behavior ultimately brought about the changes in late prehistoric society that are my focus here.

I assume in this book that the principal motivating factor at work in creating change is self-interest—the desire of individuals to ac-

[36]

cumulate wealth for its own sake, for the security it can bring, and for its use in gaining status, prestige, and sometimes power. This desire seems to be a virtually universal human drive. This idea is well suited to archaeological investigation, since wealth is well documented in the material evidence.

2 Europe in 1000 B.C.

The centuries around 1000 B.C. were a time of profound change in economic patterns in continental Europe, effected particularly by the new abundance in the production and circulation of bronze objects. With the growth in the production of bronze, more disposable wealth became available. This new wealth provided a means for some individuals to increase their status and authority, giving them a new power over their peers. Several aspects of economic organization, including settlements and population, subsistence patterns, manufacturing, trade were greatly affected by the new wealth available, and at the same time they directly influenced the accumulation and distribution of that wealth.

The distribution of settlement sites of the late Bronze Age compared with that of preceding periods indicates an increase in the clearing and conversion of forest into arable and pasture land, apparent in many parts of Europe. There were more and larger settlements and cemeteries in this period than in preceding ones, suggesting a substantial increase in population of most regions. During the late Bronze Age, too, for the first time many settlements were occupied for several centuries, rather than for only a couple of generations. That people could remain settled longer in one place indicates the development of techniques for preserving the fertility of the land, such as crop rotation, fallowing, and use of manure.

Communities were coming into much closer and more frequent contact with one another and becoming part of a Europe-wide economic system. An important change occurred in the manufacture of pottery and bronze objects. Previously, forms and styles were regional, but in the late Bronze Age a high degree of standardization developed. For example, pottery vessels from sites in cen-

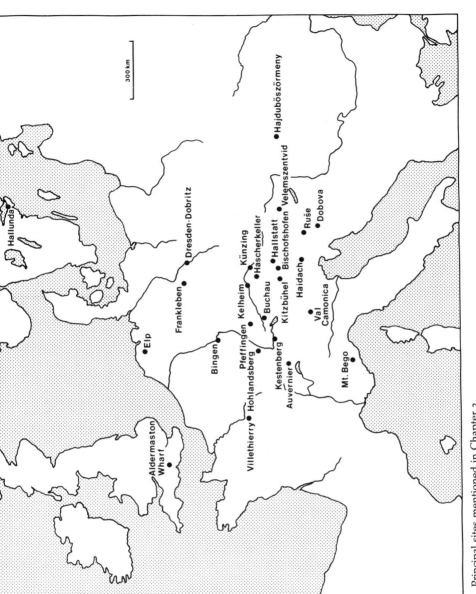

3. Principal sites mentioned in Chapter 2.

tral France, Switzerland, southern Germany, and Bohemia, are very similar. This change reflects an increase in communication among potters and among bronze workers, exchange of information, and sharing of patterns and techniques of production. And it demonstrates that the European economy became much more closely integrated during this period.

This increasing integration is reflected in the growing bronze production. Copper and tin had to be transported from mines, brought together for alloying, and distributed to communities that wanted metal. The increased quantity of metal in hoards, in graves, and on settlements from this time shows that more metal was in circulation. Commerce also increased in materials other than bronze. Graphite became popular for decorating pottery and was actively traded; amber from the Baltic regions was traded in ever greater quantities; glass beads were produced and widely traded for the first time; and much more gold was in circulation than ever before.

LANDSCAPE, POPULATION, AND SETTLEMENTS, 1000–800 B.C.

The landscape of the final millennium B.C. and that of today differed primarily in degree of forest cover. Although much land was cleared of forest from early Neolithic times on, a lot of the continent remained covered by thick forests of the mixed oak type. The precise extent of cleared and forested areas is difficult to ascertain, but we can form a good impression from distribution maps of known archaeological sites in studied regions, for example, of southern Bavaria during the early Iron Age (Kossack 1959:pl. 149). Such maps suggest that some areas were already substantially cleared of forest and inhabited by agricultural communities, that many river valleys were occupied, and that between settled regions there remained large expanses of unsettled land, most likely forested. Even at the time of the Roman conquest in the second half of the last century B.C., the continent was still largely covered by original forest.

Although precise estimates of late prehistoric European population are extremely difficult to make, educated guesses do provide a useful sense of scale for purposes of discussion. McEvedy and Jones (1978:67) suggest a population of one million in Germany about 700 B.C., compared with approximately eighty million today.

Almost all settlements in Europe north of the Alps in the late

Bronze Age were on the scale of farmsteads and very small villages, although estimates of the populations of some communities are high. For example, Reinerth suggests two hundred for Wasserburg Buchau (1928:38), Bersu estimates four hundred at Wittnauer Horn (1946:7), and Wyss believes five hundred people lived at Zürich-Alpenquai (1971a:104). The evidence suggests, however, that such estimates are too high and that the populations of communities before 800 B.C. rarely exceeded fifty and probably only very exceptionally one hundred. Most of the high estimates are based on settlement structure evidence—a poor basis in the context of Europe north of the Alps, where building was done almost exclusively in timber and where weather conditions required frequent rebuilding. Archaeologists often assume that all of the structures revealed on prehistoric settlements were in use at the same time. But this assumption is unreasonable for those European settlements that were occupied for several generations. The settlement at Elp in the Netherlands illustrates the problem. The site plan drawn up by excavators (Figure 4) shows some thirty buildings, which traditionally would be interpreted as dwellings and barns of several different family units. Yet radiocarbon dating and careful excavation and observation revealed the site to consist of a single farmstead, the main building of which had been rebuilt numerous times over the settlement's roughly five-hundred-year duration. This experience at Elp should teach us that a settlement plan does not show the size of a community at any one time, but rather the total number of structures that ever stood on the site. Because interpretation of settlement evidence is questionable, graves provide a much more reliable—though not completely unproblematic—basis for estimating population size of a community.

When cemeteries have been completely excavated and it can be assumed that one cemetery was used by only one community and, conversely, that that community used only the one cemetery (an assumption that appears to hold true for prehistoric Europe), workable estimates of population can be obtained by using the formula

$$P = \frac{De_o^o}{t} + k,$$

where P is the average population of the community, D the number of individuals buried in the cemetery, e the average life expectancy at birth, t the number of years that the cemetery was in

[41]

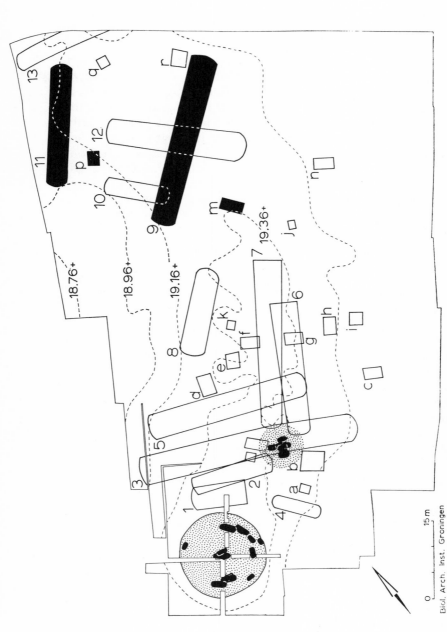

4. Schematic plan of the late Bronze Age settlement at Elp in the Netherlands. The long house-and-barn structures and smaller outbuildings of the first phase of occupation are shown in black. Those of other phases (undifferentiated) are just outlined. The outbuildings (small rectangular structures) comprise sheds and drying racks. Stippled areas to the left are cemeteries. Four-digit

Biol. Arch. Inst. Groningen

0   15 m

use, and *k* a correction factor of 20 percent to compensate for graves destroyed before discovery and missed by the excavators. Average life expectancy is difficult to determine for specific communities represented in the cemeteries, but a rough average of thirty years is not unreasonable for Iron Age Europe. (In reality, life expectancy varied according to time period, region, social status, and other factors.) Based on this formula, the following population figures are suggested for some late Bronze Age communities represented in the cemeteries. These figures are intended only to convey an impression of size, rather than to give a precise count.

Community	Approximate population
St. Andrä	5–10
Grünwald	5–10
Unterhaching	20
Gernlinden	30
Kelheim	45

Among the cemeteries that have been excavated, none suggests a population even close to one hundred. Of the sample cemeteries here, Kelheim, Gernlinden, and Unterhaching are among the largest of central Europe from this period. Most cemeteries are the size of St. Andrä and Grünwald and presumably represent the burial place of a single family. The larger ones were probably burial sites of communities consisting of a few families.

There are three common topographical situations for settlements of this period: level, dry land, the shores of lakes, and hilltops. Flatland settlements, the most numerous of the three types, were often located on the fertile and easily worked loess soils, frequently on the terraces overlooking river valleys. The chief characteristic of their location is proximity to fresh water and fertile fields. The settlements situated in the swampy lands bordering lakes were found particularly in Switzerland and southwest Germany and are of special archaeological importance because their waterlogged environments are excellent preservers of organic materials. Like the flatland settlements, these communities were agricultural in orientation, as indicated by finds of plant remains and agricultural tools. Hilltop settlements first became common during the late Bronze Age and are characterized by often very substantial fortifications of earth, timber, and stone. These fortifications and the hilltop siting indicate a primarily defensive function, although most of these

[43]

settlements were, apparently, occupied rather than places of refuge in times of danger.

While hilltops offered natural defense, supplemented by substantial earthworks, many lakeshore and flatland settlements were defended by fences. At the Wasserburg Buchau a palisade system of some thirty thousand logs, dating over a span of three hundred years, surround the settlement (individual logs may have functioned for twenty to thirty years).

Excavated settlements in the three kinds of locations were quite similar in internal structure, size, and economic activity; there is no indication of an economic specialization associated with a particular topography. The surface area of excavated settlements ranges from under 1,000 square meters to several hectares, with no apparent correlation between size and location. In measuring size, we are again faced with the problem of determining which parts and how much of the settlement area were in use at any one time, and this issue can only be investigated during the excavation of each settlement.

Dwellings, barns, and other structures were built according to either of two construction techniques. One used two rows of usually six vertical timbers sunk into holes in the ground to support the walls and roof (Figure 5). The other employed horizontal timbers placed on the ground, forming the foundation, with other horizontal logs resting on top to form the walls, as in log cabins in early America. We have been able to learn a great deal about building techniques and materials from excavations of lakeshore settlements, where many foundations have survived in the waterlogged environment. Although in most cases no wood has survived the damp climate of central Europe, recognizable postholes still exist where the vertical-post method was used and exist even in hilltop and flatland settlements. The log-cabin technique has for the most part left very little or no trace, except at some of the lakeshore sites. At many settlements where this method was used, the only evidence of it consists of fragments of wall plaster with impressions of sticks and logs against which it was packed, surviving in the ditches around the settlement and in the pits dug into the subsoil for grain storage and other purposes. In fact, the majority of settlements from this period are known only by their pits.

From the evidence of these foundations, we can get a sense of the scale of buildings. They range from very small structures, probably sheds and drying racks, of only a few square meters, to what were probably one-room huts of 25 or 30 square meters, to large

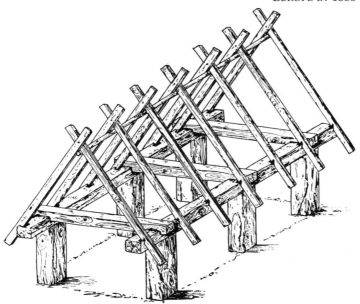

5. Characteristic frame of a building from a late Bronze Age settlement in central Europe. This drawing is based on the typical pattern of postholes found at such settlements. Length of building, about 5 m.

buildings of 100 square meters and, at Elp and other north European settlements, more than 200 square meters. These very large structures comprised both dwelling areas for human occupants and barns for animals, a pattern that still holds in much of northern Europe today. The mean size of the more substantial structures on settlements is between 30 and 60 square meters, which may indicate the average house size of the period. In Britain houses were about the same size as those on the continent but were round instead of rectangular.

Practically all settlements housed agricultural communities. The flatland settlements were usually situated directly on the agricultural land. The inhabitants of the lakeshore and hilltop settlements were slightly removed from their fields but still close to the good agricultural soil. The plant remains and animal bones recovered archaeologically on all such sites are essentially similar, and there was no apparent difference in manufacturing and trading activities.

There is no evidence that any settlement or group of settlements

[45]

had priority over others in terms of population, manufacturing activity, trade, or wealth and power. Communities were largely independent, interacting only to trade for bronze and a few nonessentials such as glass beads and graphite. The only economically specialized communities were those engaged in mining in the mountainous regions of Europe.

In Europe during the late Bronze Age, substantial man-made walls first appeared in large numbers in hilltop settlements. Along with this evidence of an increased need for defense, there is indication of widespread violence in the abundance of destruction layers (thick deposits of charcoal indicating settlement-wide conflagrations) at numerous lowland settlements. The use of weapons also increased, and their forms suggest more serious fighting. All this evidence for increased violence can be understood in light of the growing quantities of material wealth possessed by individuals and communities.

Some investigators have emphasized the scale of the defensive works around the hilltop settlements and have argued that strong central leadership must have been necessary to direct the construction and hence that there must have been highly developed social differentiation. Experimental studies of earthwork construction demonstrate, however, that the number of hours of labor required may have been fewer than expected. The fortifications built around late Bronze Age settlements were well within the capability of an agricultural community of twenty to thirty individuals to erect easily in their spare time, so that there was no need for special social hierarchies.

SUBSISTENCE ECONOMY

Only after communities have established means of procuring food can other activities such as manufacturing and trade and accumulation of wealth be carried on. Most prehistoric European communities after the Neolithic period relied on a mixed economy of farming and livestock raising. Gathering wild plants and hunting played a part in food provision throughout prehistoric and medieval times. Little quantitative information is available about relative proportions of faunal and floral remains at settlements, and we cannot ascertain the relative importance of animal versus vegetable products in the diet.

Plant Foods

The following cultivated plants are well represented on settlement sites of the late Bronze Age. This list is based largely on the work of Udelgard Körber-Grohne (1981) and Werner Lüdi (1955).

Cereals
    wheat (*Triticum*)
        emmer (*T. dicoccum*)
        einkorn (*T. monococcum*)
        spelt (*T. spelta*)
        club (*T. compactum*)
        bread (*T. aestivum*)
    barley (*Hordeum*)
    millet
        broomcorn millet (*Panicum maliaceum*)
        Italian millet (*Setaria italica*)
    oats (*Avena*)
Garden crops
    horsebean (*Vicia faba*)
    pea (*Pisum sativum*)
    lentil (*Lens*)
    poppy (*Papaver somniferum*)
    flax (*Linum usitatissimum*)

There is evidence also that apple and pear trees were being cultivated by this time, rather than their fruit simply being harvested in the wild. A rich abundance of wild plants is represented, too, on settlements, including hazelnuts, cherries, plums, grapes, strawberries, raspberries, blackberries, and beechnuts. Many other plants, such as goosefoot (*Chenopodium*), cleavers (*Galium*), and sorrel (*Rumex*), that have been but are not today considered as food sources are also well represented.

It is evident that a wide range of plants was being cultivated and numerous species of wild ones used to supplement the diet, either out of necessity or because of a desire for variety. Körber-Grohne's distribution map illustrating relative proportions of various domesticated species of plants at thirty Bronze Age sites shows that there is no clear geographical concentration of any of the plant species (1981:205, fig. 23). In some individual pits on settlement sites many different species are represented, indicating that single communities were growing a wide range of plants for food. For example,

[47]

four postholes of what is thought to have been a grain-storage structure at the settlement of Langweiler, near Düren, West Germany, contained 1,402 grains of barley, 225 spelt or emmer wheat, 13 spelt spicule bases, 27 spicule bases of emmer, 129 fragments of wild oats, 13 spicule bases of oats, and 4 of Italian millet. At Elp, the average of three samples of grains examined was 57 percent emmer wheat, 43 percent barley, and some broomcorn millet and wild oats. At Wasserburg Buchau, the cereal grains were 80 percent spelt, 4 percent emmer, 10 percent barley, 5 percent dwarf wheat, and 1 percent einkorn. Millet, horsebean, pea, poppy, and flax were also present. The settlement at Ichtershausen, near Arnstadt, yielded 815 cubic centimeters of emmer wheat grains, 140 cubic centimeters of einkorn, 450 cubic centimeters of barley, and 39 grains of lentil. These four examples indicate the range of species and combinations at individual sites. Of all species of domesticated plants represented on Bronze Age sites in central Europe listed by Körber-Grohne, emmer wheat is by far most common, being present at twenty-one of thirty sites. Barley is represented at eleven of the thirty sites. Methods of processing may have substantially affected distribution and preservation of vegetable remains.

Technology of Agriculture

Most tools were made of wood and hence survive only under exceptional circumstances. Little evidence of the complex agricultural process remains. There are, however, three aspects that are fairly well represented archaeologically—use of the plow, use of the sickle, and organization of fields. Changes in amounts of wealth available to communities, particularly amounts of metal being produced and accumulated, directly affected these three aspects of the food-production process and were in turn affected by changes in the methods and efficiency of food production.

There are no clear remains of plows from the beginning of the final millennium B.C. preserved in central Europe, although plows were used probably on a fairly regular basis by 1000 B.C. and perhaps by 2000 B.C. in many parts of the continent. We do, however, have a good picture of the kinds of plows in use and the ways they were used from remains of slightly later plows preserved in Denmark and other parts of the Northern European Plain and from rock carvings in the French and Italian Alps and southern Sweden.

No metal plow parts that antedate the late Iron Age are known. Presumably the share on these early plows consisted only of wood, perhaps hardened by charring.

Ards, plows without moldboards, are well represented among the finds in Denmark and other areas of northern Europe from the first half of the final millennium B.C. and in Bronze and Iron Age rock carvings (Figure 6) of northern and southern Europe, in the Bohuslän region of southern Sweden, at Val Camonica near Brescia in the Italian Alps, and at Monte Bego in the Maritime Alps. Dating of the plows is based on pollen recovered with them, often collected from crevices in the wood. The rock carvings are dated by the chronology of other items represented in associated carvings, particularly weapons and boats. The form of the ards shown in the rock carvings of northern and southern Europe is the same as that of ards recovered in Danish bogs, suggesting that similar ards were used throughout much of the continent. The images of the animals used to pull the plows, of their arrangement at the front of the beams, and of the activity of humans working with the teams are also similar in rock carvings from various regions, again suggesting widespread practices. Most of the carvings show ards being pulled by two animals yoked together at the end of a beam; in most cases the animals' horns are those of oxen. In almost all the images one human figure holds only a handle at the top end of the plow. In many representations another human figure walks in front, apparently leading the team.

6. Drawing of a rock carving in Litsleby, Bohuslän, Sweden, dating to the late Bronze Age and showing a crook ard similar to the specimens found in bogs in Jutland. This representation shows the plow with a horizontal sole and a long curved beam extending between a pair of yoked oxen. The man's hand holds onto a handle at the back of the vertical stilt of the plow. For further discussion of this and related representations see Glob 1951.

[49]

Peter Glob (1951) distinguishes two types of ard, both of which were in use from at least the late Bronze Age. The crook ard, of which the Walle specimen is a nearly complete example, is made from the crook of a tree, with a branch forming the long beam and the larger part from the trunk or from a larger branch forming the share. Additional pieces of wood are added to form the stilt, the handle, and the tie hook. The second type is the bow ard, represented by the well-preserved Døstrup ard (of Iron Age date), has a separate piece of wood forming the share, inserted through the end of the beam and supported by the curved stilt. The difference between these two forms is mainly structural and not apparently chronological or functional.

Best represented of the tools of agricultural production is the sickle. It was the only metal agricultural implement in use during the late Bronze Age and thus the only one that consistently survives in the European environment. The plow was used to prepare the ground for planting; the sickle was used for harvesting the produce.

In Neolithic times sickles with flint teeth were made in Europe and elsewhere. The first metal sickles appeared in Europe not at the beginning of the Bronze Age but at the start of the middle Bronze Age, and it is not until the late Bronze Age, after about 1200 B.C., that metal sickles became common in Europe. The vast numbers and widespread distribution of sickles in this late period indicate that a great quantity of bronze metal was being directed to their production. Except for bronze axes used for clearing farmland and for other woodwork, sickles were the first investment of bronze metal in the technology of agricultural production.

Sickles have been found in hoards, in settlement deposits, and even in a few graves of the late Bronze Age. They have been most abundantly represented in hoards, in both new and broken condition, all over Europe. Some hoards contained only sickles, some contained sickles and axes, and some contained a range of bronze objects and scrap that included sickles (Figure 7). The hoard at Frankleben, near Merseburg, East Germany, contained more than 230 bronze sickles. Many hoards contained more than 25 sickles. In some hoards all the sickles were new; in others, all were broken. Most of the latter hoards were most likely collections of metal belonging to metalworkers, who may have been itinerant but more probably in this period were settled and kept part of their stock safely underground. New sickles were products awaiting trade to

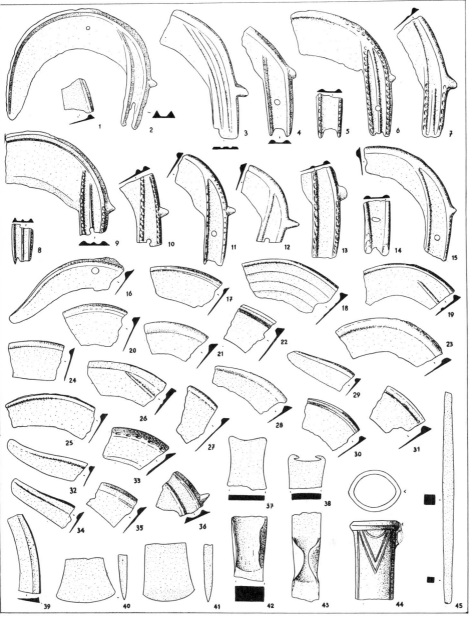

7. Part of the hoard of bronze objects from Winklsass, Bavaria, West Germany. The objects shown here include sickles (1–36, 39), axes (37, 38, 40–44), and a chisel (45).

farmers; broken ones were part of what the metalworker received in exchange, raw material for future castings.

Sickles have also been found at settlements, especially in the southwest German and Swiss lakeshore sites. At some sites, where preservation has been enhanced by the waterlogged conditions, wooden handles for the sickles also survive. Some are sophisticated in form, designed to protect the fingers from injury by plant stalks.

Molds for casting bronze sickles have been found at settlements all over Europe—usually parts of two-piece molds of sandstone with the form of the sickle cut out from one face and the other face flat to press against the first. The wide distribution of these molds indicates that the sickles were cast throughout Europe rather than manufactured at special centers. It is likely that every community of more than one or two families had someone able to cast bronze to produce tools and other everyday items.

Bronze sickles were an essential element in agricultural technology, indicating a new dependence on metal for subsistence production. They were used chiefly to cut the ears of grain off the stalks and, if the stalks were later to be harvested for thatch, to cut the stalks at the base. (Axes, which were important for clearing land, were common throughout the Bronze Age, but many more have been found on late Bronze Age sites than on earlier ones.)

Fields are plots of land marked off for agricultural purposes. They are most commonly rectangular, often nearly square. The earliest evidence for the development of fields appears now to date from early in the third millennium B.C. at the South Street long barrow in Wiltshire, southern England. Evidence suggests that it was not until about the end of the second millennium B.C. that field systems were common in northern Europe, particularly in southern Britain, the Netherlands, and Denmark. The principal evidence for field systems consists of earthen banks and sometimes stone walls surrounding rectangular parcels of land. The distribution of archaeologically identifiable field systems does not represent their original extent but rather reflects exceptional circumstances of preservation. The surviving evidence of prehistoric field systems of southern Britain and northwestern Europe is situated largely on land that, because it is only marginally agricultural, was not subjected to later plowing, which would have destroyed the earlier traces of field boundaries.

The demarcation of fields by means of boundaries reflects an intensive and long-term use of agricultural land. A considerable investment of time and energy is required to construct field boundaries so that specific parcels of land are set off from the surrounding territory. This investment of effort in establishing bounded fields implies a more intensive utilization than do open fields, and hence more careful scheduling, since no fields can be farmed repeatedly for more than a few years without exhausting the soil. Thus a system of fallowing is also implied, and crop rotation and the application of manure to the enclosed fields are likely concomitants. Not all field boundaries were as substantial as earthen mounds or stone walls, such as those surviving in Britain and northwestern continental Europe. They could also consist of light fences made of branches and thus might not show up archaeologically even under optimum conditions of preservation.

Domestic Animals

The most common domestic animals of the period were cattle, pigs, sheep, goats, horses, and dogs. The faunal remains from settlement sites indicate that cattle and pigs were the main sources of meat protein. Pigs were most abundant in many parts of the forested regions north of the Alps where the cool, damp forest environments were particularly favorable to them. Cattle were the predominant species on other sites, particularly in the open grasslands of eastern Europe and on the Northern European Plain.

While pigs were raised exclusively for meat, cattle were useful in a variety of ways, chiefly as traction animals for plows, for their milk and other dairy products, and for leather. Manure was also an important product. Sheep were raised principally for wool in most parts of Europe, as the evidence in the faunal remains attests, but were used for food as well. Goats were kept mainly for milk but also for meat. Horses were used for meat and probably also for traction, but probably not for riding at this time. Dogs may have been kept mainly as pets, for guarding settlements and herds, and for tending sheep, but they were eaten as well.

A small proportion, usually 2 to 10 percent, of the animal bones found on all settlements are of wild animals. Red deer are most common, and they were probably often killed when they raided crops, although they were likely hunted in the forests as well. A variety of other species were also hunted and eaten, including roe deer, boar, bear, elk, and hare—a range similar to what is offered today by central European restaurants specializing in game meats.

Fish and birds are also commonly represented among faunal remains.

The subsistence pattern represented by the faunal remains is similar to that indicated by plant remains. A wide variety of species was used, primarily domestic but including some wild types as well. No single species was distinctly predominant throughout Europe, nor was the diet of any one community restricted to a single or even a small number of species. The pattern is one of wide range and diversity, suggesting a certain amount of flexibility and adaptability in the diet.

It is from the late Bronze Age that we have the earliest clear evidence of stalls being used for winter tending of livestock. The pattern is most evident in the lands bordering the North Sea, where the long, rectangular houses with human dwellings at one end and animal stalls at the other were first built on a regular basis; these became common throughout the Iron Age and Middle Ages. The stalls maintained substantial numbers of animals through the winter, whereas before the animals had to fend largely for themselves, or most were slaughtered at the start of winter and only enough to maintain the herd were cared for. The use of stalls meant a considerable investment of time and energy in the animals. Larger buildings had to be constructed to accommodate the livestock, and fodder had to be grown, harvested, and stored to feed the animals through the winter. The return on investment was realized in the maintenance of healthy animals, which could be productive beginning at the first spring weather, and in large supplies of manure for spring and summer plantings.

MANUFACTURING

Material Culture in the Late Bronze Age

In all aspects of material culture continuity can be demonstrated between the late Bronze Age and earlier periods. Besides an increased variety, the main new feature of late Bronze Age material culture was a greater homogeneity of forms and styles of decoration throughout large parts of Europe, indicating increased communication among crafts workers.

Pottery vessels were used for many purposes, including preparing and serving food and beverages and storing foodstuffs and other items. Pottery recovered on settlement sites is relatively plain and coarse, that found in graves finer and more highly decorated. The vessels most abundantly recovered on settlements are bowls and dishes, cups and beakers, and large vessels with high, wide bodies and wide mouths for storage. These types of vessels correspond closely to those used in Europe into modern times. Most of them were already present in the preceding phases of the Bronze Age, but during the late Bronze Age large storage vessels for the first time became common on settlements. The most common ceramic form found in graves is the biconical vessel with cylindrical neck and flaring rim, usually used to hold the cremated remains. Bowls, cups, and beakers are also common in graves.

Baked clay was used also for items besides pottery. Loom weights, which hold taut the vertical strands of thread on vertical looms, were made of clay, as were spindle whorls. Two-piece molds for casting bronze objects were often ceramic. Animal figures and rattles of different forms were also made of fired clay.

Bronze objects have been found mainly in hoards and in graves. Most excavated settlements have yielded some, but except for those recovered on lakeshore settlements they are usually only small and fragmentary. Unlike iron and aluminum in the Western world today and iron in the late La Tène period (100–1 B.C.), fragmentary bronze objects were usually not discarded, but kept for remelting and recasting.

Four categories of bronze objects can be distinguished: jewelry, tools, weapons, and vessels. Jewelry is the most common form, particularly dress pins, pendants, bracelets, fibulae, neckrings, and finger rings. Jewelry has been found frequently in graves and, in both complete and fragmentary condition, also in hoards. Most numerous among tools found are axes and sickles. Knives, hammers, chisels, gouges, saws, anvils, awls, tweezers, razors, and keys have also been encountered often. Tools have been found most abundantly in the hoards; they also have occurred in graves and in some cases, particularly at the lakeshore sites, in settlement deposits. Of the weapons, the most commonly found are spearheads. Arrowheads are also abundant, but whether they were used primarily for fighting or for hunting is unknown. Swords are relatively common and have been found most often in richly outfitted graves. Helmets, shields, and cuirasses have been found less frequently. Axes may have had a double function as weapon and tool; no clear criterion has been discovered for distinguishing one from the other, and perhaps the same objects were used for both purposes. Bronze vessels have been found mainly in hoards and in graves.

Bone and antler were often used for implements and ornaments. Common on settlement sites where these substances are well preserved are hammers and hoes made of antler, and spearheads, cheek pieces, knife and awl handles, combs, buttons, and ornaments of various kinds made of antler and bone.

Flakes of flint have often been recovered on settlements of late Bronze Age date. Whether they belonged to the settlements of that date or were left on the land by earlier occupants can rarely be ascertained. In many cases all or most of the flakes are not of distinctive form, nor are they retouched. In northern Europe, where there are no natural deposits of copper and tin ore, flint flakes are especially common in settlements, and flint likely played a more important role in that economy than in central Europe. Pebbles were collected from streambeds and used as hammers, pestles, and slingstones. Sandstone was the preferred material for manufacture of flat molds for casting bronze objects. Numerous fragmentary and complete molds of sandstone have been recovered on settlement sites. Sandstone and other gritty stones were also used for grinding grain.

Wood was used in the construction of buildings and protective boundaries (fences, palisades, ramparts) and in the manufacture of vehicles, particularly wagons and boats, furniture, and tools. Plows and many other agricultural implements were made exclusively of wood. Handles of sickles, axes, knives, awls, saws, and hammers were also wooden. Wooden vessels have been recovered, and wooden cups, ladles, boxes, and baskets were preserved in the boggy deposits of many Swiss lakeshore settlements.

Forged iron was coming into use during this period. It is often found as ornamental inlay in bronze objects and in composite tools with bronze handles and iron blades. A small number of iron objects from the late Bronze Age have been found, and more are being discovered. Iron slag has been recovered on several sites, both in settlement deposits and in burials. Although it was being worked at this time in many different communities in central Europe, often with relatively sophisticated techniques, iron had no major economic importance before 800 B.C.

Large-scale production and trading of glass beads first occurred in Europe in the late Bronze Age, although beads of earlier date are known. Glass beads are of several types and have been found principally in graves but also in settlement deposits. Their abundance in many regions of Europe, including the central part, attests to the growth of surplus wealth and the increasing circulation of goods around the continent at this time.

Like all of the other materials we have discussed, except glass and gold, textiles were manufactured in most communities. Abundant assemblages of textiles from the late Bronze Age have survived in the bogs of Denmark, and they provide rich information about the kinds of fabrics in use, the techniques of spinning and weaving, the types of garments worn, and the colors of the clothing. Pictorial evidence from other parts of Europe show that similar garments were worn throughout the continent. Most excavated settlements have yielded evidence for spinning and weaving in the form of baked-clay spindle whorls and loom weights. The other tools used in textile production, including looms, were made of wood and have survived only in very exceptional circumstances.

During the late Bronze Age much more gold was worked than ever before, although the metal was still rare and has been found most frequently in association with other indications of special wealth. It was used principally for jewelry and special ornaments. Gold has rarely been recovered from settlement deposits but has been found in some richly equipped graves and in a small number of hoards. Its distribution makes plain that gold was a precious substance, restricted to individuals of considerable wealth.

Organization of Manufacturing

Pottery and bronze are the most abundant materials found from the late Bronze Age. The evidence pertaining to their production is much more common than that for other materials.

Numerous excavated settlements have yielded evidence for on-site production of pottery. Kilns and firing debris have been recovered in Germany at Elchinger Kreuz near Ulm, at Breisach-Münsterberg in Baden, at Buchau in south Württemberg, and at Hascherkeller in Lower Bavaria, and in France at the Hohlandsberg in Alsace and at Sévrier in Haute-Savoie, to cite only a few examples. The best documented kiln of this period is the one at Elchinger Kreuz. It was relatively well preserved and finely excavated and reported by Emma Pressmar (1979). The kiln was nearly round and freestanding, measuring 1.45 by 1.30 meters. It was made of the local loess soil on which it also stood. The kiln was constructed in a flat-bottomed shallow pit, about half a meter deep, and was approachable on all sides. The dome, destroyed by later plowing, survived only in small fragments. Underneath the kiln were four holes for stoking the fire, crossing at right angles. The wood burned in the kiln was identified as oak from surviving fragments in the fire box. Much trash pottery (misfired and broken sherds) was found in and around the kiln, as well as in three nearby pits.

The presence of kilns and production debris at most excavated late Bronze Age settlements suggests that the majority of communities produced their own pottery rather than relying on imports. This conclusion is supported by mineralogical analyses of sherds from several different settlements. There is no evidence for centralized production of pottery.

In communities ranging in size from ten to fifty individuals, it is unlikely that a full-time specialist potter could have been maintained. In traditional small communities that have been studied by ethnographers, pottery is most often produced by persons who through experience are especially skilled at the craft but who also work at producing food. They are specialists in that they alone make pottery for the whole community, but they are also subsistence producers and hence not full-time crafts specialists. Ethnographers have found that pottery is generally manufactured when other, more pressing work is not required. On the basis of the evidence of such recent small communities, it is reasonable to hypothesize that pottery production in the late Bronze Age was done by part-time specialists who exchanged their wares for such items as additional foodstuffs and crafts products made by other individuals in the community, for example, leather, wood, and textile goods.

The striking similarity of form and decoration of pottery from widely distanced areas leads us to surmise that substantial interaction among potters of various communities must have taken place. It is likely that in addition to the part-time community potters other, migrant potters existed, who perhaps traded in the graphite that was so popular at the time for pottery decoration. Though the clays and tempering materials in the pottery tested analytically have proven to be local, sources of graphite are limited geographically, and thus it had to be imported into most regions. Since the only documented use for graphite in this period was in pottery ornamentation, it is likely that the same individuals who traded graphite introduced new pottery forms and decorative patterns.

Bronze was the principal material from which tools, weapons, and jewelry were manufactured during the late Bronze Age. It was

[58]

also the material most frequently used for luxury items, of which bronze vessels were the most abundant category. This was a period of intense expansion in bronze production; the quantities of bronze tools, weapons, and jewelry in circulation increased greatly. There was also a definite increase in the number and size of large objects such as swords and axes, which incorporated greater quantities of the metal than did other items.

The majority of the bronze produced at this time consisted of approximately 90 percent copper and 10 percent tin. There are rich deposits of copper ore in the mountainous regions of Europe, particularly in the eastern Alps, the Bohemian Mountains, the Carpathians, and in western Britain and Ireland, and many of them were mined at this time. The great burst of new wealth in central Europe and in the Carpathian Basin depended directly on the large deposits of workable copper in those regions. Tin deposits are less widely distributed, and little is known about tin-mining operations.

We find the best evidence of the actual mining of copper in the Austrian regions of Tirol and Land Salzburg. Archaeologists and mining engineers have studied mine shafts, sites at which the lode material was broken up to separate ore from rock, and smelting sites. On the basis of these studies, Richard Pittioni (1951, 1976) and his colleagues estimate that some five hundred to six hundred workers may have been employed at one time in the mines in Land Salzburg, and another three hundred to four hundred around Kitzbühel in Tirol. Labor was divided; different workers mined the ore, cut and prepared timber for gallery supports, separated ore from stone, carried ore, smelted ore, and supervised the operations. From the mines at the Mitterberg and others near Bischofshofen in Land Salzburg, about 1.3 million tons of ore were removed in prehistoric times. From all the Austrian Alpine mines Pittioni estimates that some 50,000 tons of copper were produced from the early Bronze Age through the early Iron Age. More copper was mined during the late Bronze Age than in any other prehistoric period, but it is difficult to judge exactly what amount was generated then and what during other times.

Finds from the mines consist mainly of scattered sherds of pottery and occasional fragmentary tools. Unlike the salt mines of Hallstatt and Dürrnberg, whose salt has preserved organic remains, the copper mines have yielded little evidence of the mining operations. Nor is much known about the settlements in which the miners lived.

The miners' cemeteries, however, tell something about the wealth and trading practices of the mining communities. A small miners' cemetery of sixteen graves at Lebenberg (Kitzbühel, Tirol), contained fifteen graves outfitted with typical grave goods of the period, but one, richer than the others, had in it a bronze sword and spearhead. The pattern of wealth distribution in these graves is similar to that of cemeteries elsewhere. Generally the graves are well equipped, and there is little variation in wealth, suggesting that the quantities and distribution of wealth in this mining community were similar to those in the agricultural communities. This pattern changed, however, in the next couple of centuries.

Copper ores extracted from the mines were smelted close to the mines. (Tin ores were probably treated much the same, but the available evidence is insufficient for us to say anything definite.) It is unclear where the metals were alloyed. Although numerous ingots of bronze have been recovered in hoards, on settlements, and in a few graves, virtually no copper or tin bars from this period have been found. The reason is easy to understand: copper and tin were in high demand and thus precious; as soon as they were produced, the two metals were brought together, alloyed, and passed along the distribution system.

The evidence for the distribution of bronze bar ingots in central Europe is good. They have been found in hoards, in settlement deposits, and in a few graves. The ingots are usually long and thin, with a rhomboid cross section, though there is considerable variation in shape and size. They have been found in hoards with other kinds of objects, as in the hoard from Unadingen, illustrated here (Figure 8). Similar bar ingots have been recovered on some settlements. Several graves that contained such ingots have been interpreted as burials of bronzesmiths.

The small size of the bronze bar ingots is striking, most corresponding in size to the relatively narrow bracelets of the period. In fact, ingots found in some hoards, such as the hoard from Unadingen, match closely, in size and shape of cross section, bracelets found in the same hoards, leading us to surmise that these ingots may have been intended for manufacture of such bracelets. In any case, the vast majority of known ingots would have to have been combined in large numbers to yield enough metal to produce an axe, a spearhead, or any other such object of larger size, but larger ingots have not been identified in central Europe.

In hoards, far more scrap bronze in the form of broken objects and metal cakes has been found than bronze ingots. The large

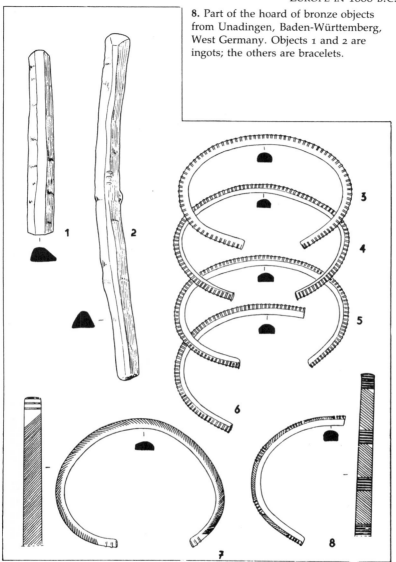

8. Part of the hoard of bronze objects from Unadingen, Baden-Württemberg, West Germany. Objects 1 and 2 are ingots; the others are bracelets.

number of these hoards, which most likely belonged to founders, relative to the number of ingots known indicates that more bronze was recycled during the late Bronze Age than at any time before or after. The majority of the tens of thousands of known hoards contained substantial amounts of such bronze scrap. Many also

[61]

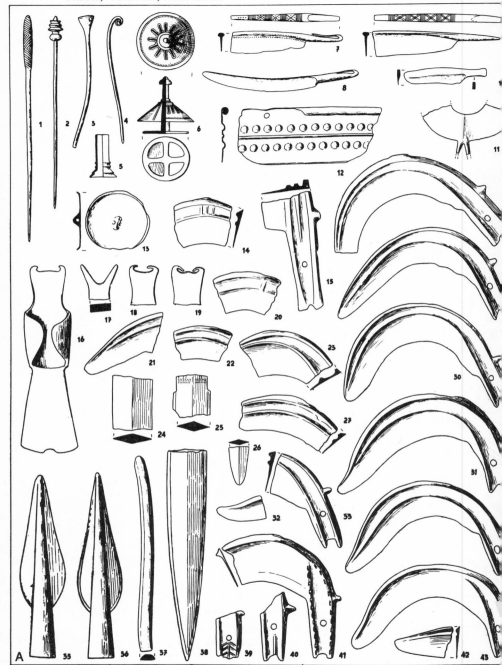

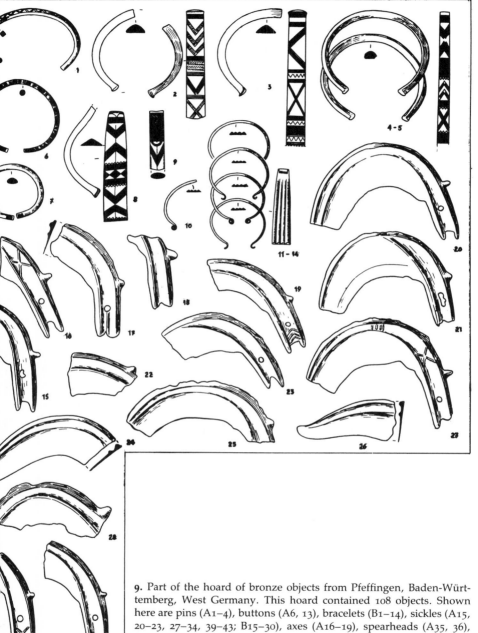

9. Part of the hoard of bronze objects from Pfeffingen, Baden-Württemberg, West Germany. This hoard contained 108 objects. Shown here are pins (A1–4), buttons (A6, 13), bracelets (B1–14), sickles (A15, 20–23, 27–34, 39–43; B15–30), axes (A16–19), spearheads (A35, 36), fragments of swords (A24–26, 38), knives (A7–10), sheet bronze fragments (A12), a razor (A11), and an ingot (A37).

[63]

contained complete, new objects, and many contained tools for working bronze.

A characteristic hoard was one found at Pfeffingen (Figure 9), which contained at least twenty-five fragmentary sickles, five fragmentary bracelets, a tip of a sword, an axe with damaged blade, two broken knives, a broken razor, and a fragment of a sheet-bronze vessel. In addition to these broken items, the hoard contained a bronze ingot, six new sickles, two complete spearheads, four complete pins, two complete knives, nine complete bracelets, and several ornaments. This hoard and others like it are best interpreted as caches of bronze metal objects that belonged to bronze workers and that were buried in the ground for safekeeping. The bronze worker may have lived nearby and made this deposit his permanent storage, or he may have been an itinerant worker and left this material along his route, planning to return to pick it up after a side trip. The broken objects, which would have been obtained by the metalworker through trade of new objects with his customers, represent scrap metal for recasting. The new objects represent his wares for exchange. The new and scrap material may have been stored separately in the hoards, perhaps in leather or cloth bags, but this separation is lost to us today since most hoards are found accidently, not excavated under systematic conditions.

Hoards provide important information about the circulation and production of bronze objects. Their abundance and richness in scrap indicates a widespread effort to conserve metal. Broken objects were not thrown away but passed back to metalworkers for recycling. Since copper and tin both required a great investment of energy to mine, smelt, alloy, and transport, bronze had substantial value. This pattern of reusing metal is reflected in the general dearth of it found on settlement sites and is very different from attitude toward iron in the late La Tène period (100–1 B.C.), whose major settlements are littered with the metal. Except at lakeshore sites in Switzerland and southwest Germany, large objects such as axes and knives have rarely been found on settlements. The only bronze objects recovered frequently on settlement sites are small scraps, such as fragmentary pins, which do not represent much metal and could easily have been lost. The probable reason that so much bronze survives from the lakeshore settlements is that objects were lost much more easily in the wet and boggy environments than on dry land, not that lakeshore communities held bronze to have less value or could afford to dispose of it more readily.

[64]

The great demand for bronze and the efforts to conserve it are also reflected in the burials. While the proliferation of hoards in Europe and the numerous objects found in them indicate the existence of a vast amount of metal in circulation, the quantities of metal placed in graves did not increase appreciably during the late Bronze Age. Scrap metal hoards are rare from preceding periods, both because there was less metal available then and because little effort was made to conserve and recycle the supply. The mining evidence from the late Bronze Age indicates that new metal was constantly fed into the system, but the demand for bronze was growing even more rapidly because of increased production of basic tools for food production such as sickles and axes and of metal-consuming elite goods such as swords, helmets, and vessels. Available metal, as a result, had to be kept and reused.

Some scholars have suggested that specific quantities of bronze metal had a relatively fixed exchange value at this time. Many hoards contained fragments in shapes that would not break off sickles in normal use but were, rather, produced by deliberate cutting from larger objects. These fragments suggest the existence of some kind of weight standard. The hoard of Winklsass, for example, contained about twenty small, rectangular fragments cut from sickles (Figure 7).

We have good information about where bronze working took place. The principal evidence consists of the presence on settlement sites of casting molds, droplets of bronze, crucibles, and remains of furnaces used to attain the temperatures required to melt bronze. Any one of these items is usually indicative of on-site bronze casting. Such remains of the bronze-working process have been recovered on most excavated settlements of more than a single farmstead.

Alpenquai, Wollishofen, and Grosser Hafner on the Zürichsee; Stadtboden and Mörigen on the Bielersee; Cortaillod and Auvernier on Lake Neuchâtel; and Estavayer-le-Lac and Corcelettes on the Murtensee—all of these lakeshore settlements of Switzerland yield evidence of bronze casting. The hilltop settlements often yield remains of bronze working—for example, the Hohlandsberg in Alsace, France, the Runder Berg in Württemberg, Germany, and a series of sites in Switzerland. Many flatland settlements also produced furnace remains, molds, and casting debris, such as those in the Saône valley studied by Bonnamour (1976), at Hascherkeller in Bavaria (Figure 10), at Velemszentvid in Hungary, and also in the more peripheral regions of the continent such as

[65]

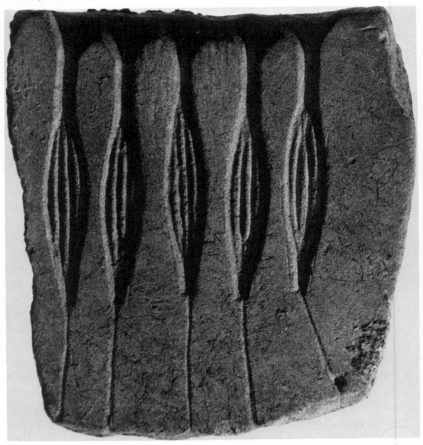

10. Sandstone mold from the settlement of Hascherkeller in Bavaria, West Germany, used for casting bands for finger rings. Maximum length, 11 cm.

Hallunda in Sweden and Aldermaston Wharf in southern Britain. The abundant finds of bronze-working activity on many settlements of the period support Albert von Brunn's suggestion (1968) that every community of any size had among its members a crafts worker who produced the bronze objects required by that community.

We have as yet little evidence for the existence of major bronze production centers. That bronze casting was so widespread indicates that most bronze objects were manufactured locally in settlements throughout Europe. Where the actual remains of furnaces survive, they indicate small-scale working of the metal, involving perhaps one metalworker or possibly two working together, but certainly no more. One possible exception may be the site of Velemszentvid in western Hungary, but not enough has been published about the old excavations there to indicate how extensive bronze working may have been. The scale of the evidence for metalworking, however, and the character of the bronze objects produced on most settlements suggest that the local bronze workers, like potters, were not full-time specialists but rather peasant crafts workers who spent part of their time, probably during slow periods in the agricultural year, working metal.

Two types of bronze objects appear to have been produced: common, everyday objects and rarer luxury items. The most common metal objects, tools and jewelry, were cast in molds, usually flat, with a form cut out of one piece and a flat surface on the other half of the mold. Some molds were more complex, as, for example, the composite molds with plugs used for casting socketed axes. These everyday objects were produced on most settlements and are found in both hoards and graves. The tools most commonly represented by molds found on settlements are sickles and axes (the two that played the principal role in agricultural production). Knives are also common and were probably all-purpose kitchen tools. Most of the jewelry items produced on the sites, to judge by the molds recovered, were rings and dress pins.

During the late Bronze Age a new way of working bronze was developed, that is, the hammering of sheet bronze into objects. The hammered objects required much more time and skill to make since large sheets had to be hammered from lumps of metal. Objects of hammered bronze were frequently elaborately ornamented with bosses and patterns of fine lines. This type of bronze work was usually used for weapons, particularly helmets, and vessels. Unlike the utilitarian objects such as tools or everyday personal ornaments like rings and pins, which were cast in great numbers from molds, hammered bronze objects were unique, each being manufactured separately. These objects of limited manufacture were affordable only by wealthy individuals, and have been found in relatively few graves, where they are associated with other indications of special wealth, such as swords and gold ornaments. Experiments by Coles (1977) revealed that most of the defensive weaponry made of sheet bronze was much too thin to have been militarily effective and must have been intended only for show.

Bronze appears to have been produced on two organizational

levels: a local one, for everyday cast tools and jewelry for local use, and a cosmopolitan one, for the elaborate luxury goods destined for a widespread wealthy clientele. Local production probably took place on all settlements of any size in Europe. Luxury items were most likely produced by a small number of workshops, the locations of which are unknown. Because of the vast quantities of bronze objects found, especially in hoards, in the region of the Upper Tisza and the Carpathians, however, many investigators look to that area as a center of production. Many of the finely hammered, ornate luxury goods, particularly vessels, from this period were found concentrated in those regions and in the lands around the Hungarian Plain.

Evidence from graves gives us some basis for conjecture about the wealth of bronze workers. Those graves that contain tools of the trade—anvils, awls, and ingots—are interpreted as smith's graves. Compared with others in the same cemeteries, these graves were usually well equipped, particularly with bronze objects, suggesting that bronze workers were able to accumulate some amount of disposable wealth. In no case, however, do graves containing bronze-working tools belong to the richest group of burials.

Life was probably quite different for the smiths who worked in hammered bronze. They were probably full-time specialists who had to learn and practice the extraordinary skill evident in the ornate vessels and helmets they produced. The crafts workers who made the elaborate sheet bronze and those who made the other items, such as swords and fittings for wagons, that occur in the richer burials, had more opportunity to accumulate personal wealth than the part-time bronze casters who worked in the small communities. The latter group worked to serve local needs, and it is unlikely that they made more than their communities needed. The specialist bronze worker, on the other hand, with customers beyond the local community, had no such limitations on quantity. He may have produced a surplus of goods and of wealth.

In addition to these two categories of bronze workers a third probably existed—specialist bronzesmiths who brought ingots and scrap into settlements, repaired broken objects, manufactured new ones in communities that had no smith, introduced new styles, and taught local bronze casters new techniques. Such individuals may have been responsible for making the molds for local, part-time bronze casters; making the molds surely required much more skill than casting objects in them. As Wyss points out (1967:4), an itinerant smith, in order to do bronze castings, would have required only a good hearth, with the addition of bellows, crucibles, and molds, all of which he may have carried with him. The activity of such itinerant smiths, complementing the work of part-time casters in the villages, would account for the remains of bronze working that we find throughout the continent.

The hoards that contained usable tools for bronze working as well as scrap and new objects—for example, the hoard at Haidach in Austria (Figure 11)—have been interpreted as caches stored by itinerant smiths. The tools—gouges, chisels, punches, and often anvils and hammers—were used for making objects ordered by a village. These hoards seem less likely to have been the possessions of craftsmen-farmers who lived in the villages. Residents would have been less likely to bury their tools in the ground, since repairs or replacement of broken tools might have been needed quickly at any time. Many hoards have contained objects of far-ranging origins. Some of the Dutch hoards, for example, contained items manufactured in Britain, objects from central Europe, and other items made locally. It would have been much more possible for an itinerant than a resident bronzesmith to acquire materials of such varied origins.

Several researchers have addressed the question of slavery in prehistoric Europe but have identified no evidence that slavery existed before the end of the Iron Age. It is unlikely, therefore, that metalworkers in the late Bronze Age were slaves or otherwise bonded persons working for the benefit of others.

Bronze tools and everyday jewelry produced in most villages were probably exchanged for agricultural goods and household products (leather, wooden utensils, cheese, honey, textiles) within the village community and perhaps with members of other communities in the vicinity. These exchanges were probably part of regular village circulation systems established over generations. The common, locally made tools and jewelry were unlikely to have been introduced into the larger trade system, except as scrap when the items were no longer useful. We can see this pattern of local exchange reflected in the distributions of most types of the ordinary jewelry, particularly dress pins, fibulae, and bracelets, found in numerous graves and hoards. Concentrations of specific types of objects are limited to particular regions. Those areas of distribution often measure between 100 and 500 kilometers across and perhaps indicate the activity of one itinerant metalsmith in a series of villages. Within these regions there were numerous (perhaps

[69]

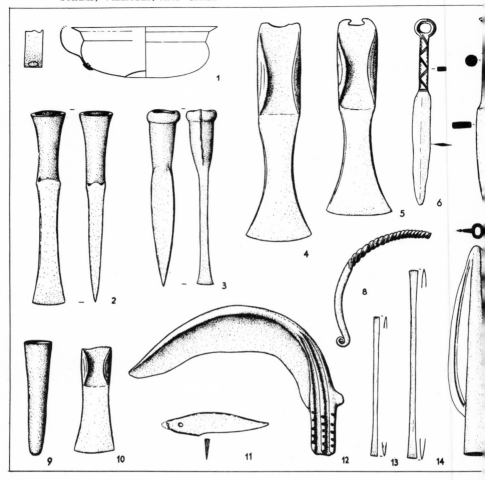

11. Hoard of bronze objects from Haidach, Carinthia, Austria. Shown here are a sheet bronze cup chisels (2, 3, 7, 13, 14), three axes (4, 5, 10), two knives (6, 11), a sickle (12), a spearhead (15), a spe (9), and a fragmentary neckring (8).

twenty, perhaps one hundred) resident, part-time bronze casters, who came into contact with the itinerant smiths and who all produced similar, though not identical, objects. More important than the distribution of bronze objects by the itinerant smiths was their introduction of new forms and perhaps new techniques to the local metalworkers, who in turn began producing the new items and distributing them within the network of their own villages.

[70]

The distribution of the products of the specialized sheet-bronze workers and sword makers was more complex. Evidence indicates that in contrast to everyday items, specific types of vessels and helmets, for example, were not confined to any local area or even single region of Europe, but rather spread throughout the continent (Figure 12). Whether the objects were made and then transported, or the bronze workers traveled to prospective customers and produced items on order is uncertain. The latter possibility is suggested by the existence of a series of hoards that contained elaborate sheet-bronze objects. The hoard from Hajuböszörmeny in northeast Hungary contained hundreds of bronze objects, among them two sheet-bronze cauldrons, a cup, and a situla (sheet-bronze pail); that at Unterglauheim contained an identical situla and two ornamented gold bowls; and one from Dresden-Dobritz contained a bucket, a sieve, two bowls, and thirteen cups. These hoards may represent assemblages of objects intended for trade to wealthy individuals by the specialist sheet-bronze workers. Possibly they were buried for safe storage and for some reason never retrieved.

An important aspect of bronze production is the removal of the metal from circulation. Bronze was valuable, and therefore people were careful to save scraps. Little bronze—only small fragments of objects—has been found on dry-land settlements. Only on the lakeshore settlements have larger amounts of bronze been recovered; in this environment objects were probably easily lost. Bronze objects found on settlement sites can all be regarded as accidental deposits.

Bronzes were, however, intentionally placed in graves. Between one-half and one-quarter of the excavated graves in most cemeteries of this period in Europe contained bronze objects. They consist for the most part of small items such as pins, bracelets, and knives; usually only one or two such items occurred in a grave. Richer graves, which contained large bronze objects such as swords, helmets, and vessels, are few in number. In total, relatively little metal was removed from circulation by inclusion in burials.

The majority of central European hoards are best interpreted also as intentional deposits of usable bronze. Those that survive to the present day must comprise only a small proportion of the number of hoards once buried. Most were probably recovered by the individuals who buried them, and the stored objects used in production and trade. Those known today were never recovered, perhaps

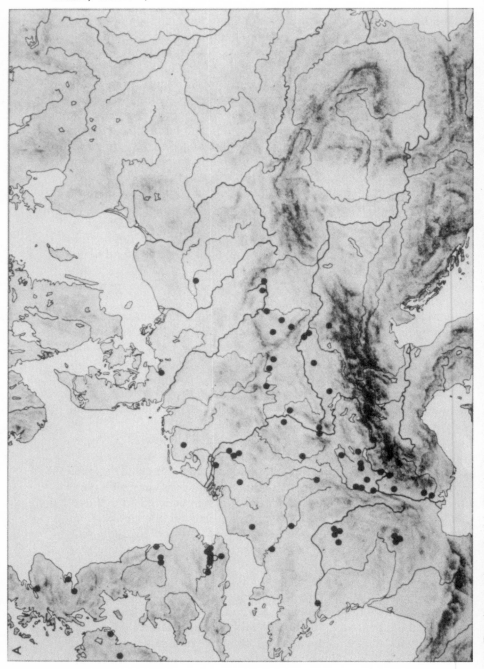

because of the plans or health of the individual or because of economic, political, or military changes that occurred.

"Votive offerings" constitute another category of intentional deposits of bronze metal. They are distinct from other kinds of hoards in the character of the objects in them and in their locations. Most of the votive finds are swords, although other special objects, such as vessels and helmets, have also been recovered. These objects, which are found especially in bodies of water such as rivers and swamps, are believed to have been offered to deities in much the same way offerings were made in Greek and Roman societies about whose religious practices we are better informed. These finds are concentrated, for example in the Rhine at Bingen and in the Inn near Mühldorf. More specimens of some types of objects (such as the Hemigkofen and Erbenheim types of flange-hilted swords) have been recovered in water than on land.

Of more concern here than their religious purpose, however, is the economic function of these offerings. Throwing bronzes into rivers and ponds had the same result as placing them in graves; it removed them permanently from circulation. Thus at the same time that much metal was recycled in the hoards, a significant amount was also disposed of in votive offerings (though not as much was being deposited in graves during this period as at other times). This disposing of bronze made necessary the constant production of more metal. If objects were kept in use, passed on from generation to generation, and recycled when broken or worn out, the demand for new supplies of metal would not have been high, just enough to satisfy demands. If objects were systematically removed from circulation, however, a steady supply of new metal would have been needed.

Removal of bronze from circulation also kept the value of the metal high. If it had not been removed, much of Europe would have been flooded with bronze (since metal production was increasing during the late Bronze Age), and its value would have dropped. That decrease in value would have hurt especially those individuals who had accumulated exceptional wealth in the metal. Some investigators have suggested that metalworkers deposited some of the hoards to take excess metal temporarily out of circulation so that its value would remain high or increase. Any individual who had accumulated wealth in bronze might have buried part of it for safekeeping or to keep others unaware of how much bronze he possessed. Such an interpretation might explain the many hoards that were never recovered. Perhaps the quantities of

[73]

metal placed in graves and thrown into water were insufficient to offset the massive ongoing recycling efforts and the increased production at the mines, and hence the metal never became scarce or rose in value. Moreover, attention was at this time being diverted to a new metal—iron. Perhaps the combination of recycling efforts and the advent of iron, particularly around 800 B.C., resulted in a waning of interest in bronze and subsequent lack of increase in its value. Persons who had buried bronze objects in the hope that their value would increase were frustrated in that hope and hence never recovered their metal.

TRADE

The late Bronze Age was a time of enormous expansion of trade (I am using the word *trade* in its widest sense, that is, to mean the peaceful exchange of goods) and of contacts among various communities throughout Europe. The most important material traded was bronze. During this period virtually no communities were without bronze. For the first time metal agricultural tools, such as sickles and axes, and other kinds of tools were made in substantial quantities. And even more abundant in the archaeological record are bronze ornaments—jewelry, ornate weapons, and vessels.

Communities depended on trade for only two commodities: luxury items and bronze. Otherwise, they were self-sufficient. Nonetheless, there is evidence on settlement and cemetery sites for trade in a wide range of goods. Graphite was extensively traded throughout central Europe, particularly after 1000 B.C. (in central European cemeteries about one-third of ceramic vessels are decorated with graphite, which suggests the scale of this trade). Glass beads and amber from the Baltic regions were also traded throughout the continent. (Were it not for the fact that many amber beads were probably destroyed in cremation fires, the quantities recovered from the late Bronze Age settlements would probably be much larger.) Seashells from the Mediterranean were imported into central Europe as jewelry.

Salt was probably widely traded during this period; radiocarbon dating has shown that the mining of salt began at Hallstatt at this time. Cattle and hides may have been trade items, particularly in the Northern European Plain, where there is evidence of intensive cattle raising and also of importation of bronzes from central Europe. Wool also may have been traded; many settlements have yielded evidence for what may have been surplus production of wool. Sets of bronze drinking and serving vessels found in a few richly appointed graves and in some hoards indicate that wine was probably imported from the Mediterranean world for consumption by wealthy individuals. There is, however, no clear evidence for trade of foodstuffs, except possibly of cattle southward from northern Europe. Food was most likely imported only by the non-self-sufficient copper- and tin-mining communities.

Much of the trading activity was probably carried on by merchants traveling on foot with their goods packed on their backs. The size of many of the bronze hoards corresponds closely to the amount of metal a person can carry. Although we know that packhorses and wagons were used at the time, we cannot estimate to what extent on the basis of present evidence. Boats were also used, but again we do not know how important they were to trade.

DISTRIBUTION OF WEALTH

From about 2000 B.C., some individuals began to accumulate material wealth, primarily in the form of bronze objects. This trend is evidenced in early Bronze Age hoards, particularly in series of rich graves in north central Europe characterized by the burial at Leubingen in East Germany, and reached a high point in the late Bronze Age. That the desire to accumulate wealth was developing is apparent in the manufacture of new kinds of objects, many of them exceptionally finely crafted and decorated, intended primarily for show. Large objects of sheet bronze, particularly vessels and helmets, are the most numerous of these, but we also find larger, frequently more ornate swords and more gold vessels and ornaments than before. Wealth was also invested in usable, economically productive items; tools for agriculture, bronze working, and carpentry proliferated. Bronze was an attractive and useful metal that was valuable because it was difficult to make. The investment of time and energy in the process of creating both useful and ornamental objects from bronze boosted their value even higher.

The production of new quantities of wealth in bronze, gold, and other unusual substances was accompanied by increases in both violence and attempts to defend against it. For the first time, many hilltop settlements were fortified with substantial systems of walls to protect their new wealth. Late Bronze Age swords are much more numerous and heavier than those of the middle Bronze Age (Figure 13). Swords and the more common spearheads were important for defense and offense. This increase in the need for defense is evidenced also in the fact that at this time keys first were used in Europe. The advent of keys implies that something warranted being locked up for safekeeping, a need that was not appreciable before.

Cremation was the standard burial practice throughout most of Europe during the late Bronze Age. Usually ashes and bones were placed in an urn, accompanied by a modest number of other ceramic vessels and often a bronze pin, ring, knife, or other small object, although the details of the practice varied considerably. Cemeteries range in size from a few graves to several hundred. The cemetery at Kelheim, with 268 graves (and probably more undiscovered), is among the largest known. Most cemeteries conform to a general pattern of distribution of wealth, with a small number of burials richer than the rest and the majority containing one to six objects. In most cases, the richer graves are characterized by having contained more of the same kinds of objects as were found in the other graves, not by having held special items.

A small number of very rich graves vary from this pattern. These were the graves of individuals who were able to amass a great deal more wealth than most other Europeans and invest some of it in unique luxury items. They contained both larger-than-average quantities of objects and also special items. The burial at Hart an der Alz in Lower Bavaria is a good example. The grave contained the cremated remains of a man who had been buried with a wagon outfitted with bronze parts. The other grave goods were eight ceramic vessels, seven of them of exceptionally fine quality; a bronze bucket, sieve, and cup; a sword; three arrowheads of bronze; a knife; a bracelet; and a gold wire ring. Wagons were very rare at this time; bronze vessels were exceptional in graves, particularly in sets of three; and swords and gold ornaments were not found in many graves.

Interestingly, these distinctions in the richest graves have no parallels in settlement structures, as far as present evidence indicates. No exceptionally large, especially fine, or richly outfitted buildings have been identified as the special residences of the wealthiest individuals.

The distribution of wealth in the graves of the majority of cemeteries is probably a fair indication of what the distribution of wealth

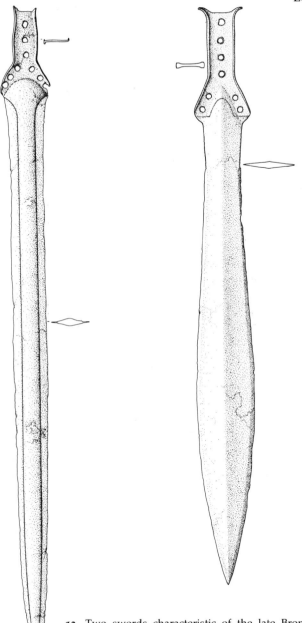

13. Two swords characteristic of the late Bronze Age, from Ludwigshafen-Mundenheim (*left*) and from Uffhofen (*right*), both in West Germany.

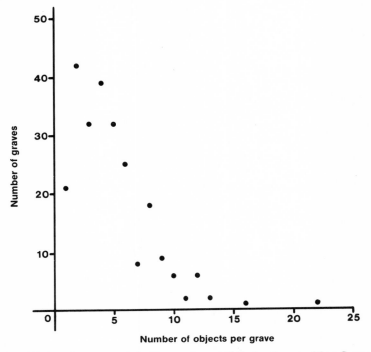

14. Distribution of grave goods in the cemetery at Kelheim, Bavaria, West Germany. Of the 268 graves, 244 are represented. The left part of the graph shows that most graves contained between one and eight objects (for example, 42 graves contained just two objects). Only a few graves had in them more than eight. The most goods in any grave was twenty-two (dot farthest to the right).

was among members of the agrarian communities of the time (Figure 14). A few individuals were able to acquire more wealth than most, but that wealth was figured in quantity rather than kinds of possessions.

3 Emergence of Centers of Production and Trade (800–600 B.C.)

The most important change that occurred at the beginning of the early Iron Age was the development of Europe's first towns. They emerged as a result of the growth of large-scale commercial extractive industries and of trade systems to carry the resulting products. Extraction and processing of salt and iron were already under way by the middle of the late Bronze Age (about 1000 B.C.), but between 800 and 600 B.C. production of these substances far exceeded earlier levels. Two of the first towns—Hallstatt in Upper Austria and Stična in Slovenia—best exemplify these changes.

HALLSTATT

Hallstatt is situated at the northern edge of the Austrian Alps about 50 kilometers southeast of Salzburg (Figure 16). The modern town lies 511 meters above sea level on the lake of the same name. An extensive prehistoric cemetery and prehistoric mines have been found in a narrow mountain valley 350 meters above the town and just west of it. This valley—the Salzbergtal—is situated on top of an enormous deposit of rock salt and is surrounded by Alpine peaks reaching nearly 3,000 meters above sea level (Figures 17 and 18). Because of the mountains towering over it, the valley receives little sunlight, and the soil is thin and poor for farming.

During medieval and modern times miners working in the salt mountain have encountered remains of prehistoric mining activity. The most spectacular find, made in 1734, was of the body of a miner completely preserved by the salt. Contemporary records note that even the man's coat and shoes survived intact. Between

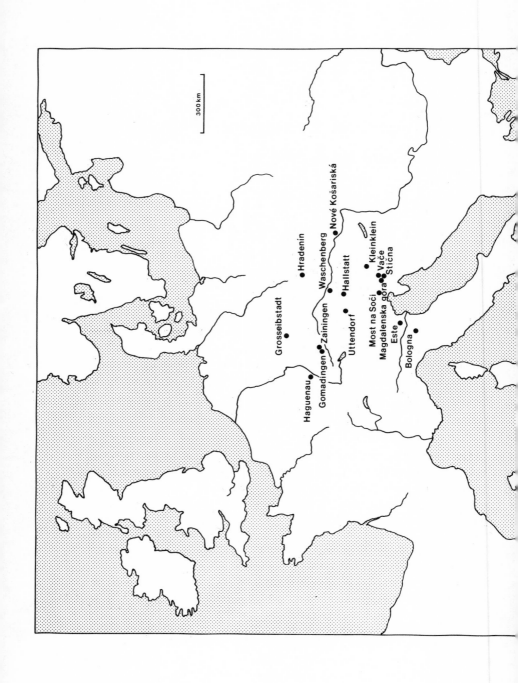

300 km

Hradenín

Nové Košariská

Waschenberg

Kleinklein

Hallstatt

Vače

Stična

Grosseibstadt

Zainingen

Most na Soči

Magdalenska gora

Uttendorf

Este

Gomadingen

Bologna

Haguenau

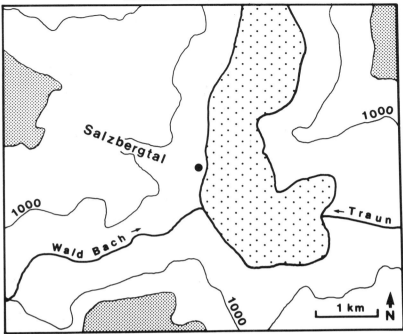

16. The environs of Hallstatt. The center of the modern town is indicated by the black circle. The Salzbergtal, in which the great cemetery and the prehistoric mine shafts have been found, is situated above the town to the west (see Figure 17). Lake Hallstatt (dotted area), into which the Traun River and the Wald Brook flow, is at an elevation of 508 m above sea level. The line marking the elevation 1000 meters above sea level is labeled; land above 1500 m is stippled.

1846 and 1864 Johann Georg Ramsauer, director of the Hallstatt mines, supervised the excavation of 980 prehistoric graves in the Salzbergtal. Later researchers opened additional burials; more than 2,000 graves have been discovered so far.

Only a few isolated objects of the Neolithic period and early and middle Bronze ages have been found at or around Hallstatt; there is no trace of a settlement or of mining before the late Bronze Age. The first evidence of organized mining activity on the site dates to about 1000 B.C. In 1830 a hoard was found in the Salzbergtal containing bronze cakes, at least twelve chisels, axes, spearheads, sword blades, at least five axes, and horse bits, most of the objects partly melted and bent out of shape. The total weight of the metal was at least 50 kilograms. (The pieces were quickly dispersed into museums and private collections, hence the exact quantities are

[81]

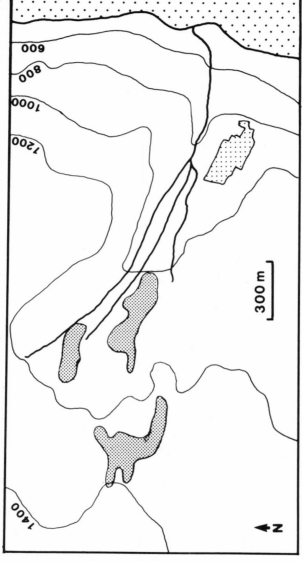

17. Schematic plan of the Salzbergtal. Dotted area at the right is Lake Hallstatt. The contour lines, labeled in meters above sea level, show the steepness of the landscape. The three principal areas of the prehistoric mining operations are indicated by stippling in the left half of the plan. The area of the great cemetery is shown in the lower right. A brook with three branches cascades down the slope, running from west to east through the center of the plan. Based on plan in Barth 1980a:69.

18. Photograph of the Salzbergtal, looking from east to west toward the high Alps in the background. The great early Iron Age cemetery was located in the open expanse of land to the left of the building in the center foreground. The buildings farther up in the valley are part of the modern salt-mining operations.

unknown.) This substantial assemblage of bronze found high in the Austrian Alps far from any known settlement reflects the commerce then developing at Hallstatt.

The Mines

Mining equipment found in the northern group of galleries (cuttings into the rock salt) at Hallstatt has been dated by radiocarbon to the period of 1000–800 B.C. There is, however, little evidence for human activity outside the mines during this period, apart from the large hoard. No associated settlement has been found, and burial in the great cemetery did not begin until about 800 B.C. The lack of late Bronze Age burials suggests that no permanent community had been established at Hallstatt before 800 B.C. Perhaps this early mining was done by individuals who mined one season of the year and spent the rest of their time farming elsewhere.

Tools recovered in the prehistoric mines tell us much about the methods employed. The miners chipped away at the rock salt with long, pointed bronze picks hafted to wooden handles. Wooden mallets and shovels were used to break up and collect chunks of salt, which were then carried up to the surface in animal-skin knapsacks that often had elaborate wooden frames. Illumination was provided by burning splints of fir and spruce. Timbers felled on the wooded mountainsides served as supports and as walkways in the galleries. Miners' caps and jackets made of fur, leather, wool, and linen have been found, as well as bone whistles for signaling inside the mountain. Food debris of beef, pork, wheat, barley, millet, apple, and cherry indicates what the miners ate as they worked.

The technology applied at Hallstatt in the late Bronze Age was the same as that used in copper mining—the galleries were steep, sloping, and narrow. After 800 B.C., however, the miners, having through experience gained an understanding of the nature of salt deposits, developed more efficient methods specifically for extracting that mineral, which employed a broad, flat, horizontal gallery system. Also, in the early stages of mining, the salt was broken into small fragments for carrying out. Later, miners devised a far more efficient way of prying from the mine walls large blocks of salt weighing more than 10 kilograms.

A total of 3,750 meters of prehistoric galleries have thus far been identified at Hallstatt, from which about 2 million cubic meters of salt were removed. New discoveries are made regularly by modern miners and by archaeologists working with them. The ancient galleries are no longer open—pressure of the mountain itself closed them after they were abandoned. Objects from the prehistoric mines are found today encased in the rock salt.

The Cemetery

The cemetery at Hallstatt provides evidence concerning the size, wealth, and commercial contacts of the mining community. For approximately eleven hundred graves we have good information about burial rites and grave goods; the other thousand or more graves opened are not well documented. The cemetery dates from about 800 B.C. to 400 B.C. and represents a community of between two hundred and four hundred people, much larger than most communities of the period. The skeletal remains and grave goods associated with them indicate that men, women, and children— not just adult males as was once believed—lived and worked at Hallstatt. Early Iron Age salt mining at Hallstatt was most likely a family occupation carried on by successive generations, as it was during the eighteenth and nineteenth centuries.

The grave goods indicate the range of trade contacts of the community and the wealth accumulated through commerce in salt. Most of the objects, including pottery, pins, bracelets, and weapons, were produced in Upper Austria and southern Bavaria, within a 30-kilometer radius of Hallstatt, but many others came from farther away. Some pieces of jewelry and several bronze helmets originated south of the Alps in Slovenia, as did the hundreds of glass beads and three glass bowls. Situlae, ornate situla lids, and some small ornaments were made in Italy. The numerous amber beads came from the Baltic coast. Ivory used for pommels on several swords originated in Africa and arrived at Hallstatt by way of Italy.

The Hallstatt cemetery is not only one of the most varied in its trade goods but also one of the richest. Many exceptional objects occur more frequently at Hallstatt than they do elsewhere; these include bronze and iron swords, some with ornate ivory-and-amber pommels, defensive armaments such as helmets and breast plates, and bronze serving and drinking vessels for alcoholic beverages, especially pails, bowls, and cups. Glass, amber, and gold ornaments also are found in greater quantities than at most other cemeteries. Other special kinds of objects found only at Hallstatt were custom made and emphasize the exceptional character and wealth of the community. Numerous bronze axes ornamented with cast figures of animals and humans on the back of the blade have been recovered, and five exquisite bronze bulls from Hallstatt have no exact counterparts elsewhere (Figure 19).

Comparison of numbers of goods in the Hallstatt graves with those found at the late Bronze Age cemetery of Kelheim is instructive (Figures 14 and 20). Only 12 of the 244 well-documented graves at Kelheim (4.9 percent) contained more than ten objects; at Hallstatt 84 of the 962 well-documented graves did (8.7%), nearly twice the percentage at Kelheim. There is a broader range of grave wealth at Hallstatt, and the richest burials at Hallstatt contained more objects than the richest at Kelheim. (Most of the pottery recovered in the course of excavations at Hallstatt was thrown away. If pottery were included in the graph of Hallstatt grave goods, the difference between Hallstatt and Kelheim would be even more striking.) These are characteristic features that distinguish cemeteries of early commercial communities from cemeteries of agrarian settlements.

Emergence as a Commercial Center

Salt had been produced on a small scale in several regions of Europe since the Neolithic period, but at early Iron Age Hallstatt,

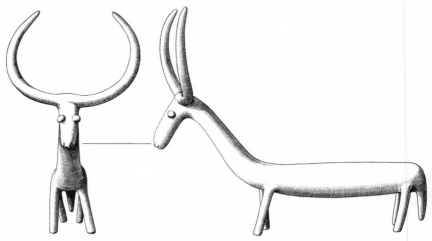

19. Bronze bull from Grave 12 at Hallstatt, excavated by the Duchess of Mecklenburg. Length, 14.2 cm.

[86]

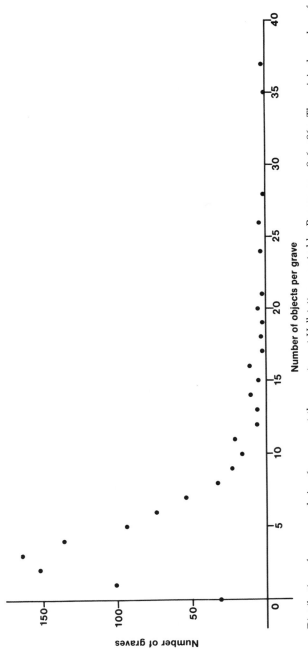

20. Distribution of grave goods in 962 graves at the cemetery at Hallstatt, excavated by Ramsauer, 1846–1864. The original number of objects was surely much larger; Ramsauer did not save most of the pottery he found, and many of the graves had been disturbed before excavation.

salt extraction became a major industry for the first time. Salt had two principal uses: as a condiment to enhance the flavor of foods and as a preservative for meat and fish. The beginning of large-scale extraction and trade of salt at Hallstatt and at other locations, such as the Moselle region of eastern France and along the Saale River in East Germany, suggests that much more salt was being used than before. And this increased use had a major impact on commerce. First, more non–food producers living in places removed from agricultural lands—for example, salt miners at Hallstatt and copper miners in the Tirol—could be sustained with supplies of preserved meat. Travel by merchants may also have been facilitated by the availability of more preserved foodstuffs, especially in winter and early spring when fresh foods were not available. Second, farming communities with access to salt could preserve meats and fish during the summer and fall for consumption during the lean seasons. Thus the possibility of nutritional deficiency and starvation during late winter was reduced. As a result the whole agricultural system became more secure, and farmers could devote more of their energies to producing surpluses for trade. Agricultural and crafts surpluses stimulated commercial enterprises such as salt production at Hallstatt, copper mining in the Alps, and iron smelting in the Alpine foothills (discussed below).

Hallstatt salt was traded mainly to communities in Upper Austria and southern Bavaria, but more distant trade contacts are indicated by the foreign imports. Boats were used to carry salt across Lake Hallstatt and down the Traun River to the lands north of the Alps, and packhorses bearing saddlebags transported salt over the mountains. The purpose of precapitalist commerce was usually to obtain specific desired imports rather than to dispose of exports for profit, as in modern capitalist societies. Hence merchants based at Hallstatt probably carried salt to places where they could exchange it for food, clothing, bronze and iron tools and weapons, and the wide range of ornaments represented in the burials.

We can easily imagine why, once commercial salt production at Hallstatt began, it grew. What is less obvious is how it got started in the first place. In experiments with replicas of the picks used at Hallstatt, Othmar Schauberger, a geological engineer in Upper Austria, found that it would have taken about twenty-eight days for two miners to cut through one meter of rock salt. The salt deposits at Hallstatt are overlaid with thick layers of weathered salt and sedimentary debris, and this material had to be tunneled through before miners reached the pure mineral. Three to five years of mining were probably required to penetrate this outer zone. Hence in the early stages at Hallstatt some other supply of wealth must have been tapped to provide the miners with food, equipment, and recompense before any commercially valuable salt was extracted.

Hallstatt is just 40 kilometers east of the extensive late Bronze Age copper mines at Bischofshofen; and, as mentioned above, copper mining techniques were initially used at Hallstatt: apparently, the first salt miners of Hallstatt had been copper miners before. The concentration of metal hoards in the river valleys north of the copper mines at Bischofshofen—the Isar, the Inn, and the Salzach—indicates that individuals or communities along the major trade routes leading away from the copper sources were wealthy. Such riches in the form of bronze metal—first available in great quantity about the beginning of the last millennium B.C.— may have been what enabled entrepreneurs to finance the initial stages of salt production at Hallstatt, thereby catalyzing the expansion of an industrial community soon to become one of Europe's first commercial towns.

STIČNA

New communities larger than any earlier ones also developed during the eighth and seventh centuries B.C. across the eastern Alps from Hallstatt in Slovenia, the northernmost and westernmost republic of Yugoslavia. The best-documented site there is Stična, and other communities at Magdalenska gora, Most na Soči, Novo mesto, Šmarjeta, and Vače were similar. All of these were hilltop settlements fortified with walls. Cemeteries with at least six thousand graves at Stična and seven thousand at Most na Soči suggest that some of these communities had more than five hundred members. Little excavation has been carried out on the settlements—Most na Soči is currently under investigation, and some work was done at Stična in the late 1960s. Our information about these sites comes mainly from the cemeteries.

In contrast to Hallstatt, where the mountainous environment offered little besides salt, Slovenia has a fertile and hospitable landscape that has been occupied continuously since the early Stone Age. Numerous late Bronze Age cemeteries, such as Dobova, Pobrežje, and Ruše, and many rich hoards demonstrate the wealth of local communities around 1000 B.C. As was the case at Hallstatt, these fortified hilltop settlements were established during the eighth century B.C. for a specific commercial reason—the exploitation of high-grade iron ores, hematite and limonite, that occured in rich surface sedimentary deposits (Figure 21). Slovenia has been an important east Alpine iron source since 800 B.C., and its central role in the development of early iron metallurgy and of commerce is reflected in the well-equipped burials (Figure 22). Its significance in the Roman period is recorded in ancient literary sources, and it has remained a major iron production center into the twentieth century.

The Cemetery

Stična, situated in the foothills of the Alps 30 kilometers east-southeast of Ljubljana, is the largest of the hill forts (Figure 23). The settlement, enclosed by earth-and-stone walls, measures about 800 by 400 meters and is located on a low, flat-topped hill. About 140 burial mounds, or tumuli, are still visible in the valley around the hill fort (Figure 24). Although only limited excavations

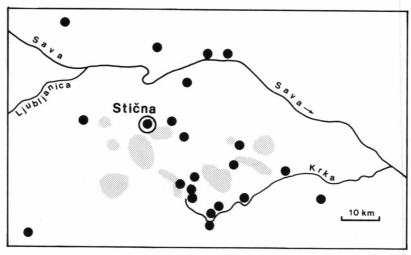

21. Schematic map showing density of surface iron ore deposits and evidence for prehistoric iron production in Slovenia. Stippled areas are sedimentary deposits containing iron ores. Black circles are prehistoric iron-smelting sites. The site of Stična is labeled. Based on Müllner 1908:53.

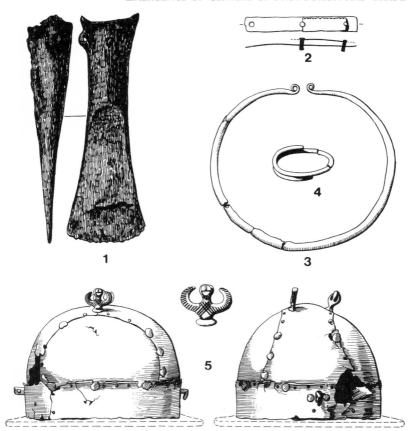

22. Objects from Magdalenska gora Grave 3 in Tumulus IV excavated by the Duchess of Mecklenburg. These objects are probably from the seventh century B.C. They are: (1) an iron axe; (2) fragmentary belt plate; (3) a neckring; (4) small ring; (5) a sheet bronze helmet with ornate winged figure.

have been carried out on the settlement, the graves have been explored. In the years between 1905 and 1911 the Duchess of Mecklenburg directed the excavation of eleven mounds containing 186 graves. Excavations carried out between 1946 and 1964 by Jose Kastelic and Stane Gabrovec on the largest mound, which was 60 meters in diameter and 6 meters high, yielded 183 graves along with detailed information about the structure of the burial site. Other graves that were opened unsystematically have also produced important goods.

As at Hallstatt, at Stična the graves provide information about

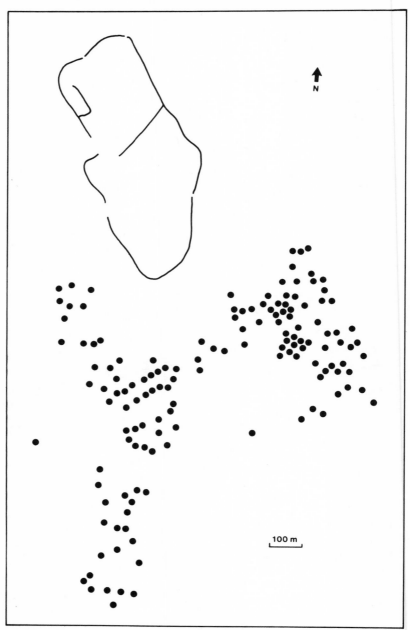

23. Plan of the site of Stična in Slovenia, showing the course of the walls around the hilltop settlement (*upper left*) and the burial mounds (black circles) still visible.

24. A typical burial mound of the early Iron Age, Tumulus VII at Stična. The excavators on the left side of the mound and the buildings to the right provide scale.

the commercial organization of the community and about its wealth. Since Stična was situated in an agriculturally productive area, its populace was not dependent on importation of food, as the community at Hallstatt was. At Stična farmers lived side by side with merchants and metalworkers. Yet Stična was also a center of trade like Hallstatt. Great quantities of amber beads from the Baltic Sea coast have been found at Stična; about one-third of all burials contain them, frequently more than 100 grams of amber in a grave. Bronze was abundant in the form of jewelry and luxury items such as vessels and helmets, indicating large-scale importation of metals from copper and tin mines to the north. Numerous luxury imports from Italy, particularly bronze and ceramic vessels to hold liquids, are represented. Finds in the graves also demonstrate the presence at Stična of major local industries, including iron production (weapons, tools, ornaments), bronze casting and hammering (jewelry, vessels, defensive weapons), and manufacture of glass beads and vessels. Figure 25 shows objects uncovered from graves in Slovenia which indicate the kinds of manufacturing occurring at this time.

Distribution of wealth in the graves at Stična is similar to that found at Hallstatt. The average quantity of grave goods at Hallstatt is larger, however, probably reflecting the involvement of nearly all individuals in salt production for commerce, whereas at Stična most people were farmers, and only a small proportion of the populace was engaged primarily in commercial industries. The richer graves at Stična, like those at Hallstatt, contained weapons, bronze vessels, and numerous personal ornaments.

Emergence as a Commercial Center

Stična's development as a commercial town resulted from its production and trade of iron. Small iron objects were common during the latter half of the late Bronze Age (1000–800 B.C.). Bronze pins, rings, and weapons were often inlaid with iron for decoration during this period, and iron knife blades (in bronze handles), iron ring jewelry, and iron awls were often found in graves and settlement deposits of the tenth and ninth centuries B.C. After 800 B.C. iron objects were placed in graves much more frequently, and for the first time larger objects such as spearheads, axes, and swords were made of iron. The principal advantage of iron over bronze was the commonness throughout central Europe of iron ores; in

[94]

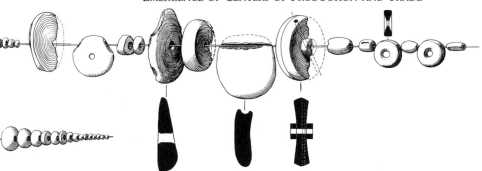

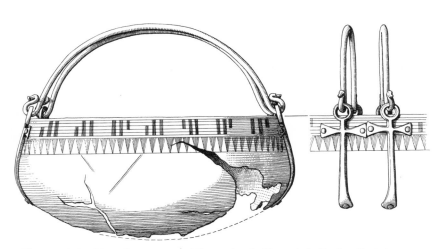

25. Characteristic objects from graves at the centers in Slovenia indicating the intensive commerce and manufacturing activities during the early Iron Age: (*top*) amber beads, (*center*) glass beads, (*bottom*) kettle of sheet bronze.

contrast, the ores of copper and tin were much more limited in distribution. Once they learned the techniques of smelting and forging iron, many communities took advantage of the vast quantities of metal in their own territories. Iron was particularly important during the early Iron Age for weapons (swords, spearheads, battle-axes, arrowheads) and for tools (axes, knives, hammers, chisels, gouges, awls). The many tools that became available with the expansion of iron metallurgy played an important role in the general intensification of production that developed in early Iron Age Europe.

Communities in Slovenia were quick to exploit the rich iron ore that occurred locally in surface deposits. Stična and the other hill forts were established at the same time that iron objects became much more common in the graves of the region. Huge deposits of iron slag have been found on many of the hill forts, including Stična, and slag has been found in graves at Magdalenska gora, Toplice, and Vače. Unfortunately, we have little direct evidence of workshops in which iron was smelted and forged because of the lack of large-scale settlement excavations. The only well-documented iron workshop in central Europe from the early Iron Age is at the Waschenberg in Upper Austria, a very small village in which iron smelting and forging were carried out on a modest scale. Although Slovenia was well endowed with iron ore, some nearby regions, particularly the lowland Adriatic lands of northeast Italy, were not. At the large cemetery at Este, about 60 kilometers southwest of Venice, iron objects became common during the eighth century B.C. There are no major local sources of iron ore in the vicinity of Este, and it is likely that the iron objects were imported from commercial centers in Slovenia such as Stična.

The growth and wealth of Stična and the other early towns of the area were based principally on their commercial production of iron, but the trade of other goods came to play a part as well. Amber from northern Europe was transshipped at the commercial centers and carried on to northern Italy. The Greek geographer Strabo, writing at the time of the birth of Christ, listed as trade goods from Slovenia to northeast Italy iron, slaves, cattle, hides, resin, pitch, wax, honey, cheese, and gold. Jaroslav Šašel (1977) argues persuasively that Strabo's discussion refers specifically to the early Iron Age.

Wine was probably the main import into Slovenia from Italy, as Strabo informs us; olive oil and other Mediterranean foodstuffs were also traded. Luxury objects from Italy have been found in many graves at Stična and elsewhere in Slovenia—for example, ceramic oinochoes (jugs) and kraters (two-handled vessels used for mixing beverages), bronze figurines, and an Etruscan bronze tripod at Novo mesto. Imports from the east Mediterranean region, including a polychrome glass bottle from Egypt and an ornate bronze bowl from the Levant, both recovered in graves at Stična, probably arrived by way of Italy. Further evidence for interactions between communities in Slovenia and Italy is the common production in the two regions of numerous very similar objects, including fibulae, pins, and pottery. Slovenia and northeast Italy also shared in the development of situla art, a special artistic tradition in which scenes of festivals and games were portrayed on sheet bronze buckets and belt ornaments. The trade in iron was an important component of these contacts. The communities at Stična and other sites in Slovenia also traded with the Hallstatt salt miners, as is demonstrated by numerous iron objects, bronze ornaments, and glass beads of southeast Alpine origin found in the Hallstatt graves.

SPECIALIZED PRODUCTION AND THE FORMATION OF TOWNS

These earliest commercial towns of Europe north of the Mediterranean all emerged at about the same time and under similar circumstances, although the substances in which each community specialized were different. An experimental stage of production can be demonstrated at both of the two major locations—in the earliest salt mining done between 1000 and 800 B.C. at Hallstatt, before the establishment of the permanent community there, and in the production of small numbers of minor iron items in Slovenia during those two centuries. The expansion of the industries after the first experiments depended on the changing economic conditions of the late Bronze Age.

The growth of Hallstatt and Stična was directly dependent upon the extensive trade systems that were established throughout central Europe during the late Bronze Age, when large amounts of metal as well as luxuries such as amber and glass beads were circulating widely. The even greater quantities of trade goods found at early Iron Age sites indicate that trade had continued to expand. The growth of the towns also depended on the ability of agrarian communities to produce goods for exchange. The increased agricultural efficiency documented during the late Bronze

Age enabled farmers to generate more surpluses for trade. At the same time, the expansion of commercial systems stimulated farmers to produce such surpluses because more attractive exchange goods became available. Improved agriculture also meant that more people who were not farmers—miners, metalworkers, and merchants, for example—could be supported. These changes were mutually reinforcing and also contributed to the overall intensification of trade and production that occurred during the early Iron Age.

The commercial enterprises were begun by individuals who perceived the possibilities of gain in the industrial production of salt and iron and who had at their disposal the wealth with which to finance the initial stages of extraction. These entrepreneurs were motivated by the desire to acquire additional wealth in the form of the wide range of luxury goods then in circulation—such fine bronze objects as ornate cauldrons and helmets, gold jewelry, and ornaments of amber, glass, and ivory—as well as the security, status, and power that accompany wealth. They were able to enlist the services of miners by promises of material gain through trade. Many historical and ethnographic examples demonstrate such beginnings to commercial ventures: during the Industrial Revolution, for instance, many people left the drudgery and loneliness of farm life for growing commercial centers where they could earn cash (which made accessible some of the luxuries of the time) in exchange for their labor.

The success of the early mining at Hallstatt led to rapid growth of the community. When the population reached between two hundred and four hundred, the town stopped growing. The main limiting factor may have been the difficulty of supplying the community with food and equipment, all of which had to be transported in by boat and then up to the mountain valley by packhorse or human power. All of the tasks involved in salt extraction—mining in the galleries, felling and shaping timber for supports, and processing mined salt for trade—required special skills developed through experience. Significantly, there are no groups of very poorly equipped burials in the Hallstatt cemetery that might be those of exploited laborers. Rather, the distribution of grave goods implies that the work was profitable for everyone engaged in the venture.

Similarly, at Stična some individual must have realized the commercial potential of iron and induced metalworkers to produce more of it. As production grew, more specialists had to be supplied with food, tools, and recompense for their efforts. Farmers could have been attracted to the growing commercial centers by the material wealth available, some of which was distributed to them in exchange for food and other farm products. The growth of the town depended on the willingness of people—specialist metalworkers and farmers—to work harder in order to generate surpluses for exchange. The more intensive production aimed at trade led to the growth of the larger communities.

OTHER PARTS OF EUROPE

Hallstatt and Stična represent special developments in early Iron Age Europe and were not typical. The vast majority of communities remained agrarian, similar to those described in chapter 2, though they were increasingly affected by the commercial changes originating in the new centers. More luxury goods became available, and communities were stimulated to produce greater surpluses in order to acquire them. A small series of richly outfitted graves equipped with swords, helmets, cuirasses, and bronze vessels was found at Kleinklein in the Sulm Valley of Steiermark, Austria, dating to the time of the beginning of iron production there. In that region iron metallurgy did not lead to the formation of larger communities but only to the enrichment of a few individuals. The rich graves of the Bylaný group of burials in Bohemia are also connected to early iron production, again without the associated formation of towns. Similar graves were found at Grosseibstadt in Bavaria. Special burials at Nové Košariská in Slovakia are noteworthy for their enormous numbers of ceramic vessels (up to 80) and elaborate burial chambers, but they do not contain either weapons or bronze luxury items and are associated exclusively with small settlements. The existence of groups of richer-than-average graves at these locations suggests that some persons elsewhere in Europe were reaping the material benefits of intensified production and commerce, but at these small settlements the commercial development was not great enough to stimulate the growth of towns.

The cemetery of a copper mining community of this period has been investigated at Uttendorf on the northern edge of the Austrian Alps about 100 kilometers west of Hallstatt. By 1977 forty-five graves had been discovered, and Fritz Moosleitner suggests there may be several times that many. Even at the greatest size hypothesized by the excavator, the cemetery would not represent a community larger than fifty persons. Unlike Hallstatt and Stična, none of the graves is exceptionally rich, though the burials are accompanied by bronze, iron, and pottery grave goods. Although the pottery indicates close connections with communities in the lands to the north, southern Bavaria in particular, the bronze objects are characteristic of southern and southeast Alpine areas. We can thus surmise that Uttendorf was supplying commercial centers such as Stična with copper. The evidence from Uttendorf is important because it shows that not all specialized mining sites developed into wealthy commercial towns in the way Hallstatt did.

Throughout most of Europe settlements were small, and there was little specialized industrial production or accumulation of wealth. In the Netherlands, for example, a detailed study by P. B. Kooi (1979) has shown that settlements took the form of scattered farms, each occupied by a single family. Throughout the Northern European Plain there were no larger communities, and the evidence indicates that there was little differentiation in burial wealth. Similarly, in western central Europe, cemeteries at Haguenau in Alsace and Zainingen in Württemberg show little differentiation among graves and represent small agrarian communities carrying on limited metalworking and trade (Figure 26). There are the occasional noteworthy graves more lavishly equipped than most—at Gomadingen in Württemberg, for example—but they do not compare with the richer burials at Hallstatt and Stična. The only communities comparable to the trading towns of the east Alpine region were forming on the fringes of the Mediterranean Sea.

Across the Alps in the Po Plain of northern Italy large towns were developing at Bologna and Este much like those at Hallstatt and Stična. These northern Italian towns also owed their existence to expanding commercial systems and new industries to sustain

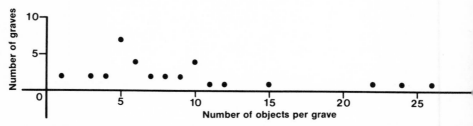

26. Distribution of grave goods in the thirty-three graves of the cemetery at Zainingen, Baden-Wü berg, West Germany.

them. During the sixth century B.C. these and other commercial centers around the Mediterranean played a special role in the development of new towns in other regions north of the Alps. A new commercial interest enters the central European sphere then—the demand by Greek cities for raw materials to sustain their expanding populations and industries.

4 Growth of Commercial Centers (600–400 B.C.)

New trading towns grew up during the sixth century B.C. in a region several hundred kilometers west of Hallstatt between the upper Seine and upper Danube rivers. The formation of these commercial centers in western central Europe was in no sense *caused* by the formation of the earlier towns to the east, but was the result of similar economic circumstances. These included the availability of stores of disposable wealth, increased agricultural efficiency permitting production of larger surpluses, active trade networks, and individual initiative to work for personal gain. During the sixth century B.C. an important new economic element entered the picture—the quest of Mediterranean societies for natural products of forested Europe.

TRADE WITH THE GREEKS

From the Neolithic period on we have clear evidence for trade across the Alps between central Europe and the Mediterranean—for example, in the *Spondylus* shells frequently found in Neolithic graves. Metal ornaments were carried between northern Italy and central Europe throughout the Bronze Age, and in the late Bronze Age many similar objects, including bronze tools and jewelry and glass beads, were found both north and south of the Alps. The bronze cup, sieve, and pail—a set of vessels used for drinking wine south of the Alps—found in the rich grave at Hart an der Alz in Upper Bavaria suggest that wine may have been imported into central Europe from Mediterranean lands as early as 1200 B.C. Beginning around 600 B.C. a variety of luxury goods originating in the

27. Principal sites mentioned in Chapter 4.

Mediterranean region appeared in central Europe, indicating a change in the commerce between north and south.

Between 800 and 500 B.C. cities of mainland Greece and Ionia established dozens of new colonies on the shores of the Mediterranean, Adriatic, and Black seas. The overarching cause behind this expansion was population growth and strain on available resources in the urban centers of the Greek homeland. Some colonies were established as new homes for Greeks as a result of overpopulation of the cities in the motherland. Some colonies, particularly in southern Italy and Sicily, were founded to produce wheat for shipment back to the Greek urban centers. Others were established for trade, in order to secure needed raw materials, particularly metals, for Greek crafts industries.

During these three centuries of colonization, Greek settlers, sailors, and merchants came into contact with many different peoples on the north coast of Africa, the southern coast of Europe, and the shores of the Black Sea. Greek trade with central Europe, which will be treated here, was typical of the commercial interactions between Greeks and other peoples as well.

About 600 B.C. Ionian Greeks from the city of Phocaea in Asia Minor established the colony of Massalia (modern Marseille) on the Mediterranean coast close to the mouth of the Rhône River. Massalia was founded specifically to handle trade between the areas producing raw materials in the interior of the continent and in Iberia and the eastern Mediterranean urban centers in need of those materials. The Rhône is the longest river flowing from the interior of Europe into the Mediterranean Sea, and it provided a convenient corridor for travel and transport. Shortly after 600 B.C. Greek and Etruscan luxury imports began to arrive in central Europe. The commerce intensified over time, reaching its peak of activity around 500 B.C.

The best represented import is fine pottery from Attica in Greece. Sherds of Attic pottery (Figure 28) have been recovered in the settlement deposits at several central European sites, such as the Heuneburg, Mont Lassois, Château-sur-Salins, the Britzgyberg, Châtillon-sur-Glâne, the Ipf, the Marienberg at Würzburg, and Zürich-Üetliberg. Two complete Attic cups were found in the Vix grave at the foot of Mont Lassois and two in the grave of Kleinaspergle near the Hohenasperg. Greek ceramic amphorae used to transport wine have been recovered at many of the same settlements and in several graves. Attic painted pottery and wine amphorae were everyday items among well-to-do Greeks and were

28. Sherds of Attic pottery recovered at the Heuneburg.

common objects of trade. Nearly all peoples with whom Greeks came into contact were eager to acquire wine and the Attic pottery used for serving and drinking it.

Bronze vessels from Mediterranean workshops were also traded to central Europe. Some types were relatively common in the Greek world, such as the trefoil-mouth jugs found in the graves at Kappel in the Rhine valley and Vilsingen just west of the Heuneburg, but most were exceptional and even unique products of Greek bronze-working skill. Most spectacular was the bronze krater from the grave at Vix, standing 1.64 meters high and weighing 208 kilograms, the largest metal vessel known from the ancient world and a product exhibiting extraordinary craftsmanship (Figure 29). The tripod and cauldron from La Garenne near Vix, and, from near the Hohenasperg, the cauldron from the grave at Hochdorf, and the Grafenbühl tripod are other unique products of Greek bronzesmithing skill. Other exceptional items of Greek manufacture include the silver and gold bowl and gold diadem from Vix and the pair of sphinxes carved from bone, ivory, and amber from Grafenbühl (Figure 30).

Luxury objects of Etruscan manufacture have also been found in

29. The Vix krater. This extraordinary vessel is made of sheet and cast bronze and stands 1.64 m high and weighs 208 kg. It was manufactured in a Greek workshop, probably in southern Italy.

30. Sphinx from the rich central burial in the tumulus at Grafenbühl. Carved of bone, it has an amber face and two gilded bronze rivets and stands 4.8 cm high. Like the Vix krater, this object was probably made in a Greek workshop in southern Italy.

central Europe. These include bronze jugs with beak-shaped spouts, bronze bowls, gold ball-shaped beads, and a ceramic mold for casting a bronze Silenus head found at the Heuneburg. There is some debate among classical archaeologists as to which objects were made by Greeks and which by Etruscans. Since crafts workers were often highly mobile, they shared ideas and techniques and frequently worked in foreign lands. In any case, Greek merchants were dealing in Etruscan products as well as in Greek ones. Silk cloth from Grave 6 in the Hohmichele tumulus at the Heuneburg and coral ornaments found at many different settlements also were brought to central Europe from the shores of the Mediterranean.

Amidst the Greek and Etruscan luxury imports north of the Alps one is struck by the absence of everyday objects common in the Mediterranean cultures. No Greek coins of this period have been recovered in central Europe. None of the many different kinds of bronze pins worn in Greece and Etruria has been found. Thus only selected objects were imported.

Other evidence besides imported goods attests to interaction between the central Europeans and the Greeks. The clay brick wall surrounding the Heuneburg is unique north of the Alps and demonstrates the application of specific technical knowledge from the Mediterranean world. It must have been built by a Greek architect or by a central European who had learned the technique in the South. The life-size stone statue carved of local north Württemberg sandstone which stood on top of the burial mound at Hirschlanden near Stuttgart is unique and shows strong influences of Mediterranean sculptors. The fast-turning potter's wheel and the domesticated chicken were also introduced into central Europe from the Mediterranean area at this time.

There is no archaeological evidence in the Greek cities for this trade with central Europe, but the reasons for this absence are clear. All of the literary evidence concerning trade indicates that Greeks were interested primarily in obtaining raw materials for Greek industries and consumption. The Greek historian Polybius, writing about trade north of the Black Sea (a region comparable in many respects to central Europe) lists as products imported by the Greeks grain, timber, fish, salt, hides, slaves, gold, amber, wax, pitch, resin, and honey (4 38. 1–5). Several centuries later Romans were importing quantities of salted pork and woolen fabrics from central Europe (Strabo 4.3.2.; 4.4.3). Such materials were probably the main trade products sought by the Greeks.

THE HEUNEBURG AND OTHER TOWNS

A few communities in western central Europe actively involved in the Greek trade developed into major centers of production and commerce. Only the Heuneburg has been extensively investigated so far.

The Heuneburg is situated on a spur of land at the eastern edge of the Schwäbische Alb on the west bank of the upper Danube in southern Württemberg (Figure 31). The roughly triangular surface measures about 250 by 150 meters in its greatest dimensions, and the surface area is about 3.2 hectares (roughly 10 acres). Since 1950,

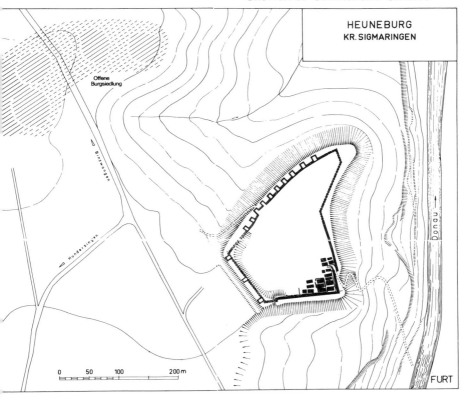

31. Plan of the Heuneburg showing the fully excavated southeast corner.

excavators have investigated a substantial portion of the southern third of the site.

The southeast corner has yielded remains of post-built, timber-frame structures ranging in size from about 25 to 90 square meters, closely packed in an arrangement not unlike that of medieval towns (Figures 32 and 33). Plans of seventeen structures have been published, fifteen with postholes along the walls and two with timber frames as foundations. A hypothetical model of the settlement includes about seventy additional buildings besides these seventeen. Of course, only complete excavation will show the true extent and character of the built-up area, but the model indicates the excavators' impressions of the settlement. If all of the buildings were dwellings (unlikely since the size and materials found inside vary) and if all were occupied simultaneously (unlikely over the 150-year history of the site), then the population might have been

[109]

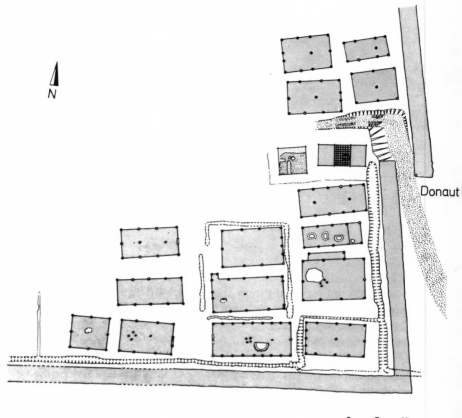

Donaut

0   5   10m

32. Detailed plan of the structures in the southeast corner of the Heuneburg, showing rec
tangular building foundations, interior hearths, drainage ditches, and the gate on the side
overlooking the Danube River ("Donautor").

around 450. If instead we assume that a third of the buildings
served some purpose other than dwelling and that only half of the
structures were occupied at one time, then the population might
have been between one hundred and two hundred, a much more
reasonable guess.

About 400 meters northwest of the Heuneburg, underneath four
large burial mounds, another settlement was discovered, with
wood-frame buildings, fences, drainage ditches, and traces of
crafts such as weaving and bronze casting. This outer settlement
was founded at about the same time as the Heuneburg (around 600

33. Artist's reconstruction of the buildings in the southeast corner of the Heuneburg.

B.C.) and ended shortly after 550 B.C. Thus for the first half of the occupation of the Heuneburg, a contemporaneous settlement existed a few hundred meters away. The southeast corner of the Heuneburg was densely built up for a century or longer. When the outer settlement was abandoned, the land was used for burial of residents of the Heuneburg.

The Heuneburg is distinct from other settlements in its region in the density of debris from various occupations and in the evidence for long-distance trade and manufacturing. Every part of the settlement investigated has yielded such remains, in contrast to the much sparser cultural materials from other sites.

The site is also special in the quantity of luxury imports in the settlement deposits and in the graves around the settlement. About one hundred sherds of Attic pottery have already been recovered, most dating from 540 to 480 B.C. They came from a wide range of vessels used for serving and drinking wine, including kraters (for mixing wine with water and spices), jugs (for pouring), and cups. Fragments of ceramic amphorae in which Greek merchants transported wine have also been found, and they match amphorae at the port of Massalia. Coral was brought from the

[111]

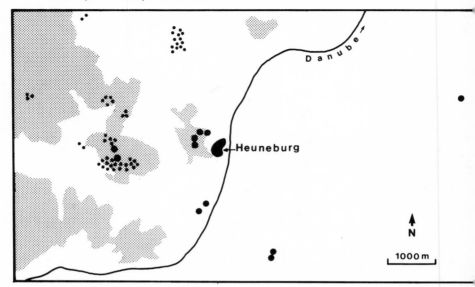

34. The Heuneburg and vicinity. Exceptionally large burial mounds are represented by large b
dots, smaller mounds by smaller dots. Land more than 600 m above sea level is indicated
stippling. Based on Kimmig 1968, inside front cover.

Mediterranean to the Heuneburg for use as jewelry. A partly
worked coral branch attests to production at the Heuneburg of
beads and inlay for bronze jewelry. The mold for casting a bronze
head raises more complex questions. Was an Etruscan bronze
caster working at the Heuneburg? Were local metalworkers using
Etruscan-made molds to cast attachments for vessels? Amber from
the Baltic shores of northern Europe, glass beads from the southeast Alpine area, and bronze jewelry from different parts of the
continent attest to trade with other lands, but the commerce with
Greeks in the Mediterranean was most important for the development of the town.

Exceptionally rich burials are associated with the Heuneburg.
About seventy burial mounds are known around the site, surely
only a small fraction of the original number, most of which have
been obliterated by plowing (Figure 34). Eleven mounds are unusually large. One was converted into a fortress during medieval
times! These huge tumuli held wealthy graves complete with burial
chambers of hewn oak planks and such sumptuous grave goods as
four-wheeled wagons, gold necklaces and bracelets, bronze ket-
tles, and ornate iron daggers with bronze sheaths, as well as the
usual bronze jewelry, iron tools, glass beads, and pottery.

[112]

LUXURY TRADE, SURPLUS PRODUCTION, AND THE EMERGENCE OF TOWNS

By the time the colony of Massalia was established in 600 B.C., trade between Mediterranean merchants and indigenous peoples of southern Gaul had been going on for several decades. Greek and east Mediterranean pottery predating Massalia has been found on a number of sites in the region. Hence communities in southern France already knew of foreign merchants trading along their coasts, and the Greeks who established Massalia were aware of trade possibilities there. There was always contact between communities on the Mediterranean coast of France and the interior areas of the continent, and direct connections between Massalia and central Europe did not take long to form. Greek traders rarely traveled inland, and so it is likely that central Europeans went to Massalia or maintained relations through intermediaries along the Rhône valley. The initial establishment of trade relations was probably carried out through exchange of gifts, the tangible results of which we see in the Greek bronze vessels in the graves at Kappel, Vilsingen, Kastenwald, and Grächwil, all dating to the first half of the sixth century B.C.

The forests and rich agricultural lands of central Europe offered in abundance the resources sought by east Mediterranean cities. Greek merchants could offer attractive luxury goods in exchange, particularly wine, bronze vessels, and painted pottery. The motivating force in the establishment and growth of these trade relations was the desire on the part of central Europeans to acquire Mediterranean luxuries. Compared to the indigenous central European material culture, the vessels and ornaments available from Greek traders were sophisticated and exotic; possessing them was a fine way for central Europeans to show off to their compatriots. Wine had its own special charms for those who could get it.

Enterprising central Europeans—perhaps persons already in leadership roles, perhaps others—encouraged their fellows to produce surplus goods for trade. Ethnographic studies show that without specific incentives and leadership, peasant communities generally do not produce surpluses. With the strong subsistence base and already developed systems of crafts production and regional trade, surplus production would not have been difficult if communities were motivated by the prospect of return goods. Producers may have been rewarded directly with imported luxuries or indirectly with feasts and gifts of local origin.

[113]

The entrepreneurs who organized the trade benefited from the exotic luxury items and from the heightened status that accompanied the possession and distribution of such luxury wealth. Some of the imports were handed out to those producing trade goods for them. Why some individuals were successful at mobilizing their communities to produce greater surpluses for trade while others were not is a matter of personality and ability. Persons from other communities were attracted by the wealth at the growing centers, and some moved to them to share in the production for trade and in the rewards. More producers meant larger surpluses, more imports, and greater populations. The Heuneburg exemplifies the results of such growth.

As the volume of trade expanded, the entrepreneurs managing the trade and its attendant production became more important to the Greek merchants. Special custom-made luxury articles produced in the latter half of the sixth century B.C. in Greek workshops, such as the Vix krater and the Grafenbühl sphinxes, attest to the Greeks' strong interest in keeping the central European trade going. The presence on the upper Seine of the Vix krater, an enormous object of exceptional Greek workmanship, has been interpreted as indicating that Greek relations with the community at Mont Lassois were of special importance to Greek merchants. The great krater has generally been viewed as a political gift, following statements by Herodotus about similar objects presented by Greeks to potentates in other parts of the ancient world. It is possible, however, that the krater was commissioned by a wealthy central European entrepreneur who wanted an extravagant foreign vessel commensurate in size and ornamentation with his or her self-esteem.

The new emphasis on production of goods for trade led to reorganization of local economies. Specialized industries were developed to generate products far in excess of local needs, as in the earlier instance of salt mining at Hallstatt and iron production at the centers in Slovenia. Depending on what products were most important in the Greek trade—and we can only guess which were—this higher level of production may have been carried out at centers such as the Heuneburg or at smaller production sites where the natural resources were found.

The cultural impact of this change in economic orientation is most apparent in the formation of the commercial towns. As commerce in western central Europe intensified, the character of its settlements changed. Before 600 B.C., the landscape was dotted with small agricultural communities—farmsteads and very small villages—all roughly similar in economic activity. As trade grew between 600 and 480 B.C., a few large commercial and industrial centers such as the Heuneburg came to dominate the landscape, producing for the smaller communities some goods (bronze tools and ornaments, perhaps iron tools) that those smaller communities had previously made themselves. The existence of these commercial towns was dependent solely on southward trade. After Greek demand for central European goods dropped around 480 B.C., these towns dwindled in size and were abandoned. At about that time the Po Valley of northern Italy became a source for the goods sought by Greek traders. Once the Greek luxuries were no longer traded north of the Alps, the persons who had been producing surpluses for trade lost their incentive to do extra work. Communities reverted to producing only enough for their own consumption and limited trade.

Greeks had no other interest in central Europe beyond acquisition of materials through trade. They made no attempt to gain political and economic control over continental Europe as the Romans did five centuries later. Nor did the Greeks in any sense bring about the formation of the commercial towns. Rather, this development resulted from the efforts of the central Europeans to produce more tradable goods so that they could acquire the Mediterranean luxuries.

Although trade with the Greeks brought about very important cultural changes in central Europe during the sixth century B.C., this commerce may not have been very significant economically to Greece. The number of Greek imports in central Europe is not large. The several hundred sherds of Attic pottery recovered at the Heuneburg and at Mont Lassois represent only a small fraction of the pottery from the Etruscan city of Vulci in central Italy, for example, where nearly a thousand complete vessels of black-figure Attic ware were found.

With few exceptions, evidence north of the Alps for trade with Greeks is confined to the area of western central Europe discussed here. Very few Mediterranean imports have been found outside this region, and commercial towns developed only here. The exceptionally rich graves occurred principally in this area, as did special crafts products such as gold neckrings. Elsewhere north of the Alps, settlement patterns, economic organization, and distribution of wealth were similar to those of around 1000 B.C.

Some investigators have suggested that the Heuneburg and similar sites were political centers of their regions. It is unlikely that this was the case, at least following accepted modern definitions of the word *political*. The Heuneburg was a focus of economic activity for at most 150 years. Only for half that time were exceptionally rich graves associated with the site and were Greek imports arriving regularly. The evidence points to rapid development of a trade center and an equally rapid demise within an area of small, segmentary communities. The community at the Heuneburg was tied to smaller sites through networks of regional trade within the great system of surplus production for trade with the Mediterranean societies. But there is no evidence to suggest that sites like the Heuneburg fulfilled the role of political centers in the sense that Near Eastern cities or Mycenaean towns like Mycenae, Pylos, and Knossos did. The Heuneburg has yielded no trace of large-scale storage facilities, administrative buildings, religious structures, or any form of palaces. No evidence of writing has been uncovered to suggest the record keeping associated with political capitals. To judge by the evidence of manufacturing and trade at the Heuneburg and the distribution of locally made and imported objects in its hinterlands, the relations between larger commercial communities and small hamlets were purely economic.

CHANGING PATTERNS THROUGHOUT EUROPE

Elsewhere in Europe less dramatic changes were taking place with the general increase in trade, continued development of iron metallurgy, and increasing complexity of society.

Settlements

The principal settlement forms throughout Europe remained the farmstead and hamlet, though in some regions besides Slovenia and western central Europe economically specialized and sometimes larger communities developed. A very prosperous, though small, community of copper miners and traders is represented by a cemetery of fifty-six graves at Welzelach in the Alps of the Austrian Tirol. The population of the community was fewer than twenty, and there is no evidence for any economic activity other than mining, processing, and trading of copper metal. The graves show considerable wealth among these metal producers. On the Hellbrunnerberg, a hill 5 kilometers south of Salzburg, was a settle-

[116]

ment contemporaneous with the Heuneburg and also involved in long-distance commerce. No systematic excavations have been carried out on the settlement surface, but erosional deposits show a wide range of foreign products, especially from western central Europe and the northern coasts of the Adriatic Sea. The community at the Hellbrunnerberg may have played a major role in the development of salt trade from the newly begun mines on the Dürrnberg mountain.

Biskupin was a large settlement in Poland that has been exceptionally well preserved because of its situation in a bog. On the basis of the density of wooden structures on the settlement, the area of which is about 1.3 hectares, investigators have proposed population figures as high as 1,200. Such a number is certainly much too high. At Biskupin, as at Wasserburg Buchau, the extraordinary preservation of wooden buildings, many probably dating from different phases of occupation, is deceptive. Without an associated cemetery, a good population estimate cannot be made, but I think between fifty and two hundred is a reasonable guess (see also Piggott 1965:202). Rajewski (1959:96) notes that no storage pits were used at Biskupin because of the wet subsoil; hence it is likely that many of the structures were intended for food storage rather than for dwellings. None of the graves near Biskupin was especially richly outfitted, nor is there evidence for unusual trade or manufacturing. The crafts in evidence at Biskupin were domestic ones to satisfy the needs of the community.

In parts of eastern Europe fortified hilltop settlements housed communities in which trade and surplus production played a larger role, for example in the Kalenderberg area of southeastern Austria, at Smolenice in southwest Slovakia, at Závist in Bohemia, and at several sites in the Lausitz region of East Germany and Poland. These eastern European fortified hilltop settlements were frequently accompanied by cemeteries containing a few graves richer than most, but the differences in wealth were small compared to those at the towns of western central Europe. Wealthier graves were distinguished only by larger quantities of pottery, often of finer quality, as at Sopron-Burgstall in Hungary and Nové Košariská near Bratislava in Moravia. Differences in wealth were expressed in a local, traditional manner, not in exotic imports or new elite goods such as gold neckrings, daggers, and bronze vessels. Even the largest cemeteries, such as Szentes-Vekerzug with 192 graves, Tápiószele with 455, and Chotín with 476, reflect small communities with fewer than one hundred members.

Many of the fortified settlements in eastern Europe have been referred to in the literature as *Fürstensitze* (literally "princely residence") and compared to the commercial centers of western central Europe. The internal areas of some, such as Biskupin, Smolenice, and Závist, were densely built up, as at the Heuneburg. Many yielded evidence of manufacturing in iron, bronze, textiles, and pottery, as well as participation in some long-distance trade. None, however, shows the evidence for personal accumulation of wealth apparent in the rich graves at the trading towns in western central Europe. At the east European sites, tumuli vary in size, and the wealth of tumulus graves compared with that of flat graves suggests that individuals buried in tumuli had more status. In some cases, as at Sopron-Burgstall in western Hungary, wealthier graves were distinguished by the quantity and ornateness of their pottery. But at no other sites do we find the extraordinary burial wealth of the western central European centers.

South of the Alps in the Po Plain of northern Italy, Bologna grew to become the focus of economic activity. Its expansion was the result of increasing commerce stimulated by the foundation of the Greek port city of Spina at the mouth of the Po River around 520 B.C. At Bologna and Spina the cemeteries show patterns remarkably similar to those at the Heuneburg, Mont Lassois, and the Hohenasperg, with some extraordinarily rich graves containing much Greek painted pottery and many Etruscan bronze vessels.

Economy

There is no evidence to suggest a major change in subsistence patterns in Europe at this time. The same plants and animals formed the basis of the diet, and no great changes are apparent in the technology of agriculture. The tip of an iron plowshare found at Gussage All Saints in southern Britain may date to the fifth century B.C., and if so provides evidence of early adoption of iron for plow parts.

At the commercial centers of western central Europe specialized metalsmiths were producing both elite goods (gold jewelry, ornate daggers, bronze vessels) for the wealthy and everyday jewelry for the populace of the region. Aside from this special role of metalworkers at the commercial sites, the greatest changes in manufacturing were increases in iron production and the introduction of the fast-turning potter's wheel.

During the sixth and fifth centuries B.C. iron came into general use for the first time and replaced bronze as the principal material for tools and weapons, though bronze continued to be the most common material for jewelry, ornaments, and vessels. Several iron-working sites provide information about the context and scale of smelting and forging. At a small hilltop settlement on the Waschenberg near Wels in Upper Austria were found nine pits in which local iron ore was smelted and a workshop where the metal was forged. A smelting furnace was discovered at Hillesheim in the Rhineland-Palatinate. In both instances, iron was produced from its ore by very small communities. Because iron ore, unlike copper and tin, is widespread in Europe, virtually every community could produce its own metal implements once the techniques of smelting and forging became generally known. Hence specialized metal-producing and metal-trading communities did not play the same role that they did during the Bronze Age. Heavy iron hammers, tongs, anvils, chisels, and ingots from the Býčí Skála cave in Moravia are representative of the tools used by blacksmiths at the time.

The development of iron-working technology opened the way for improved efficiency in many areas of production. Once the technology—carburization of iron to form steel and heating and quenching to control hardness and brittleness—was understood, iron could yield a much sharper and harder cutting edge than bronze. The wide availability of surface iron ores meant that the quantities of metal accessible to communities for conversion to tools was much greater than before. As more iron tools were made, all kinds of production could be carried out more efficiently—house construction, building of wagons and ships, clearing of forested land, and crafts work in wood, bone, and amber.

The fast-turning potter's wheel came into use in Europe during this period, introduced from the Mediterranean world. This device made possible the more rapid manufacturing of pottery. Its impact on the central European economy was less than that of iron technology, and not until the end of the Iron Age were the full effects of this new machine realized.

Distribution of Wealth

Most cemeteries of this period show the typical Iron Age pattern of wealth distribution: most graves have few goods, a small number have many, and there are some in between. The rich burials at the commercial centers of western central Europe differed from others in three important respects.

First, they were distinguished by their location. The rich burials were situated at the center and bottom of exceptionally large burial mounds, with poorer graves arranged concentrically around them higher up in the tumulus. This situation made clear the primacy of the individual interred in the center relative to the lesser souls buried in circles around him or her. The tumuli which contained these wealthy graves often were very large. The Hohmichele tumulus at the Heuneburg was 13 meters high and 65 meters in diameter, that at the Magdalenenberg at the edge of the Black Forest nearly 100 meters in diameter. The Magdalenenberg, the most thoroughly excavated of these large mounds, contained 126 plain graves around the rich central burial (Figure 35). The complexity of the structures built for the rich graves is well illustrated by the recently excavated tumulus at Hochdorf near Stuttgart. That mound had a stone wall around the outside, a circular mound of earth underneath the tumulus, and an elaborate chamber built of alternating layers of split timbers and large stones. Nearly all of the rich graves contained rectangular burial chambers built of hewn oak planks.

Second, the rich graves at the commercial centers had many more, and more varied, objects in them than graves in most other parts of Europe. The graph illustrating numbers of grave goods in burials in the Grafenbühl tumulus demonstrates this point, even though the rich central burial was robbed during the Iron Age. Fibulae, bracelets, beads, and pottery are all considerably more numerous in the rich graves.

Third, the rich graves contained categories of objects that never occurred in plainer graves, particularly gold neckrings, gold bracelets, four-wheeled wagons, bronze vessels of foreign and local origin, and ornate daggers. Even though most of the rich graves were robbed within decades after burial (Hochdorf is an important exception), the grave goods that the robbers left behind still provide a picture of the extravagant material culture possessed by these individuals. Particularly striking are the unique objects such as the Vix krater and the bronze cauldron with reclining lions on its rim, gold fibulae, a gold-trimmed sheath, gold-covered shoes, and a bronze couch, all from Hochdorf, and an ivory lion's foot from a couch stolen from Grafenbühl. These extraordinary objects, most of them of Mediterranean origin, characterize the rich burials of western

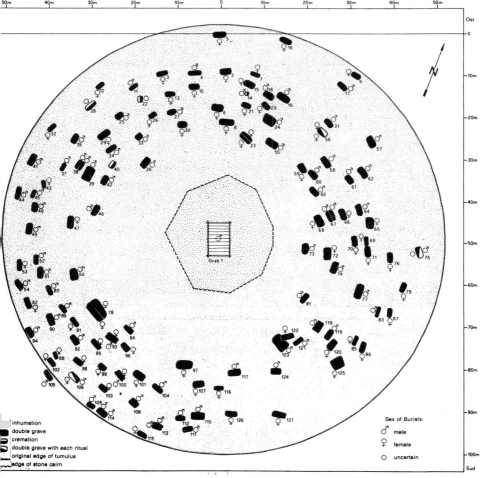

n of the tumulus of Magdalenenberg. The central burial was placed in a finely made wooden
r covered over with an enormous cairn of stones. The later graves were arranged concentrically
the central tomb.

central Europe and attest to a sumptuous lifestyle on the part of the
elite and to access to the most extravagant products of Mediterranean workshops.

The gold neckrings so characteristic of these rich burials are of
special importance because they provide a link between the new
towns and the rural countryside (Figure 36 and 37). These rings
occur in the richest graves at the centers, but also in less rich

[121]

36. A typical neckring of sheet gold, this one from rich grave 1 in the Römerhügel tumulus. Diameter, 23 cm.

burials. The rings are all similar, though not identical, and were probably made in one workshop or in a very limited number of workshops at the towns. They were symbols of status (suggested by the ring around the neck of the figure represented in the Hirschlanden statue as well as by their regular occurrence in the richest graves), probably worn on special occasions by persons of wealth and importance in the social hierarchy. The rings in the lesser graves may have been worn by local officials in the countryside who coordinated the rural production systems for the Mediterranean trade.

The well-established chronology of grave goods and objects from settlements in western central Europe enables us to trace the increasing wealth of the richest graves during the course of the sixth century B.C., to the growth of trade with the Greeks. The rich graves of the first half of that century, such as at Kappel and Vilsingen, contained gold ring jewelry, four-wheeled wagons, and rather plain imported bronze vessels. They did not contain imported luxuries of unusual character or large numbers of imports. The graves richest in local luxuries and foreign exotica date to the final quarter of the sixth century B.C.—the fabulously wealthy graves of Vix, Grafenbühl, and Hochdorf. The Attic pottery, Greek wine amphorae, and coral found in these graves show that this was also

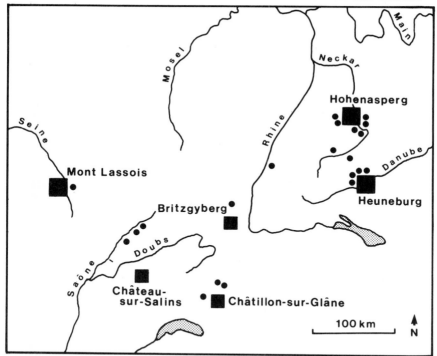

37. Distribution of sheet gold neckrings in western central Europe. Gold neckrings are represented by black circles. The three large black squares represent the principal commercial centers: the Heuneburg, the Hohenasperg, and Mont Lassois. The three smaller black squares represent commercial sites—the Britzgyberg, Château-sur-Salins, and Châtillon-sur-Glâne—that are thought to have been less significant.

the time of most intensive trade. In other parts of Europe such extremes of wealth were lacking.

During the fifth century B.C. another series of richly outfitted graves that shared many features of those of the sixth century B.C. towns appeared in the middle Rhineland, the Marne region of France, and Bohemia. These graves were also characterized by large tumuli, wooden burial chambers, gold ring jewelry, imported and local bronze vessels, weapons, and wheeled vehicles (now two-wheeled chariots instead of four-wheeled wagons). Yet there were important differences between these graves and their earlier counterparts. The later rich graves did not contain any extraordinary imports comparable to the Vix krater, the Hochdorf cauldron, or the exotic couches from Hochdorf and Grafenbühl. Nearly all

[123]

the imported vessels in the rich graves of the fifth century B.C. were everyday objects in Etruria, from which most such vessels came. Most significantly, the later rich graves were scattered quite evenly over the countryside, not concentrated at any particular centers. No centers of population, manufacturing, or commerce developed during this time, and so those rich graves are not of direct concern to this book.

INFLUENCE OF TOWNS OF THE SIXTH-CENTURY B.C.

The main function of the Heuneburg and the other centers of western central Europe was to coordinate the production of goods for trade with Greeks. The towns were not inhabited solely by specialists, however; farmers also resided in them. The Heuneburg was similar to the early medieval trading ports of northern Europe—Haithabu, Helgö, and Birka—in that all developed as centers of trade and of production for trade. In each case, the commercial centers declined rapidly when the long-distance trade was interrupted. At the early medieval entrepôts, as at the Heuneburg, there is no evidence that the commercial foci were political centers.

Though the interactions between central European communities and Greek traders led to a spectacular cultural blossoming for a time in western central Europe, the effect on later development of European society was minimal. There is no indication that any political ideas were transmitted from Greeks to central Europeans, nor that Mediterranean artistic or architectural themes were maintained in central Europe after the end of the commerce. Not until several centuries after the fast-turning potter's wheel was introduced did this device come into general use. Styles of ornamentation in temperate Europe changed as a result of familiarity with Mediterranean crafts, but the southern themes were transformed, not simply borrowed. In sum, the interactions with Mediterranean societies, specifically Greeks, during the sixth century B.C. had little lasting effect on cultural life in temperate Europe after the century or so during which the trade was carried on.

5 Raids and Migrations into Southern Europe (400–200 B.C.)

During the fourth and third centuries B.C. there were no commercial towns in central Europe comparable to the Heuneburg, nor groups of exceptionally rich graves. Salt mining at Hallstatt ceased around 400 B.C. Stična, Magdalenska gora, and the other centers in Slovenia declined during the fourth century B.C. at the same time that new elements appeared in the material culture which suggested that peoples entered from north of the Alps and settled in the region. After the decline of the commercial centers, the settlements of Europe once again consisted of similar farmsteads and hamlets throughout the countryside. The entrepreneurial energies of ambitious individuals were focused on raiding, looting, and also settling new lands, rather than organizing production systems for commerce.

EXPEDITIONS INTO ITALY AND EASTERN EUROPE

Beginning around 400 B.C. bands of central Europeans set off on expeditions to the Mediterranean lands, principally Italy. Most of these expeditions were military in nature, but some were relatively peaceful, and they were the first events involving central Europeans which were recorded in classical historical documents. The tribal names of the invading peoples and their material culture indicate that those who crossed the Alps into Italy came mostly from eastern France, southern Germany, and Switzerland.

The incursions shocked the indigenous Italic populations principally because of the audacity and ferocity of the attacks. Livy, our richest source, writes:

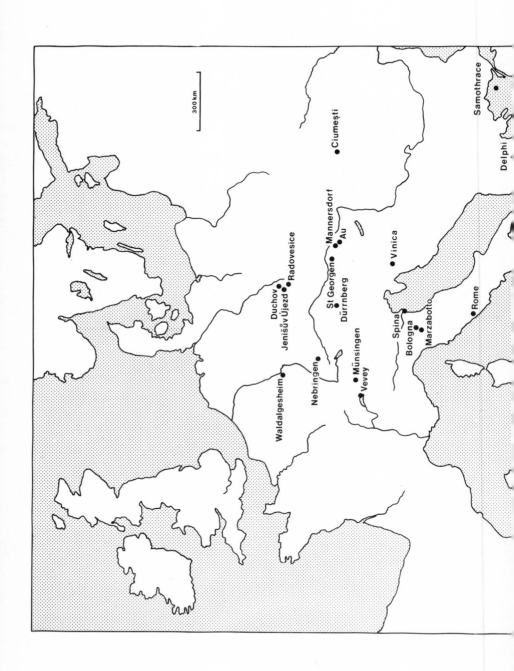

300 km

Samothrace

Delphi

Ciumeşti

Mannersdorf

Au

Vinica

St Georgen

Radovesice

Duchov

Dürrnberg

Jenišův Újezd

Rome

Spina

Bologna

Marzabotto

Münsingen

Nebringen

Vevey

Waldalgesheim

The story runs that this race [the Gauls], allured by the delicious fruits and especially the wine—then a novel luxury—had crossed the Alps and possessed themselves of lands that had before been tilled by the Etruscans; and that wine had been imported into Gaul expressly to entice them, by Arruns of Clusium, in his anger at the seduction of his wife by Lucumo. [5. 33]

[The Gauls] . . . crossed the Alps through the Taurine passes and the pass of the Duria; routed the Etruscans in battle not far from the river Ticinus, . . . and founded a city there which they called Medi-olanium. [5. 34]

Livy mentions several tribal groups who came into Italy, including the Cenomani, the Libui, the Salluvii, the Boii, the Lingones, and the Senones. All were apparently successful in routing the inhabitants of the northern Italian lands. In about 390 B.C. central European warriors attacked the city of Rome.

As they marched swiftly and noisily on, the terrified cities armed in haste, and the peasants fled; but they signified with loud cries, wherever they came, that Rome was their goal. [5. 37]

They entered Rome, killed many of its inhabitants, pillaged what they could find, and set fire to the city. Only the Romans who sought refuge in the citadel survived the attack. As they looked down on their city,

Wherever the shouting of the invaders, the lamentations of the women and children, the crackling of the flames, and the crash of falling buildings drew their attention, trembling at each sound, they turned their thoughts and their gaze that way, as though Fortune had placed them there to witness the pageant of their dying country. [5. 42]

Diodorus of Sicily describes the invasion of Italy in the following words:

. . . the Celts who had their homes in the regions beyond the Alps streamed through the passes in great strength and seized the territory that lay between the Apennine mountains and the Alps, expelling the Tyrrhenians who dwelt there. [14. 113]

The account given by Dionysius of Halicarnassus of the reasons behind the central European incursions is worth recounting at some length, since it provides several useful pieces of information.

> The reason why the Gauls came into Italy was as follows. A certain Lucumo, a prince of the Tyrrhenians, being about to die, entrusted his son to a loyal man named Arruns as guardian. Upon the death of the Tyrrhenian, Arruns, taking over the guardianship of the boy, proved diligent and just in carrying out his trust, and when the boy came to manhood, turned over to him the entire estate left by his father. For this service he did not receive similar kindness from the youth.
>
> It seems that Arruns had a beautiful young wife, of whose society he was extremely fond and who had always shown herself chaste up to that time; but the young man, becoming enamoured of her, corrupted her mind as well as her body, and sought to hold converse with her not only in secret but openly as well. Arruns, grieving at the seduction of his wife and distressed by the wanton wrong done him by them both, yet unable to take vengeance upon them, prepared for a sojourn abroad, ostensibly for the purpose of trading. When the youth welcomed his departure and provided everything that was necessary for trading, he loaded many skins of wine and olive oil and many baskets of figs on the waggons and set out for Gaul.
>
> The Gauls at that time had no knowledge either of wine made from grapes or of oil such as is produced by our olive trees, but used for wine a foul-smelling liquor made from barley rotted in water, and for oil, stale lard, disgusting both in smell and taste. On that occasion, accordingly, when for the first time they enjoyed fruits which they had never before tasted, they got wonderful pleasure out of each; and they asked the stranger how each of these articles was produced and among what men. The Tyrrhenian told them that the country producing these fruits was large and fertile and that it was inhabited by only a few people, who were no better than women when it came to warfare; and he advised them to get these products no longer by purchase from others, but to drive out the present owners and enjoy the fruits as their own. Persuaded by these words, the Gauls came into Italy. [13. 10. 14–17]

Pliny in his *Natural History* (12. 5) offers a different account of the migration, but with a similar basis. He describes a Helvetian named Helicon, who worked as a craftsman in Rome for a time, then returned home across the Alps bringing with him wine, oil, a fig, and a grape. Enamored of these southern fruits, the Helvetians and their neighbors crossed the mountains into Italy.

The archaeological evidence for these incursions comes primarily from cemeteries in Italy. At Bologna, the major commerical center of the Po Plain during the fifth century B.C., large gravestones of this period bear carved scenes of combat, with one party wielding weapons of central European character. In the cemeteries at Bologna grave goods of central European type became common around 400 B.C., and the name of the community was changed from the Etruscan "Felsina" to Celtic "Bononia." Many men's graves contained iron weapons similar to those in use north of the Alps, whereas in earlier graves such weapons were unusual. Iron jewelry was placed in both men's and women's burials, whereas previously jewelry had been mostly bronze. Similar changes are apparent in cemeteries throughout the Po Plain and in the Apennine hills to the south, for example, at the well-studied sites of Filottrano, Marzabotto, and Montefortino. Burial practices and grave goods at small cemeteries in the Apennines also suggest that the persons buried may have been of central European origin, as at San Martino in Gattara and Casola Valsenio.

Central European emigrants also played a part in the political chaos that prevailed in the Balkan lands of southeast Europe after the collapse of the Hellenistic Empire in the first half of the third century B.C. The literary evidence concerning that region is less complete than that for Italy, and much of the archaeological evidence is problematical. The whole of the ancient Mediterranean world was shocked by the Celts' attack, unsuccessful though it was, on the rich Greek treasury at the sanctuary site of Delphi during the winter of 279–278 B.C. In all of Greece only a handful of objects, including an iron sword from Dodona, chain mail from Samothrace, and fibulae from Delos, can be attributed to the invaders who swept through the land and attacked Delphi. Since the central Europeans did not settle in Greece as they did in Italy, they left behind much less evidence of their presence.

Cemeteries throughout Hungary, Yugoslavia, and Romania provide evidence for new settlements of central Europeans beginning shortly after 400 B.C. and especially in the period 300–200 B.C. Much of the central European material in the graves arrived through trade and through borrowing of ornamental motifs, but some was brought by immigrants. The graves in most cemeteries in these regions were similar in character to those north of the Alps.

PLUNDERING FOR WEALTH

The tribal names mentioned by Livy, Dionysius, and Polybius, and the style of jewelry items and weapons placed in graves of immigrants in Italy all point to western central Europe as the origin of most of the newcomers. They came principally from the regions in which most of the Greek and Etruscan luxury imports of the sixth and fifth centuries B.C. have been found. The incursions into the Mediterranean lands can be understood largely as a direct result of the disruption of the commerce between western central Europe and Mediterranean societies.

During the first decades of the fifth century B.C. the intensive trade between central Europe and the Greeks ceased. The principal cause of this change was probably the establishment around 520 B.C. of two major Greek port cities at the mouth of the Po River, Adria and Spina, founded to open up the rich lands of the Po Plain and the forested foothills of the Alps to Greek commercial exploitation. The agricultural wealth of the region was much praised by the ancient authors, and in the valley and the mountains all of the raw materials and processed goods were available which had previously been obtained from western central Europe. The Po Valley was closer to the Greek cities that needed the resources, and less overland and river transport was required to move materials from the Po Valley to Greek cargo ships than from western central Europe. Aside from the logistics, political configurations unknown to us may also have played a part. Perhaps the central European potentates were no longer satisfied with bronze kraters and ornate couches and were beginning to demand too much in return for the produce of their lands. The latter part of the sixth and first part of the fifth centuries B.C. were periods of great strife between Greeks, Etruscans, and Carthaginians in the Mediterranean Sea, and this turmoil may also have played a role in the shifting of Greek trading interests from the Rhône to the Adriatic. Whatever the causes of the shift, the archaeological evidence shows that shortly after 500 B.C. the Greeks stopped trading with western central Europe and began large-scale commerce with communities in the Po Valley.

The disruption in the flow of luxuries arriving by riverboat and packhorse from the South was catastrophic for those who had grown accustomed to regular supplies of wine, oil, painted pottery, and fancy bronze vessels. Besides losing their accouterments of the good life *à la méditerranéen*, they also lost their preeminent positions of power in the control of the luxury trade and of the local commercial systems.

The accounts of Livy, Dionysius, and Pliny, though apocryphal in detail, agree on one point that is probably true—the main motivation for the central Europeans' incursions across the Alps into Italy was their desire for the "delicious fruits and especially the wine" (Livy 5. 33) which they had learned were available there. (We need to understand "fruits" in a broad sense to include nonedible luxury goods as well as wine and exotic foodstuffs.)

Individuals who perceived an opportunity to gain wealth, status, and prestige organized bands of warriors to seize that wealth. Raids into Italy in the early fourth century B.C., including the assault on Rome, were apparently conducted by war parties organized by ambitious individuals, similar in conception and execution to the historically documented Viking attacks on northern European communities during the ninth through eleventh centuries of the Christian era. We know little about the size of the raiding bands. Livy and the other historians exaggerate the numbers of the attackers so as not to discredit their own ancestors, the unsuccessful defenders. The ancient accounts imply that communities in the Po Plain and the Etruscan centers of central Italy were unprepared for the invasion. Livy states that the Gauls marched along at a fast pace. The raiding parties need not have been very large to effect the surprise and damage that they did. Groups of several hundred men armed with spears and swords could have inflicted the damage and caused the panic described.

Northern and central Italy were prosperous lands and offered rich plunder to the intruders. Many graves at Bologna, particularly in the Certosa cemetery, at Marzabotto, and at the port city of Spina contained many Etruscan bronze vessels and gold and silver ornaments and much Greek pottery. Such objects were standard equipment for tombs of well-off individuals during the fifth century B.C. and show the kinds of materials ripe for plundering. Early European literary sources show that it was customary for the leader of a war party to receive the lion's share of the loot. He let his men gather what they wanted from the defeated communities. Given the swiftness and ferocity of the attacks and the standard of material wealth in Italy, these intruders were probably very successful in their ventures.

[131]

It is difficult to distinguish in the archaeological record between small war bands of armed men and larger groups immigrating into new lands. Evidence from Italian cemeteries could be interpreted in terms of the taking of native wives by central European conquerors—central European weapons are represented, but much of the rest of the material culture is local Italic in character. In southeast Europe the evidence does not suggest massive immigration, but rather the diffusion of cultural styles, partly through trade and partly through copying. Within central Europe there is no evidence for substantial depletion of population at this time. The countryside was densely covered with small settlements and associated cemeteries during the fourth and third centuries B.C. Thus most of the movements probably consisted of raids by small groups of warriors, not large tribal migrations. Sometimes the successful warriors returned to their homes enriched with their booty; other times they took local wives and settled in the new lands.

Many Italian graves of the late fourth and early third century B.C. which had iron weapons of central European character were richly equipped. For example, Grave 953 in the Benacci cemetery at Bologna contained an iron sword, iron javelin, iron spearhead and spear shoe, bronze helmet, diadem of gold leaves, iron bracelet, four large bronze vessels (jug, two cauldrons, bowl), five bronze kyathoi (ladles), and a bronze strigil. This grave is striking both for its large number of objects and for the set of weapons, the set of drinking vessels, and the gold ornaments. Similar graves have been found at other sites in northern Italy. These rich graves of central European character in Italy were considerably wealthier than well-outfitted ones of the same period north of the Alps. Personal fortunes of central Europeans were now made by raiding in Mediterranean lands, not trading at home in central Europe. After the period of pillaging during the first part of the fourth century B.C., some central Europeans settled in northern Italy to live in the fair climate where wine and other southern delights were readily available.

The raids on Greece left very little archaeological trace because the intruders there were constantly on the move. In Hungary, Yugoslavia, and Romania, where at least some groups from central Europe settled, there is little evidence for the accumulation of personal wealth, unlike in northern Italy. The indigenous peoples of these regions did not possess the rich material culture that northern Italian communities did, and their settlements were thus not such attractive targets for attack. Even the richest graves, such as that at Ciumeşti in northwest Romania with an ornate helmet, chain mail shirt, and bronze greaves, did not exhibit the opulence of the wealthy burials of central Europeans in Italy.

THE FOURTH AND THIRD CENTURIES B.C. IN CENTRAL EUROPE

Settlements

The burial pattern in most of Europe at this time consisted of flat inhumation graves, usually with a few dozen graves in a cemetery as at Nebringen, Vevey, and Au an der Leitha, but occasionally with more as, for example, the 138 graves at Jenišův Újezd in Bohemia, 216 at Münsingen-Rain in Switzerland, and 350 at Vinica in Slovenia. Even these large cemeteries represent small communities of between twenty and one hundred people. One of the few thoroughly studied settlement complexes of the period is at Radovesice in Bohemia, which was probably typical of the larger settlements (Figure 39). It consisted of a group of two to four hamlets with a total population of between thirty and eighty. There is no evidence for the existence of larger agglomerations, such as Stična and the Heuneburg of the earlier period, and fortified hilltop settlements were less common than they had been. Iron and bronze working and pottery manufacture were carried out in the small communities. The few objects of particularly fine workmanship, such as swords and helmets, and of precious substances, such as gold, amber, and glass, were widely distributed throughout the continent, not concentrated at particular centers of wealth.

Economy

Little information is available about subsistence practices during these centuries, but the data we have suggest no substantial changes. Material culture was relatively uniform across continental Europe, indicating more interaction than previously between metalworkers and potters. Burial patterns were homogeneous, and combinations of goods placed in graves were also similar throughout central Europe. This uniformity of burial practice and material culture is particularly striking in the sets of weapons placed in men's graves. Very few central European burials were exceptionally rich.

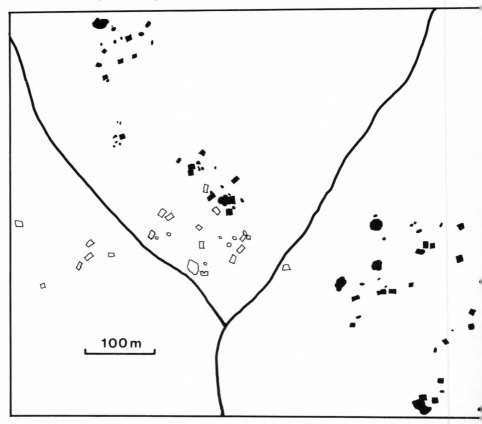

39. Plan of the settlement complex at Radovesice near Teplice in Czechoslovakia. The black struc dated to the early part of the late Iron Age, the open structures to its middle phase. Based on th Waldhauser 1979:119, fig. 2.

Iron was much more common in graves during this time than between 600 and 400 B.C. (Table 1). In many cemeteries 50 to 75 percent of the men's graves contained weapons, including long iron swords, iron spearheads, iron parts for wooden shields, and sometimes iron helmets (Figure 40). Many belt hooks, rings for attaching weapons to belts, and fibulae were also made of iron. Graves found in different regions included blacksmith's tools among their equipment. A grave discovered in 1954 at St. Georgen in Lower Austria was that of a fifty-year-old man buried with iron tongs, an iron hammer, and an iron file, as well as a pair of shears and a fibula, both also of iron. Metalsmiths' graves were usually

Table 1. Quantities of iron in graves of 600–400 B.C. and 400–200 B.C.

	Number of graves	Percent with iron	Average number of iron objects per grave
600–400 B.C.			
Magdalenenberg	133	24.8	0.41
Mühlacker	40	27.5	0.30
400–200 B.C.			
Jenišův Újezd	138	68.3	1.47
Münsingen	218	39.0	0.94

fairly well outfitted, suggesting that smiths held some status in their communities.

Although iron had by this time replaced bronze for tools and most weapons, bronze was still the principal material for many luxury items such as jewelry and vessels. Bronze was employed mostly for fibulae and bracelets, both of which were very numerous in the graves. Luxury goods such as vessels and helmets were less common than they had been during the period between 800 and 400 B.C. There was a general decrease in the range of objects made of bronze and in the amount of fine craftsmanship applied to them.

We know little about the pottery industry of this period since few settlements have been extensively researched and few kilns found. Most of the objects placed in graves were made of metal, and ceramics were poorly represented. The fast-turning potter's wheel was coming into general use in central Europe, but in the North handmade pottery still predominated. The pottery of this period was plainer and less colorful than earlier ceramics.

In sum, the quality of crafts products, except iron implements, declined during the fourth and third centuries B.C. Metalsmiths developed skills for producing high-quality steel objects, but devoted less effort to ornamentation and elaboration of other materials, such as bronze and pottery. The evidence relating to trade suggests a lack of commercial and manufacturing centers. Materials that were especially heavily traded during the early Iron Age—bronze, glass, graphite, amber, gold—continued to circulate, but less than before. Interaction with Mediterranean societies all but stopped. The southern imports that have turned up in graves, such as the bronze pails from Waldalgesheim in the Rhineland and Mannersdorf in Austria, were isolated specimens. In

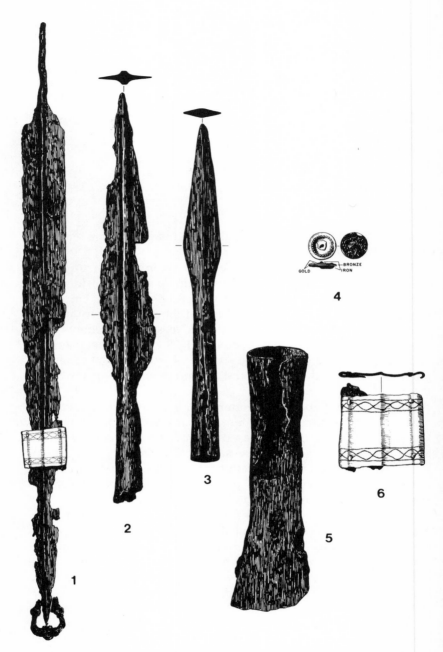

40. Weapons characteristic of graves of the fourth and third centuries B.C., these from Grave 19–20 in Tumulus V at Magdalenska gora. The grave contained a sword (1), two spearheads (2,3) and an axe (5), all of iron, as well as an ornamented bronze clasp from the scabbard (6) and a small gold ornament (4), probably from the chape at the base of the scabbard.

this landscape of dispersed settlement, small-scale trade, and limited local crafts, the Dürrnberg stands out as an exceptional site.

The Dürrnberg

Salt production and trade remained important economically in central Europe even after the breakdown in Mediterranean trade and the demise of the commercial towns. Around 400 B.C. salt mining at Hallstatt declined, but the slack was taken up by miners on the Dürrnberg at Hallein in Austria, 40 kilometers west of Hallstatt. The salt deposits in the Dürrnberg mountain are part of the same geological formation as those at Hallstatt, and the miners' equipment recovered from the two places is similar. In contrast to Hallstatt, the Dürrnberg is not situated in an inaccessible and inhospitable location. It is on the Salzach River, and at the base of the mountain along the river is flat valley land suitable for agriculture. The Salzach has long been a major artery of commerce, and a modern highway runs through the valley today. The situation of the Dürrnberg was thus more favorable than that of Hallstatt because of the good agricultural and pasturage land and more efficient transportation and may have been the main reason for that community's replacing Hallstatt as the principal salt producer in Iron Age Europe.

At the Dürrnberg remains of the miners' settlements as well as their graves have been found. The scale of the settlement and burial areas indicates that the community was made up of several small units consisting of three to five families each, hence with ten or twenty adults per unit. The structure and contents of the graves suggest that no one unit was wealthier or of higher status than others; there were richer and poorer graves, but no breaks in the continuum of wealth (Figure 41). The richer graves were not separated from others, as they were at the centers of western central Europe. According to physical anthropological analyses of the skeletal remains, the bones bear signs of great physical stress, supporting the notion that the persons buried in the graves at the Dürrnberg were the same ones who did the mining. There is no evidence for slavery, or for any other kinds of underclass, either in the cemetery or in the settlement. The miners were profiting from the rewards of their own labors.

As was the case at Hallstatt, at the Dürrnberg the graves were richer than those at most other cemeteries. Besides the charac-

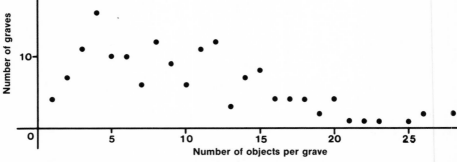

41. Distribution of grave goods in 163 burials of the fourth and third centuries B.C. at the Dürrnbe near Hallein in Austria.

teristic iron weapons in men's graves and bronze jewelry in women's, the Dürrnberg burials contained large quantities of imported amber beads, glass beads, and gold ornaments. Imports indicate connections with western central Europe, Bohemia, Slovenia, the Baltic coasts, and Italy, as well as with lands closer to the site, and show that the salt trade from the Dürrnberg was both intensive and extensive.

Distribution of Wealth

The patterns of wealth distribution in graves during this period (400–200 B.C.) were similar to those in most cemeteries in early Iron Age Europe. As the graphs (Figures 41 and 42) show, the majority of graves contained few objects, and only a few graves contained many, the characteristic pattern for most of late prehistoric Europe. Unlike the very rich graves at the commercial centers of the early Iron Age such as Hallstatt, Stična, and the Heuneburg, the wealthiest graves of the late Iron Age contained only a few dozen objects, and they rarely had in them any objects exclusive to the richest. The few exceptions date to the very beginning of the late Iron Age (first half of the fourth century B.C.), such as the unique grave at Waldalgesheim, which contained a highly ornate gold neckring and two matching bracelets, a bronze pail imported from central Italy, and bronze ornaments from a two-wheeled chariot, and Grave 44/2 at the Dürrnberg, which had in it two gold bracelets and other gold ornaments, an iron sword, two iron spearheads, a

[138]

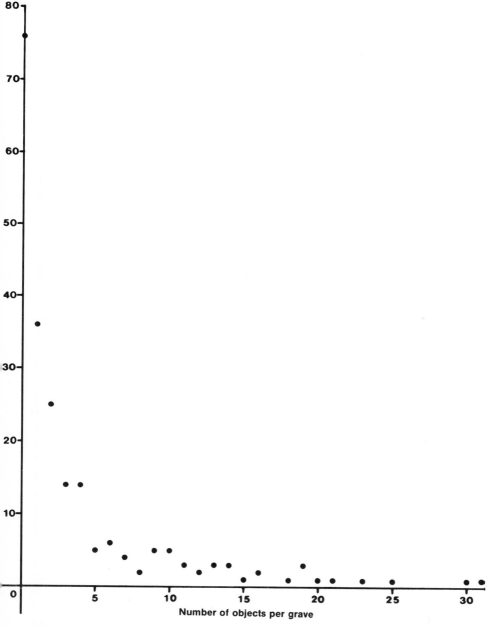

42. Distribution of grave goods in 216 burials at the cemetery of Münsingen-Rain in Switzerland.

bronze helmet, bronze pail, bronze bowl, and bronze canteen, an Attic kylix, and iron parts from a wooden wagon. After the fourth century B.C. such graves were very unusual.

The increase in the numbers of weapons placed in graves seems to indicate a new emphasis on warfare and on men's roles as fighters, though the significance of weapons as burial goods is always problematical. The pattern of more homogeneous distribution of grave wealth than during the sixth and fifth centures B.C. coincides with the new practice of flat inhumation graves instead of tumulus burials. There was, of course, some variation in size and depth of burials, and in the presence or absence of coffins, but compared to preceding centuries, when huge mounds were erected for some individuals and elaborate wooden chambers built, about the same amount of energy was invested in the preparation of each grave of the late Iron Age.

The decline in the production of special luxury goods further reflects this lack of exceptional accumulation of wealth by individuals. Gold was much less often placed in graves than during the sixth and fifth centuries B.C., and large objects such as neckrings and bracelets were rare. Again, the late fourth century B.C. grave at Waldalgesheim was a notable exception. Individual pieces of gold ring jewelry are known from several sites, but not in the profusion they were found at the earlier commercial towns. Imported and local bronze vessels were now rarer. Surplus wealth was not being generated on the scale that it had been at the towns of the earlier period, and hence individuals could not acquire precious metals or the means to support specialized crafts workers.

A few hoards of metal objects have been found dating from this period, the most important of which is that discovered in 1882 in a spring at Duchov in northwest Bohemia. A bronze cauldron was found together with about two thousand bronze objects, mainly fibulae and bracelets. This hoard dates to the latter part of the fourth century B.C. It has been interpreted as a votive deposit and as a merchant's store. Hoards were much rarer during these centuries than during either the late Bronze Age or the last two centuries before Christ.

THE NEW ART STYLE

The intensive interactions between central Europeans and Greeks between 600 and 480 B.C. brought European crafts workers into contact with ornamented objects of Mediterranean origin, particularly bronze vessels and jewelry. During the fifth century B.C. a new style of decorating metalwork was developed in Europe, first in the middle Rhineland. This style departed from the strict geometric ornament of the early Iron Age and transformed shapes and motifs borrowed from Mediterranean crafts products into a new tradition known as La Tène or Celtic art. This style spread rapidly throughout Europe and to the British Isles and was characterized by stylized human and animal heads, Mediterranean motifs such as palmettes, and curvilinear rather than straight lines (Figure 43 and 44). Within decades the new style replaced the earlier forms of ornamentation throughout most of Europe.

43. Bronze sword scabbard from Hallstatt Grave 994. This object, recovered from one of the latest graves in the Hallstatt cemetery, shows the new use of the human form in the early La Tène Period as well as the emphasis on curvilinear and spiral decorative motifs.

44. Cast bronze handle attachment on the jug from Kleinaspergle in Baden-Württemberg, West Germany. The use of the stylized head and decorative spirals is characteristic of early La Tène art. This example occurs on a jug, the form of which is closely derived from that of the imported Etruscan jugs found in many of the richer graves in central Europe.

6 Emergence of Urbanism in Late Prehistoric Europe (200–15 B.C.)

During the final two centuries before Christ the largest communities of pre-Roman Europe developed, with populations in the several thousands. These communities were formed basically for the same reason that the commercial towns of the sixth century B.C. were formed: to increase surplus production for trade so that luxury goods could be imported. Despite the existence of at least a dozen major centers that could arguably be called cities, Europe was not an urban society before the arrival of the Romans around the middle of the last century B.C. The oppida, as these commercial centers are called, were exceptional, and their role in the economic life of most Europeans was minimal. The vast majority of people lived in farmsteads, hamlets, and small villages, and their way of life determined the character of late Iron Age society.

INTENSIFICATION OF IRON PRODUCTION

After 200 B.C. iron was produced on a large scale throughout Europe. Settlements that have been excavated have yielded vast quantities of iron tools, weapons, and ornaments. For the first time there was also abundant evidence for smelting and forging, including workshop sites and tools used by blacksmiths. The best evidence for iron working comes from Manching in Bavaria, where since 1955 excavators have recovered thousands of iron artifacts. In his study of the iron objects found there between 1955 and 1963, Gerhard Jacobi identified some two hundred distinct types of iron implements from the site. Assemblages from other oppida are sim-

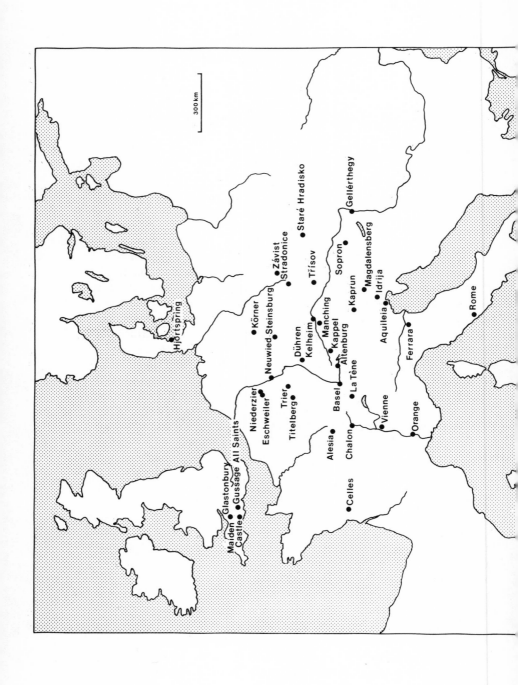

300 km

Hjortspring

Körner

Neuwied Steinsburg

Závist
Stradonice

Staré Hradisko

Gellérthegy

Tísov

Sopron

Magdalensberg

Idrija

Kaprun

Manching

Kappel

Altenburg

Dühren

Kelheim

La Tène

Aquileia

Niederzier

Eschweiler

Trier

Titelberg

Basel

Vienne

Ferrara

Orange

Rome

Alesia

Chalon

Celles

Glastonbury

Gussage All Saints

Maiden
Castle

ilar, as published finds from Stradonice, Heidetränk, Dünsberg, Velemszentvid, Staré Hradisko, and Vienne indicate.

Iron implements for a wide range of productive activities are represented. They include tools for metalworking (hammers, tongs, anvils, files, chisels, punches, burins), woodworking (axes, chisels, drills, saws, knives), leather and textile production (knives, awls, needles, weaving equipment), pottery manufacture, agriculture (plowshares, hoes, shovels, sickles, scythes, pruning knives), fishing gear, balances, toilet articles, surgical instruments, implements for the hearth, kitchen utensils, keys, harness equipment, wagon parts, and chains and rings. Iron nails become common during the second century B.C.; huge numbers were needed to hold together the timbers in the walls enclosing the settlements. Improvements in efficiency of production became possible because of the abundance of iron that could be worked into tools and because of the variety of specialized tools developed. The basic technology of tool manufacture for blacksmithing, agricultural production, carpentry, and cooking changed very little between the late Iron Age and the Industrial Revolution.

Iron was smelted and forged in both large and small communities. The evidence for smelting consists mostly of furnaces and slag deposits. The most common type of furnace was the bowl furnace, a pit about 50 centimeters deep and 30 centimeters in diameter, usually with a ceramic chimney, only fragments of which survive (Figure 46). Occasionally a bloom of smelted iron is found in pits of late Iron Age furnaces. Often the only surviving

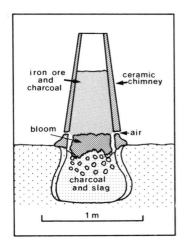

46. A typical smelting furnace of the late Iron Age. Based on a drawing in Hingst 1978:64, fig. 75.

traces of smelting activity on a site are lumps of slag and ceramic nozzles used to channel air, with or without bellows, into the furnace.

Large-scale iron smelting was carried out at some of the oppida, including Manching, Velemszentvid, and Třísov, generally outside the settlement because of the danger of fire and because of the noxious gases produced. Most of the oppida were situated close to deposits of iron ore, and those that were not, such as the Steinsburg, had to import iron in ingot form. Many smaller settlements that have been excavated have also yielded evidence of iron smelting, for example, farmsteads at Steinebach and Uttenkofen in Bavaria and hamlets at Gussage All Saints and Glastonbury in southern Britain.

In some regions there is evidence of unusually large-scale production where settlement remains indicate a small population. At the site of Msec in Bohemia, Radomír Pleiner has investigated a complex of nineteen smelting furnaces associated with a very small community. The evidence suggests that iron was produced in quantities much larger than would have been required for local use. About a thousand smelting sites have been found in Burgenland in eastern Austria, about two-thirds of which date to the final century before Christ. The settlements in this iron-rich region were small, and the metal was clearly being produced for trade. Nearby towns at Velemszentvid and Sopron-Varhely apparently served as trade centers for the Burgenland iron, using some of the metal themselves and trading some. Since iron ore is relatively abundant in Europe, the limiting factor in production was usually the supply of wood for fuel. Shortages of wood made the development of large workings at many population centers (where wood was scarce because of overexploitation) less practical than at dispersed, small-scale smelting communities in well-forested lands.

Blacksmiths' tools have been recovered at all major settlements (Figure 47). At Manching they include four kinds of hammers, three of tongs, three of anvils, and a range of files, perforators, punches and burins. Similar tools have been recovered in hoards, as at Kappel in Württemberg and Wauwilermoos in Switzerland, and in some graves such as at Celles in southwest France and St. Georgen in eastern Austria. The scale of iron extraction and tool manufacture suggests that specialists devoted full time to the industry. In smaller communities iron implements were likely forged by part-time smiths who raised food like their fellows. Smelting and forging are not difficult and do not require elaborate facilities.

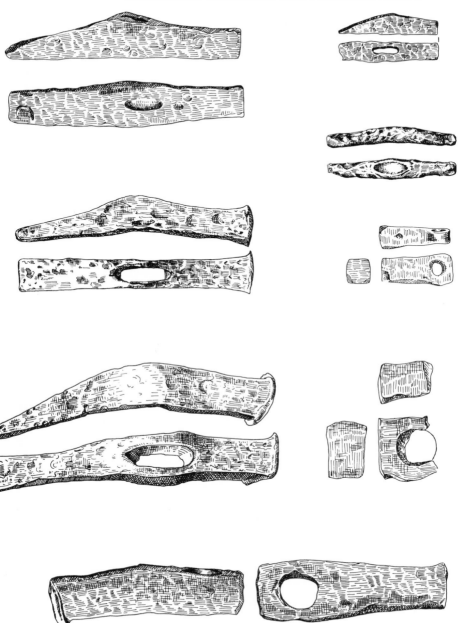

47. Iron hammers from Manching, illustrating the range of different types and sizes. Object in upper left is 15.2 cm long.

Some investigators have argued on the basis of the range of techniques required to make various kinds of objects, from plowshares to fibulae to fine swords, that smiths specialized in different categories of implements. There is little evidence to support such specialization, however. It is true that metallographic analyses of swords have shown that exceptional technical knowledge and skill were applied in their manufacture. And makers' marks on fine swords in Switzerland, in particular, including one with the Greek inscription "KORISIOS," show that sword makers were proud of their work and identified their products as their own. Yet the fact that some smiths made exceptionally fine items does not necessarily imply that they did not also make more mundane objects such as plowshares and fibulae. Many hoards, such as those from Kappel in Württemberg and Körner in central Germany, contained a wide range of objects including weapons, plowshares, and kitchen utensils. If these hoards were metalsmiths' stores, as that from Kappel almost certainly was, then their contents would suggest that one individual produced the different items. In his study of textual and archaeological evidence pertaining to smiths in early medieval Scandinavia (which was similar in many ways to continental Europe in the late Iron Age), Müller-Wille found that smiths did both fine and coarse work. Pleiner ascertained in his analyses of iron objects from this period that techniques of production were not standardized and that parts of objects varied greatly in metal quality. Even though some objects stand out as exceptionally finely made, the manufacture of iron implements was probably less standardized and specialized than is often thought.

In the late Iron Age, as in the late Bronze Age, we find burials that contained metalworking tools which can be interpreted as smiths' graves. A grave at Celles in southwest France had in it many iron objects, including two hammers, nine perforators, four chisels, a punch, a gouge, and two files. Graves 1 and 18 at Idrija near Bača in Slovenia also contained blacksmith's tools. None of these graves was particularly richly outfitted. None had imported bronze or ceramic vessels or gold ornaments. In his cross-cultural survey of metalsmiths, Robert Forbes found that in some cultures smiths have high status, in others low status, but they always are held in awe because of their special abilities. The evidence from early medieval Scandinavia and Ireland suggests that in those places smiths had relatively high status, but nowhere near the highest in their societies. The late Iron Age graves of continental

Europe similarly suggest that smiths were well-to-do, but not that they were among the wealthiest persons in their communities.

More than seven hundred double-pointed iron ingots attest to trade of the metal (Figure 48). They have been found most abundantly in southern Germany, eastern France, and Switzerland, but as far away as Brittany to the west, Denmark to the north, Provence to the south, and eastern Poland to the east. Most occurred in hoards, such as that discovered in 1963 at Aubstadt in central Germany, which contained twenty-three ingots. These ingots, which consist of relatively pure iron, may have been owned by merchants or metalworkers, but they may also have represented standards of value accumulated by wealthy persons. They could be readily transformed into weapons, tools, or ornaments, as circumstances required. The distribution of these ingots does not reflect that of iron production, but rather regional practices of storing iron in this particular form. Some centers of iron working have yielded no ingots, such as Burgenland, Noricum, Bohemia, and the Holy Cross Mountains of Poland, while others, as around Manching and in the Saarland, have yielded many.

Unlike bronze objects, few iron objects were traded within central Europe. Even in hoards that contained many different kinds of objects, such as at Kappel, all of the iron items were local forms. Iron workers apparently did not travel far to practice their craft and did not accumulate pieces from other regions.

GROWING COMMERCE WITH URBAN ITALY

Commerce between European communities north of the Alps and peoples of the Italian peninsula was greatly affected by military and political events. Roman historical records provide us with reasonably good information about developments in the northern half of Italy during the last four centuries before Christ. At least partly as a result of the sacking of the city by central Europeans around 390 B.C., the Romans began building up an army and gradually started conquering territories to the north, first in Etruria in central Italy and then across the Apennines in the southern part of the Po Plain. In 283 B.C. the Romans conquered northern Picenum, established the territory known as the *ager Gallicus* in the area between Ravenna and Ancona, and founded the colony of Sena Gallica (Senigallia). Between 225 and 222 B.C. a series of important

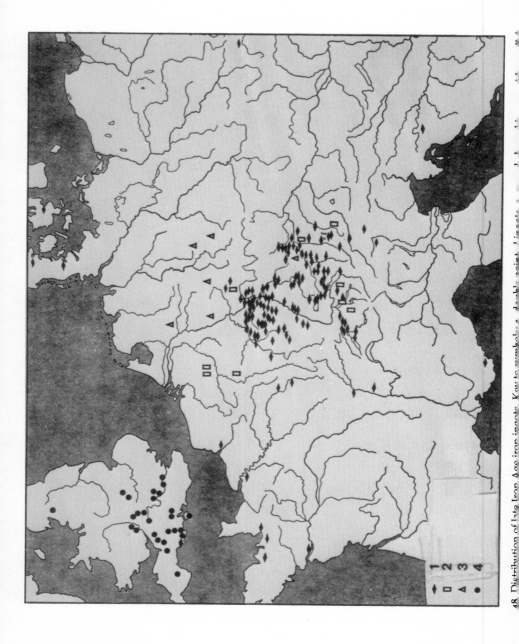

48. Distribution of late Iron Age iron ingots. Key to symbols: 1 double-point ingots; 2 sword-shaped ingots; 3 ....

battles were fought between Celtic groups and Roman armies from which the Romans emerged victorious. The presence of Hannibal and his Carthaginian army in Italy from 218 to 216 B.C. delayed Roman plans for further annexation of lands into their expanding domain, but with peace established between Rome and Carthage in 201 B.C. the way was open for further military action in northern Italy.

Bologna was made a Roman colony in 189 B.C., and in 183 B.C. Mutina (Modena) and Parma were established as colonies. By this time, having finally defeated the Celtic communities, Rome controlled all of northern Italy to the Alps, providing Roman merchants with opportunities for commerce with the lands to the north. In 181 B.C. the colony of Aquileia was established as a port at the northern end of the Adriatic Sea, specifically to serve as a base for merchants trading with the east Alpine area. By this time Roman merchants were visiting the Norican community at the Magdalensberg in Carinthia, southern Austria, to develop commercial relations with the iron producers there. In 121 B.C. Roman armies crossed the western Alps into southern France and established the colony of Gallia Narbonensis, extending north as far as Lake Geneva. This acquisition gave Roman merchants full opportunity to organize large-scale commercial ventures with communities in Gaul and brought Roman and central European cultures into more direct contact.

At the end of the second century before Christ northern Italy was invaded by Germanic bands of Cimbri and Teutoni, along with Celtic groups, who swept across the Alps from the northeast into the Po Plain, like the earlier intruders intent on seizing booty from the wealthy communities of the region. In 113 B.C. these raiding parties defeated a Roman army in battle at a location designated as Noreia, somewhere in the modern Austrian regions of Carinthia or Styria. Roman armies were again beaten eight years later at Orange in the Rhône valley. But in 102 and 101 B.C. reorganized Roman forces finally defeated these marauders in battles at Aix in southeast France and at Ferrara near the mouth of the Po in northern Italy. These Roman victories brought an end to the raids from north of the Alps which had impeded the progress of Roman expansion.

No literary documents survive which describe the early development of trade between Rome and the North. Roman wine amphorae first appeared in central Europe around the middle of the second century B.C. and are represented at several sites including

[151]

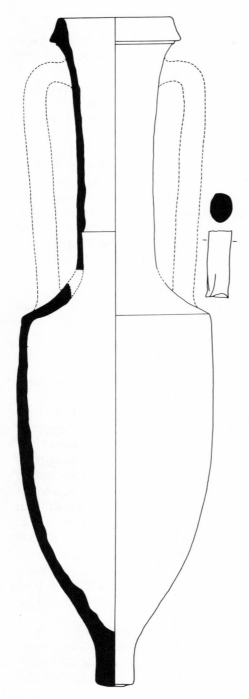

49. Drawing of a Roman ceramic wine amphora recovered at Manching. Height, about 97 cm.

Manching (Figure 49). Bronze vessels of Roman manufacture began to arrive in substantial numbers at the beginning of the final
century before Christ, and most Campanian pottery in the North
also dates to the final century of the prehistoric era. The archaeological evidence in central Europe thus shows that trade with
Roman Italy began by the middle of the second century B.C., shortly after Rome had established control over northern Italy.

The wine amphorae, the most abundant category of imported
objects in the archaeological record, have a strongly western distribution. They have been found principally in France, southern
Germany, and Switzerland. At Manching more than thirty-four
were found, twenty-nine at Basel-Gasfabrik, eight at Basel-
Münsterhügel, sixteen at Altenburg, more than fourteen at the
Magdalensberg, and four in a grave at Goeblingen-Nospelt in Luxembourg. Single specimens have been recovered at other sites. In
eastern central Europe only two are recorded from Stradonice and
just one from Staré Hradisko. The majority of sites in eastern central Europe have not yielded any. Wine was probably only rarely
transported overland in these ceramic amphorae. The large
number of amphorae in France reflects the ease of transporting
them on ships and barges on the Rhône and its tributaries. Fragments of twenty-four thousand amphorae were recovered in the
Saône River at Chalon. The smaller number of amphorae to the
east does not mean that less wine was traded there, only that
lighter containers were used, such as wooden barrels and animal
skins, both mentioned by Strabo in this connection.

Roman bronze vessels of the final century B.C. are more evenly
distributed throughout Europe, and the distribution of these small,
lightweight vessels may provide the most accurate picture of the
geographical range of the wine trade. The greatest number of them
has been recovered in the hilly lands of central Europe, south of
the Northern European Plain and between the lower Seine,
Prague, and the Alps. Among the best represented vessels are
Kappel-Kelheim-type jugs (thirteen found; see Figure 50), and
Aylesford pans (thirty-one; see Figure 51). Less common imports
include sieves, handled beakers (*kyathoi*), ladles, and basins.

The principal imports from Rome to central Europe in terms of
value and volume were probably ones that do not survive in the
archaeological record, such as wine. Wine is the item most often
mentioned by ancient writers in connection with commerce with
central Europe (Athenaeus 4. 36; Diodorus of Sicily 5. 26). The
great fondness of central Europeans for wine is a central theme of

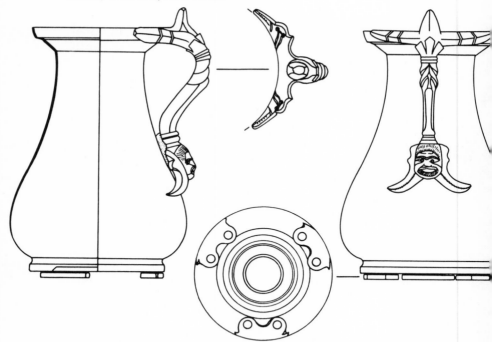

50. Drawing of a Roman bronze jug of the Kappel-Kelheim type. Height, about 22 cm.

many accounts in the classical sources, and the importance of the wine trade in the sixth century B.C. has already been discussed. As soon as the Romans conquered central Europe, they imported grapes, peaches, figs, dates, and olives, as well as oysters, preserved fish, fish sauce (*garum*), chestnuts, and salted meats. It is likely that such items were also traded before the conquest, but they have not yet been looked for in late Iron Age contexts.

The goods traded from central Europe to Roman Italy do not survive archaeologically. We are left to surmise what they were on the basis of indirect evidence. Some of the best evidence comes from the oppidum on the Magdalensberg, the largest settlement of ancient Noricum, famous in the Roman world for its high-quality iron products. Around 120 B.C. the native community at the Magdalensberg established a pact with Rome for mutually beneficial commerce. Norican merchants were permitted to reside and trade within the Roman Empire, and we know that some lived at Aquileia. As early as 186 B.C. Roman envoys were at the site, and

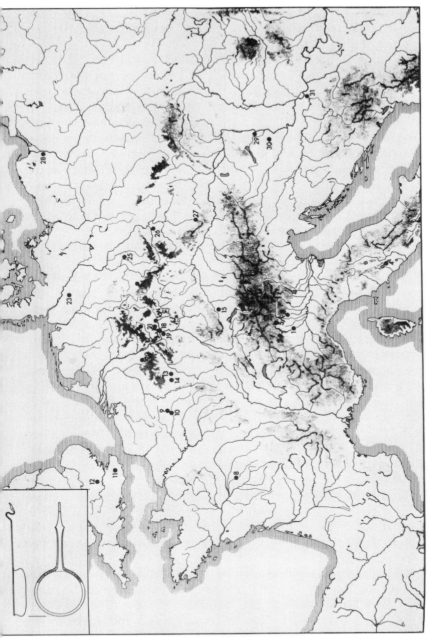

51. Distribution of Roman bronze Aylesford pans. For site names, see Werner 1978:17.

excavations at the Magdalensberg have revealed an extensive settlement of Roman merchants before the annexation of the region into the empire in 15 B.C.

The most important evidence from the Magdalensberg consists of cellars discovered in 1960 which had been used by merchants who left several hundred inscriptions scratched into the plaster walls. These inscriptions recorded commercial transactions. The style of the script indicates that the inscriptions were written sometime between 35 B.C. and A.D. 45. Thus they may have predated the annexation of the region by Rome or else followed it shortly. In either case, they provide valuable information about trade at the site. Since the inhabitants of Noricum had excellent relations with Rome from the beginning of the second century B.C., no fighting was involved in the annexation. Archaeological evidence from the Magdalensberg and the textual sources show that little change occurred in the trade patterns when the site was incorporated into the empire.

The inscriptions list goods exchanged and the quantities involved. All objects mentioned were metal tools and vessels. The tools included anvils, axes, clasps, and rings made of iron, and the vessels were jugs, basins, trays, and beakers of copper or brass. The quantities were usually in the hundreds. For example, a group of three merchants who came to the site purchased, respectively, 720 rings and 560 axes, 550 rings and 510 axes, and 560 rings and 565 axes. Another transaction involved 740 trays and 500 rings. In some cases the weights of the objects were recorded. "Sineros of Aquileia bought 110 basins weighing 15 pounds [4.8 kilograms] each." "Filenus of Rome bought 393 11-pound axes" (nearly 1,400 kilograms of axes). The cities from which buyers came were sometimes mentioned. Aquileia, Bologna, and Rome were best represented, and some merchants came from as far off as North Africa. Different times of year are cited, indicating that trading took place all year round. The names of the producers of the metal objects were those of local Noricans. Although these inscriptions refer only to metal objects, it is certain that trade in other materials was also taking place.

Another important find relating to iron trade between central Europe and Rome was made at the settlement on top of the Burgkogel, a hill near Zell am See, Salzburg, Austria. There an iron ingot weighing exactly 20 Roman pounds was found, probably for trade to a Roman merchant. The same site yielded three Roman copper coins dating between 90 and 84 B.C.

The Romans required much iron. The growing army needed large quantities for swords, spears, helmets, and other military gear. Nails and clamps were required for building bridges, forts, and barracks. Production of iron in Italy was limited, and large amounts of the metal could be obtained cheaply from central Europeans eager to trade for wine and other Italian commodities.

Leather was probably also an important trade good. The Romans needed leather for military equipment such as belts, straps, shoes, and tents. After the conquest of western and central Europe, the Romans traded for hides and leather from Scandinavia and other parts of Free Germany (the lands north and west of the Roman Imperial frontier), and it is likely that this commerce began before the conquest. Cattle are well represented by faunal remains on settlements of the period, and the iron tools recovered include many used in processing leather.

Slaves were also traded to Rome. The Roman economy depended on a steady influx of slaves. Rome acquired slaves from all parts of the ancient world, and Diodorus of Sicily refers to the existence of slaves in central Europe. An iron manacle found at La Tène in Switzerland may have been used on slaves. The connection between warfare and slavery was an intimate one in the ancient world, and the increased fighting between communities in temperate Europe during the final century before Christ may have been motivated by a desire not only to seize wealth but also to capture slaves for trade to Rome.

Strabo in his *Geography* (4. 4. 3) mentions that salted pork and woolen textiles were exported from Gaul to Italy after the conquest, and they may have been traded earlier as well. Other items traded to Italy just after the conquest were cattle, cheese, resin, pitch, wax, and honey, all of which may have played a part in the earlier commerce too.

Ships and barges were used to transport goods by river. The Rhône was the principal artery connecting the Mediterranean with interior Europe. In reference to trade to the east Alpine region, Strabo mentions transport by river and overland by wagon (4. 4. 10, 7. 5. 2), and Diodorus of Sicily refers to the use of wagons in Gaul (5. 26). In mountainous regions packhorses were the main mode of transport. Donkey bones recovered at the settlement of Závist in Bohemia have been interpreted as evidence for the use of these Mediterranean animals in the trans-Alpine commerce. A wooden frame found at La Tène was probably a saddle for holding bags or casks on a packhorse.

URBAN CENTERS OF THE LATE IRON AGE: MANCHING AND OTHER
OPPIDA

Julius Caesar used the word *oppidum* to denote the principal
centers of Gaul between 58 and 50 B.C., and the term is now applied to all the large fortified settlements of the final two centuries
before Christ in Europe. They share many features and occur in a
broad band from central France in the west to the Hungarian Plain
in the east, from the Lahn River in the north to the Alps in the
south (Figure 52). To the north, on the Northern European Plain
and in Scandinavia, smaller settlements remained the rule, with no
trace of larger communities. In Britain, large hill forts, such as
Maiden Castle, Danebury, and Hengistbury Head, were constructed that shared some features with the continental oppida,
but they probably did not house such large populations. Along the
Atlantic coast of France smaller communities existed. To the east,
in modern Ukraine, Romania, and Bulgaria, some larger agglomerations of population are known, but the scale of industrial and
commercial activity was not as great as at the central European
oppida. To the south, the Alps remained settled by mountain peoples who lived in small communities. In Italy, as in Mediterranean
France and coastal Yugoslavia, urban life-styles and economies
characterized the Romanized lands.

All of the settlements designated as oppida were enclosed by
walls built of earth, stone, and timber and were much larger than
sites of earlier periods. The wall at Manching enclosed 380 hectares
of land, at Staré Hradisko 40, and at Třísov 21. By comparison, the
Heuneburg comprised 3.2 hectares. Most oppida were established
on hilltops, though some—Manching, for example—incorporated
natural defensive features. Many were densely settled for a century or longer. Little systematic research has been conducted in the
interior areas of most, though many collections exist from early,
unsystematic diggings, and so it is unclear whether all or only
some had large populations.

The earliest evidence for occupation of these huge sites dates to
around the middle of the second century before Christ when town-
like communities developed at Manching in southern Germany,
Stradonice, Hrazany, and Závist in Bohemia, and at Staré Hradisko
in Moravia. Třísov in Bohemia, Steinsburg in central Germany, and
Altenburg in southern Germany were founded at the beginning of
the final century before Christ. Basel-Münsterhügel was established shortly before the middle of that century. Since large-scale

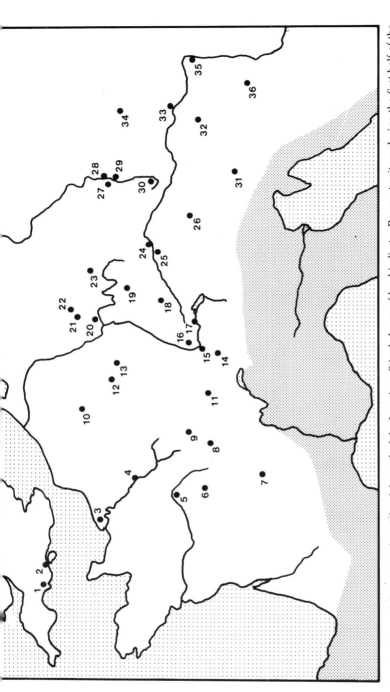

52. Locations of the principal oppida of the end of the Iron Age. Stippled area of land indicates Roman territory during the first half of the final century B.C. 1, Maiden Castle. 2, Hengistbury Head. 3, Fécamp. 4, Paris. 5, Orléans. 6, Bourges. 7, Gergovia. 8, Bibracte. 9, Alesia. 10, Namur. 11, Besançon. 12, Titelberg. 13, Otzenhausen. 14, Bern. 15, Basel. 16, Kirchzarten. 17, Altenburg-Rheinau. 18, Heidengraben. 19, Finsterlohr. 20, Heidetränk. 21, Dünsberg. 22, Amöneburg. 23, Steinsburg. 24, Stradonice. 28, Závist. 29, Hrazany. 30, Třísov. 31, Magdalensberg. 32, Velemszentvid. 33, Bratislava. 34, Staré Hradisko. 35, Budapest-Gellérthegy. 36, Szalacska. (Based on maps in Schaaff and Taylor 1975b:322 and Rieckhoff-Pauli 1980:38, fig. 1.)

excavation of these sites has been very limited, it is not possible to identify developmental phases from small villages to oppida. Earlier settlements are known at many of the sites, but the process of transformation of the smaller communities into large complexes is unclear. The period 100–50 B.C. was the high point of these sites in terms of population, industry, and trade. Some were abandoned around the middle of the final century B.C., including Manching, Staré Hradisko, and Steinsburg, and many in Gaul were conquered by Caesar's armies at that same time. Some sites, such as the Magdalensberg in Carinthia and some of the French oppida, continued to be settled several decades after the Roman conquest; some experienced their greatest periods of activity just before the birth of Christ.

The common features shared by the oppida suggest that all were established in response to similar opportunities and needs, but the variation in the dates of settlement and flourishing emphasizes the regional diversity and lack of interregional political unity. Textual and archaeological evidence suggests that the oppida were fully independent of one another. The lack of any unifying political structure was one of the reasons the Gauls were defeated so easily by Caesar's armies.

Large-scale commerce with Roman merchants and production for that commerce could be carried out only through a centralized organization in which products were brought together in one place for processing and transport, as is well documented at the Magdalensberg, to which the iron and copper or brass objects sought by Roman merchants were brought from manufacturing sites in the countryside. Roman merchants came there to carry on the trade, and did not, as far as we know, venture into the countryside. The oppida grew in size because their wealth from manufacturing and trade attracted people from the surrounding countryside. In return for producing greater quantities of trade goods, they received portions of the imports and of the items manufactured at the oppida such as glass bracelets, bronze jewelry, and iron tools.

As more people were drawn to these centers to smelt, forge, and transport iron and to raise cattle and prepare leather, more primary food producers were required to supply them. Technological innovations helped to improve the efficiency of agricultural production; the iron-tipped plow came into general use, as did shovels with broad iron heads, predecessors of modern spades. Large iron scythes became common. Rotary querns, well represented at Manching and elsewhere, increased the efficiency of grinding grain. Thus with more efficient tools, more people could be supported by fewer food producers.

Another factor in the emergence of the oppida as population centers may have been the growth in the trade of slaves to the Romans. Once central Europeans realized that human beings could be profitably exchanged, a new phase of raiding and warfare may have begun for the purpose of capturing slaves. Ancient and modern history abound with examples of neighboring peoples warring against one another to capture slaves for trade. Fearing the raids of neighboring groups, many people may have fled their farms and villages to take up residence in the oppida.

Of the roughly 40 sites identified as oppida, only a few have been systematically excavated. Especially informative plans of settlement structures have been obtained at Manching, Staré Hradisko, Hrazany, and Třísov. Many of the major sites were excavated during the nineteenth century without the benefit of modern techniques, such as Bibracte, Stradonice, and Velemszentvid, and many examined more recently have been studied from the point of view of their defensive works but not their internal organization.

The plans from Manching and other excavated sites show remains of densely clustered buildings, particularly in the form of postholes, foundation trenches, and pits (Figure 53). The structures are built on rectangular grid patterns, and buildings and streets are aligned to major axes. The rectangular arrangement suggests that the settlements were laid out according to a specific plan. At both Manching and Staré Hradisko parts of the settlements were divided by long palisades, implying that these sites were not just agglomerations of houses and workshops, but were subdivided into substantial units. Jiří Meduna has suggested that the units at Staré Hradisko were separate farmsteads, joined together within the oppidum structure. For Manching, Werner Stöckli has offered a similar interpretation for the areas separated by long palisade trenches. At Manching the archaeological evidence suggests some very large buildings and enclosures, perhaps for some communal use. The purposes to which individual structures were put are difficult to determine because in most cases the land has been plowed hundreds or thousands of times since the late Iron Age. Most of the objects recovered came from the pits and from the overlying humus layers, and they are difficult to associate with specific buildings that once stood on the settlement.

All of the major oppida have yielded evidence for iron produc-

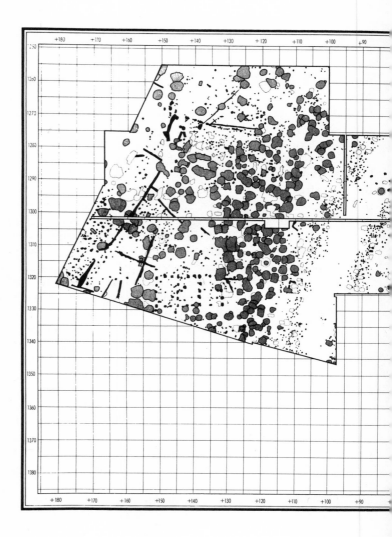

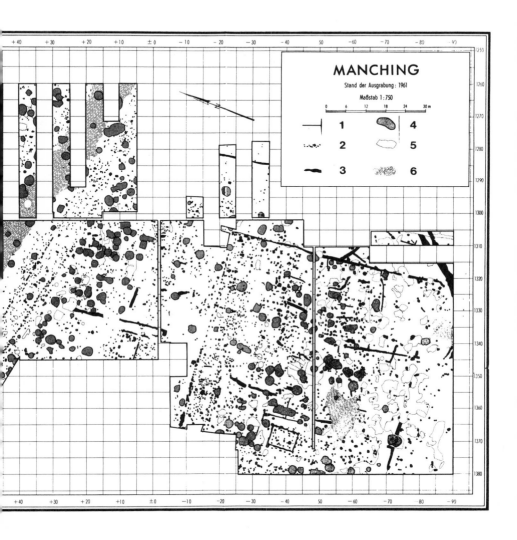

53. Plan of part of the excavated area of Manching. Key to symbols: 1, boundary of excavation. 2, postholes. 3, ditches. 4, pits. 5, shallow depressions (less than 40 cm into subsoil). 6, old streambeds and ponds. Numbers along edges of plan mark the grid system in 10 meter intervals.

[163]

tion, bronze casting, glass manufacture, pottery making, coin minting, textile production, bone and antler carving, and jewelry manufacture. The huge quantities of iron and bronze recovered show that manufacturing took place on a much larger scale than ever before. Yet the majority of the occupants were certainly not crafts workers. The tools, weapons, and ornaments found could easily have been manufactured by a few dozen specialists in the course of a century. It is likely that at least 95 percent of the population of these oppida were farmers. Agricultural implements, including plowshares, scythes, sickles, and foliage knives, were common among the finds (Figure 54). Many of the farmers may have been part-time crafts workers and traders as well, as many peasants still are today when the agricultural schedule does not demand all their energies. Joachim Werner (1961) has written about medieval long-distance trade over the Alps carried on seasonally by men who were full-time peasant farmers most of the year. In the winter they set off on long commercial ventures. Similar patterns of part-time trade are likely for the prehistoric Iron Age. Farmers probably lived at the oppida because of the greater availability of material goods and more interesting life than in the rural hamlets.

We have good evidence for several small satellite communities around the oppida. For example, at the Steinsburg such settlements have been identified just outside the walls of the oppidum and also at a distance of several hundred meters away. At Závist the outermost fortification encompassed a settlement of more rural character than that in the inner precincts. Similar rural settlements have been found at the oppidum of Gergovia, at the unenclosed settlement of Aulnat in south central France, and at Bibracte.

We can only make educated guesses about the population of the oppida, because of the lack of good cemetery evidence associated with the large settlements and lack of extensive excavation of the settlement sites themselves. In most of central Europe the practice of burying the dead in flat inhumation graves with grave goods went out of fashion around the end of the second century before Christ, and very few burials are known from the final century B.C. In the Rhineland and westward some cemeteries have been excavated, but no large ones associated with oppida. On the basis of the size of enclosed areas, density of building remains, and quantities of material recovered, archaeologists studying the oppida have made estimates of likely population sizes. Filip suggests several thousand inhabitants for Stradonice, Závist, Třísov, and Staré

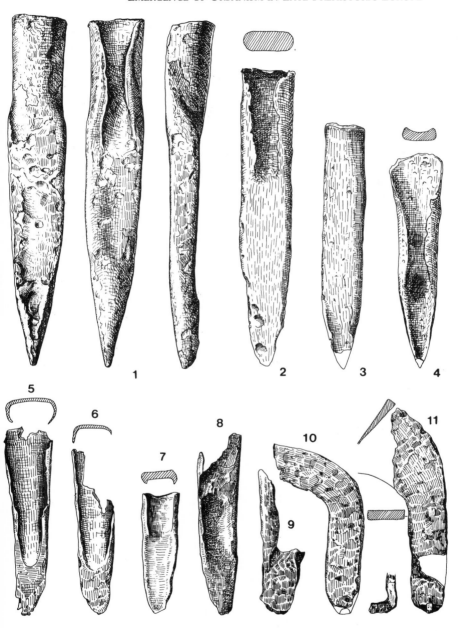

Iron plowshares (1–9) and fragments of scythes (10, 11) from Manching. The object in the upper left is 27.2 cm long.

Hradisko (1971:266). For Závist Waldhauser estimates about 3,400 (1981:116). Meduna offers a figure of 5,000 for Staré Hradisko (1971:310). From the quantities of meat represented by animal bones at Manching, Joachim Boessneck and his colleagues suggest that the minimum average number of occupants might have been around 1,700 and that the actual number was probably two or three times that many (1971:12).

The most thoroughly studied settlement of the late Iron Age is Manching near Ingolstadt in Bavaria. Manching is situated 4 kilometers south of the Danube River, but the river flowed directly by the site in prehistoric times. The site is located on a low sand and gravel terrace formed by the Danube and its tributaries. It is bounded on the west by the small river Paar and the Igel Brook and on the south and southwest by boggy land of the Feilermoos bog; to the north are the sands and gravels that originally lay on the south bank of the Danube.

Werner Krämer, director of the Manching excavations, notes that the location was selected for its situation on routes of communication. It lay on one of the major river arteries of Europe and on the natural crossing of two land routes, one along the terrace extending north-south between the marshy lowlands and the other along the south bank of the river (later the location of the principal Roman road in the region). Although Manching is not situated on a hilltop as the majority of oppida were, its setting provided natural protection. The courses of at least two brooks, the Igel on the southwest and the Riedelmoos on the southeast, were changed when the oppidum walls were built. Both streams now flow at the base of the wall outside the settlement.

The site is circular and bounded by walls more than 7 kilometers in length enclosing 380 hectares of land (Figure 55). Between 1955 and 1975, 66,906 square meters (about 6.7 hectares) of the settlement surface were excavated, slightly less than 2 percent of the area. A zone about 400 meters wide just inside the walls yielded evidence of only sporadic settlement. The excavators believe that this region, which is damp and low-lying, may have been kept as pasture land for livestock. The central, densely inhabited part of the oppidum measures about 1.5 kilometers east-west and encompasses 80 hectares. Across this area are thousands of settlement pits and postholes. As is the case in most central European settlements, only features that had been dug down into the subsoil are preserved, such as storage pits, wells, postholes, and foundation trenches. Posthole foundations have been found for a variety of

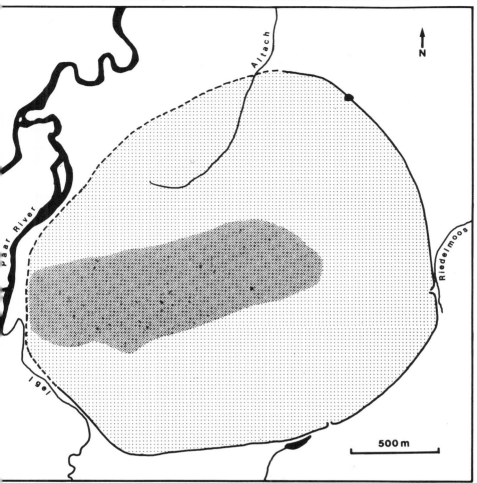

ppidum of Manching (entire stippled area). The heavily stippled area in the middle is the location
nsest settlement remains. The small river Paar flows by the site on the west, and brooks bound the
it on the other sides. The parts of the wall around the site that survive are indicated by a solid line,
it do not by a broken line. Based on Krämer and Schubert 1970, insert 5.

kinds of structures, ranging from small rectangular buildings 6 by
8.5 meters in size to huge structures of unknown purpose, one of
them 6 meters wide and more than 80 meters long. The pits,
postholes, and foundation trenches are so dense that a coherent
pattern of structures is difficult to discern, and they reflect much
rebuilding on the site during the century of its occupation. Excava-

tions from 1955 to 1961 produced about 400,000 animal bones, and between 1955 and 1967 more than 175,000 sherds of pottery were recovered. None of the evidence studied to date provides a good basis for estimating population size, but a figure of one or two thousand is a reasonable quess.

Manching flourished between 150 and 50 B.C. These dates have been established on the basis of the fibulae, weapons, and Roman imports recovered. A small cemetery dating to the beginning of the late Iron Age was found at the modern village of Steinbichel just west of the wall, and within the settlement on the parcel of land known as Hunsrucken was a cemetery dating to the middle of the late Iron Age, perhaps partly contemporaneous with the occupation of the oppidum at the end of the late Iron Age. These two cemeteries suggest that a small community existed in the vicinity before 150 B.C., but the evidence suggests a rapid growth rather than a slow development of the great settlement. No cemetery dating to the end of the late Iron Age—the time of the main occupation—has been found.

The community met a violent end. Many iron weapons, all of local forms, were found scattered over the central region of the site, including swords, spearheads, and shield umbos, most of them fragmentary. Skeletal remains of more than three hundred humans were found scattered about the settlement, and many skulls showed clear evidence of battle wounds. The character of the weapons indicates that this final battle took place sometime around 50 B.C.

Evidence for iron production is abundant at Manching. Large mounds of iron slag from smelting of the local bog ore have been found just south of the settlement in the Feilermoos bog. The numerous forging tools suggest very intensive iron working at the site. Molds for bronze casting and fragments of furnaces have been recovered. Numerous glass bracelets and beads have been found, and large chunks of unformed glass represent the raw material from which they were made.

Commerce with the Roman world is attested by fragments of more than thirty-four wine amphorae and ceramic vessels from Campania. Coin hoards in the vicinity attest to the accumulation of wealth in precious metals. One containing more than one thousand gold coins of local type was found in the village of Irsching six kilometers northeast of the oppidum, and a hoard of local silver coins were recovered buried in a pot within the settlement. Some thirty coins have been found in the settlement deposits, and pieces of ceramic molds for casting coin blanks indicate that coins were minted there. Thirteen equal-arm balances, twelve bronze and one iron, have been found at the site. Such balances, used for weighing precious metals, are well represented at other major settlements as well. Graphite imported from deposits to the east was mixed with clay for making one variety of pottery. Sapropelite, a form of coal, was brought in from mines in Bohemia and used to make bracelets.

The large amount of cultural debris at Manching, particularly the animal bones (see the chart, Analysis of faunal remains from Manching) and the pottery, suggests that the site was likely used as a fair and market center to which many people came from surrounding lands to trade and to celebrate, eat, and drink. The many people who congregated for fairs, markets, and celebrations likely discarded vast quantities of food remains, including animal bones, and other domestic debris such as broken pottery, and they probably also lost many small objects such as fibulae and low-denomination coins. Daniel Defoe's description of the Sturbridge Fair in England in 1723 provides a general impression of the phenomenon in more modern times: "As for the people in the fair, they all universally eat drink and sleep in their booths and tents; and the said booths are so intermingled with taverns, coffee-houses, drinking-houses, eating-houses, cook-shops, etc. and all in tents too; and so many butchers, and hagglers from all the neighboring counties came. . . ." Defoe makes the point that the structures were erected temporarily for the fair, then torn down afterwards. Such fairs, still common in many parts of Europe, date back well into the prehistoric period.

Evidence in support of the local market role of Manching has been found in smaller settlements such as Steinebach in southern Germany. These rural sites have yielded items such as glass bracelets and sapropelite jewelry that are unlikely to have been manufactured in each small community. Roman bronze vessels, which surely arrived in central Europe at the oppida, also have turned up in small communities. The availability of the Italic luxury goods, as well as of new items produced in specialized workshops at the oppida, stimulated central European farmers to produce extra goods for trade and individual entrepreneurs to try to eke profits out of the system.

The remains of these entrepreneurs who organized the production and circulation have not been found because a cemetery for Manching has not been discovered. Yet the coin hoards on and around the site represent one form in which the entrepreneurs

Analysis of faunal remains from Manching (data from Boessneck *et al.* 1971)

Of about 400,000 bone fragments analyzed:
  99.8 percent domestic species
  0.2 percent wild species
Estimated numbers of animals represented on the site, based on analyzed remains from excavated portions:
  50,000 cattle
  50,000 pigs
  50,000 sheep and goats
  6,000 dogs
  5,000 horses
If total occupation was about 100 years (150–50 B.C.), the number of animals alive at one time would be approximately:
  2,000 cattle
  1,500 sheep and goats
  1,000 pigs
  200 horses
  150 dogs
If annual slaughter rates were
  500 cattle
  500 pigs
  500 sheep and goats
  50 horses
then the annual meat supply would have been about 154,000 kg, an average of about 422 kg per day.

were storing their acquired wealth. In other regions the successful merchants are identifiable by their wealth of grave goods, for example, at Goeblingen-Nospelt in Luxembourg, Hoppstädten-Weiersbach near Trier, and Hannogne in the Ardennes.

A final indication of the importance of Manching in its territory is the survival today of a large annual livestock market and fair called the Barthelmarkt at Oberstimm, 3 kilometers west of Manching. Krämer suggests that this fair represents the modern version of the tradition that has been carried on continuously from late Iron Age Manching.

ECONOMY AND SOCIETY IN THE LATE IRON AGE

McEvedy and Jones (1978:18) suggest a population of around thirty million for Europe at the birth of Christ, three times their estimate for 1000 B.C. Diodorus of Sicily (5. 25) tells us that tribes in Gaul had populations between fifty thousand and two hundred thousand. Julius Caesar provides the following figures for tribes in the vicinity of northern Switzerland in the middle of the final century B.C.: 263,000 Helvetii, 36,000 Tulingi, 32,000 Boii, 23,000 Rauraci and 14,000 Latovici. He states that in the Gallic uprisings inspired by the local leader Vercingetorix in 52 B.C. the Sequani (a tribe in eastern France between the Saône River and the Jura Mountains) raised 12,000 men, the Aedui of central France and Arverni of south-central France each 35,000. If men capable of bearing arms made up one-quarter of the populations, then the Sequani would have numbered 48,000 and the Aedui and Arverni each 140,000. Strabo in his *Geography* (4. 4. 3) states that the Belgae of northern Gaul comprised fifteen tribes, including 300,000 persons able to bear arms.

Many scholars have discussed the accuracy of the figures provided by the classical writers. Since Caesar was fighting to conquer central Europe, it is likely that he overestimated rather than underestimated the native populations about whom he wrote. If Caesar's numbers were correct, the Helvetians would have been living at a density of about thirteen people per square kilometer, probably somewhat high. Sabina Rieckhoff-Pauli suggests that half of Caesar's figure would be a reasonable estimate. On the basis of archaeological evidence, Jiří Waldhauser suggests that the northern half of Bohemia was inhabited by about fifty thousand people at this time. This estimate represents a much less dense occupation than those proposed by the classical writers for Gaul. Gaul probably was more densely populated than eastern central Europe, but not as much as this discrepancy would suggest.

Settlements

Only a small proportion of central Europeans lived in the oppida, the largest of which, such as Manching, Stradonice, and Bibracte, probably had populations around one or two thousand. Most Europeans still lived in small hamlets with populations of less than one hundred. Some were single farmsteads, such as that at Steinebach in southern Bavaria. Others were hamlets or small villages consisting of two to twenty dwellings. Among sites of this category that have been excavated are Eschweiler-Laurenzberg in the Rhineland, Haina in central Germany, Zăluží in Bohemia, Mistřín in Moravia, and to the north Feddersen Wierde in Lower Saxony and Hodde in South Jylland. These small settlements were usually open and unfortified, though some had fences around them. The archaeological remains include postholes marking the walls of buildings, storage and borrow pits, and finds including pottery and objects of iron, bronze, stone, and glass, as well as floral and faunal remains of meals.

All of these small communities were agricultural, and their members probably spent most of their time producing food. Although most of the sites yield evidence of some manufacturing and trade, at none does the evidence suggest that commerce was the economic basis. Bone and antler were shaped into implements, and textiles spun and woven. Slag attests to iron production. Bronze casting is represented by partly finished objects and by crucibles. One ceramic crucible at Mistřín even contained remains of gold. The small communities were producing most of the material culture used by their members and did not rely heavily on products from the oppida. In some cases small sites were producing metal goods for export, as at Msec in Bohemia and the many sites in Burgenland. At Gussage All Saints in southern Britain a small farming community was manufacturing series of ornate chariot fittings for trade.

The material assemblages at these small sites were similar to those at the oppida, not markedly poorer. Comparison of pottery from the site of Altendorf near Bamberg with that from Manching shows that not only were the same kinds of pottery in use at the two locations, but the types even occur in similar proportions at both places. Metal objects were also alike at small and large sites. For example, at Eschweiler-Laurenzberg the hammers, chisels, needles, knives, keys, horse and wagon equipment, spearheads, and swords were indistinguishable from those recovered at Manching. At Eschweiler-Lohn, a small settlement that met a violent end, many iron weapons were recovered including shield bosses, spearheads and spear shoes, arrowheads, and swords, along with slingstones, all very similar to those at the oppida. Apparently the small communities throughout central Europe possessed state-of-the-art tools and weapons. Iron plowshares were found in two houses at the small habitation site of Zăluží in Bohemia, showing that new agricultural implements were generally available. Small communities also obtained luxury ornaments such as glass bracelets and beads, lignite bracelets, and sapropelite jewelry. Coins are well represented at the small settlements, and some were minting their own.

Houses throughout central Europe were rectangular, generally around 150 square meters in interior area, with vertical support posts along the walls. In regions along the North Sea coast a particular kind of building was employed beginning in the late Bronze Age—a long rectangular structure separated into a smaller living area for humans and a larger one, subdivided into stalls, for up to thirty head of cattle. The part of the building for human habitation was about the same size as the houses in the rest of Europe. In Britain, houses were round instead of rectangular, but similar in size and construction to those in central Europe.

Economy

Several classical authors mention food production north of the Alps in barbarian Europe. Information derived from Posidonius, writing around the beginning of the final century before Christ, emphasizes the agricultural richness and high productivity of central European lands. Strabo in the *Geography* (4. 1. 2) writes that all of Gaul except swamps and thickets was used for food production and that the land yielded cereal grains, millet, nuts, and all kinds of livestock. He mentions enormous flocks of sheep and herds of swine in Belgica and describes production of large amounts of food, especially milk and meat, particularly fresh and salted pork (4. 4. 3). Athenaeus (4. 36) was also impressed by the quantity of meat consumed by central Europeans and mentions loaves of bread and fish eaten with salt, vinegar, and cumin. Many classical authors refer to beer, sometimes brewed from barley and sometimes from wheat, along with a drink made of honey, probably what we know as mead (Athenaeus 4. 36, Diodorus of Sicily 5. 26). The classical writers knew of the wine trade and noted that wine was the preferred beverage of the wealthy.

The basic form of the wooden ard—the simple scratch plow without a moldboard to turn over the soil—remained the same throughout the final millennium before Christ (Figure 56), and the only major technological change was the addition of the iron plowshare during the final two centuries B.C. All excavated oppida have yielded iron plowshares; for example, there are forty-three specimens from the Steinsburg, nine from Manching, and nine from Heidetränk, and shares have also been recovered at many small settlements. Evidence that heavier and deeper-plowing implements may have come into use is provided by iron coulters,

[173]

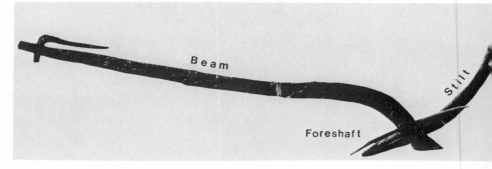

56. The Døstrup plow, from a bog in northern Jutland, Denmark. The plow is made of five pie beam, about 3 m long, is made of an alder trunk, and the hook at the front end is made of hazel wo stilt is made of lime and originally had a share of harder material, now missing. The handle at the to stilt is also of lime. The thin foreshare set between the beam and the stilt is of elder wood and show of heavy use.

such as one in the hoard from Hainbach in Land Salzburg, Austria, dating to the final century B.C. The coulter was used in heavy plowing for the initial breaking of the soil in front of the plowshare and moldboard. Iron plowshares and heavier plows with mold-boards and coulters enabled farmers to plow more land per day than the plain wooden ard. The iron shares and heavier plows could cut deeper than the ard, and so farmers were able to farm the heavier and richer soils. The moldboard turned over the soil and circulated soil minerals more effectively. Plows with moldboards also aerated the soil more completely than those without and pro-moted better drainage of the fields.

The scythe first became common during this period as well (Fig-ure 57). A scythe is in essence a sickle with elongated blade and shaft. Because of the physical properties of bronze, a bronze sickle had to be short or it would break during use. The toughness of iron permitted the use of much longer blades. Scythes are well repre-sented at the oppida and at some of the smaller settlements. At Manching twelve iron rings used to fasten scythe blades onto their wooden handles have been found, along with a number of frag-mentary blades. Twenty-eight scythe blades were recovered at the Steinsburg. Scythes were also found in many hoards, for example, at Kappel, Kaiserbrunn, and Körner. Grain can be cut much faster with a scythe than with a sickle. Development of the scythe proba-bly increased the efficiency of harvesting the cereal grains, which formed the basis of the European diet. Scythes were also important

[174]

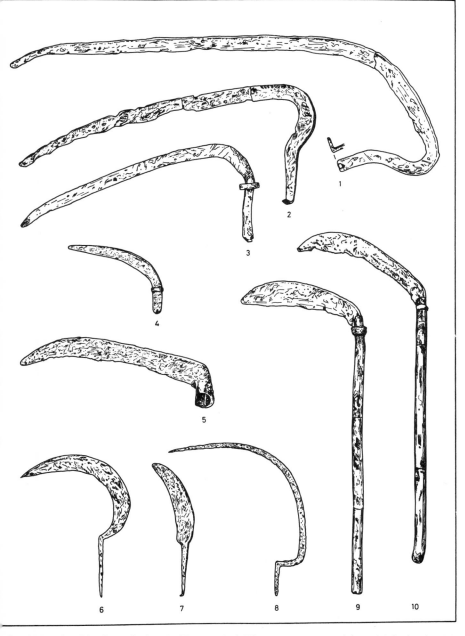

. Scythes and sickles from the late La Tène period. They were recovered from (1) Szalacska, (2) rija, (3) Oberleiserberg, (4) Kaposmerö, (5) Fort-Harrouard, (6, 7, 9, 10) La Tène, and (8) einsburg. Objects 9 and 10 include wooden handles. The blade of object 10 is 28.2 cm long.

[175]

for harvesting hay for winter fodder. Large-scale manufacture of scythes may have played a major role in the wintering of livestock to provide winter meat and dairy products and traction for plows in the spring. The keeping of larger herds may have been related to the growth in trade of live animals, dairy products, meats, and leather.

After iron, the material that provides the most information about production is pottery. Analysis of about 200,000 sherds from Manching shows that four categories of pottery were manufactured on the site, differentiated from one another in composition, technique of manufacture, and form. The uniformity of composition and shape within each of the groups suggests that pottery was made for the whole community by specialists, not by family members for individual households.

Besides trade with Italy, commerce was carried on throughout continental Europe. Copper and tin for bronze ornaments were extracted from the same ore bodies as before. After a decline for about three centuries, salt mining resumed at Hallstatt around 100 B.C. Salt extraction began at Reichenhall in southeastern Germany at about the same time, while activity at the mining community at the Dürrnberg declined, perhaps because of new competition from Hallstatt and Reichenhall. Salt springs in the hilly landscapes north of the Alps were also exploited now, and evidence of major workings has been found at Bad Nauheim and Schwäbisch Hall in Germany as well as at sites in Poland.

Gold and silver were used for jewelry and for coins. Silver was unusual north of the Alps before this period, and most of it probably came in the form of coins from the Mediterranean world, as payment to central European mercenaries serving in armies of Mediterranean societies and perhaps as bullion in trade (the Magdalensberg inscriptions mention transactions in which Roman merchants paid in coin).

Distribution of Wealth

During the second century before Christ as during most of the preceding period, material wealth was relatively evenly distributed in graves. There were only a few exceptionally rich graves, such as that at Dühren in Baden, Germany, which contained two bronze vessels and two bronze mirrors from Italy, a bronze kettle and iron stand, two gold finger rings, two silver fibulae, four glass bracelets, amber ornaments, a silver coin, and ten ceramic vessels. Cremation began to replace inhumation as the principal burial practice during the second century before Christ, and fewer objects were placed in graves. By the final century B.C. inhumation burials with grave goods were very rare. For most of central Europe, with the exception of the Rhineland and areas west of it, practically no cemeteries have been found, only isolated small groups of burials. No cemeteries have been found associated with the main occupation of Manching, for example. The explanation for this lack of graves lies in the changes in burial rite. Cremation burials without grave goods can easily go unnoticed by modern investigators. Waldhauser (1979) discusses an important grave from the interior of a rectangular enclosure of the late La Tène period at Markvartice in Bohemia. The grave, consisting of a small pit dug only into the surface humus, contained cremated remains. Had the interior of the enclosure been plowed, the grave would have been obliterated. If most graves were similarly buried in shallow pits without goods, they were destroyed without a trace by the centuries of plowing since the end of the Iron Age.

To the north of the zone in which the oppida were located, small cemeteries reflect a pattern of farmsteads and hamlets. Figure 58 shows the distribution of grave goods in one of these. The only parts of Europe in which oppida and traditional burial practices occurred are the Rhineland and areas west of it. The region around Trier, with some forty-five cemeteries dating to the final century before Christ, is particularly well documented. The graves were somewhat more richly outfitted with goods than those of the preceding centuries, but the metal and pottery objects were plainer and more standardized than before.

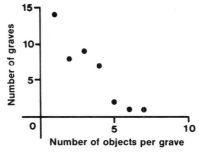

58. Distribution of grave goods in 42 burials in the cemetery at Naumburg on the Saale, East Germany.

Most of the cemeteries of the Rhineland were small and exhibited little differentiation in wealth, but there were some exceptions. One of those was the cemetery at Wederath; it served the expanding regional center of Trier, which was first Celtic and later Roman. Grave 1216 at Wederath contained a fifty-year-old man buried with his full set of iron weapons—sword, two spears, wooden shield with iron parts, and axe—as well as his razor and an iron bracelet. Buried with him was a young adult woman with a rich assemblage of glass jewelry. Eighteen ceramic vessels accompanied the two bodies. Among eleven graves in part of a larger cemetery at Hoppstädten-Weiersbach were two that had wagons among their goods and one with sixty-nine objects in it. Several exceptionally rich burials (Figure 59) have been found at Goeblingen-Nospelt in Luxembourg, associated with the great oppidum of the Titelberg, but no large cemetery has been identified yet. Four of these contained thirty-one, thirty-two, fifty, and sixty objects. Of those graves, two contained large quantities of Roman ceramics and bronzes as well as local weapons and precious metal jewelry. A few rich graves also were found in smaller cemeteries, as at the Trier-Olewig grave and Neuwied Grave 2. Graves similar to these have been found to the west and north of the Middle Rhineland, in the Champagne region of northeastern France (Hannogne) and in eastern Britain (Welwyn). These rich burials of northwestern Europe are characterized by the similarity of their contents—weapons, especially swords; drinking vessels, including those imported from the Roman world; two-wheeled chariots; and ornaments of precious metals. Table 2 shows the special elite objects that have been found in these graves.

The prominence of weapons in these graves is significant. At the end of the Iron Age, warfare became an important means of gaining wealth. Both commerce and warfare were significant in the development of the oppida, and, as Grierson has shown for early medieval times, they were not always clearly separable. A successful attack on an oppidum could yield riches in booty as well as slaves for trade to Rome. Caesar mentions the regular practice among the Gallic tribes of raiding between neighboring groups: "Before the arrival of Caesar, the knights nearly every other year either attacked another tribe or warded off the attacks of another tribe" (*The Gallic War* 6. 15). This state of affairs north of the Alps may have been greatly influenced by the development of trade with Rome beginning in the mid–second century B.C.

For the first time since the late Bronze Age, buried hoards were

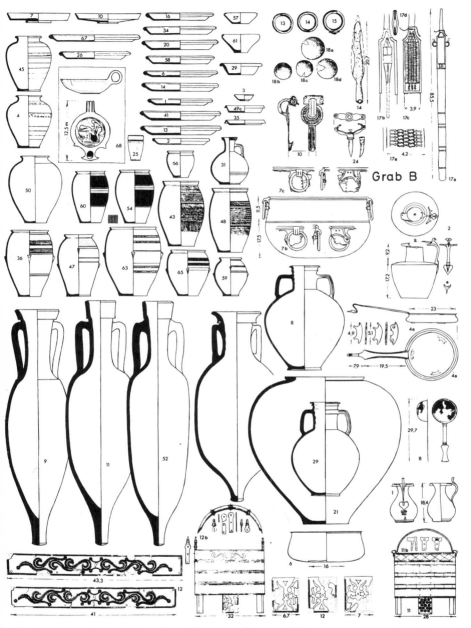

59. Iron weapons (*upper right*) and a wide range of imported Roman ceramic and metal vessels from Goeblingen-Nospelt Grave B.

Table 2. Exceptional objects in rich graves, 100–1 B.C.

Grave	Swords	Shields	Spears	Helmets	Spurs	Roman amphorae	Metal vessels
Trier-Olewig	1		2	1			
Neuwied 2	1	1	4		2		1
Wederath 1216	1	1	2				
Goeblingen-Nospelt A	1		3		1	2	3
Goeblingen-Nospelt B	1		1		1	5	8
Hannogne	1		2			1	2
Novo mesto	1	1	1	1			

numerous during the final two centuries before Christ. The same problems of interpretation pertain to these hoards, and they are variously believed to have been smiths' stores of metal, traveling merchants' caches, votive offerings, and treasures hidden in times of war. Whatever the specific circumstances of their burial, the hoards are important as accumulations of wealth—capital collected by individuals or groups and hidden in the ground. These hoards can be divided into two categories: those that contained tools and those that contained precious metals. The hoard from Kappel in southern Württemberg is a good example of the first category. It had in it 126 metal objects and a handle made of antler. Only twelve of the metal objects were not broken. The bronze items included an imported Italic jug, two Italic pails, an Italic wine ladle, two rein rings, fragmentary parts of wagons, and small ornaments. Among the iron objects were parts of several large andirons, two pairs of tongs, two hammers, eight axes, a chisel, a wedge, an anvil, a scythe blade, a sickle blade, a fragment of a sword, and fragmentary rings and attachments. This hoard constituted a considerable accumulation of metal and was probably the property of a well-to-do metalworker, to judge by the large number of smith's tools present. The Aubstadt hoard of twenty-three iron ingots contained only raw material. In the north of Europe, the Hjortspring hoard found in a bog on Als Island in Denmark comprised a boat 13 meters long, eight iron swords, wooden shields, iron and bone spearheads, iron chain mail, wooden vessels, and ornaments.

Coins were minted on a regular basis in Europe during the final two centuries before Christ. The idea of coinage was adopted from Mediterranean peoples, and the first coins minted in central Europe were modeled after gold staters of the Macedonian kings Phillip II (ruled 359–336 B.C.) and Alexander (ruled 336–323 B.C.). Beginning in the fourth century B.C., central Europeans were serving as mercenaries in Mediterranean armies, and many were paid in coin. In this way many central Europeans became familiar with coinage as a medium of exchange and an easily stored and disposable form of wealth. The most active minting and trade of European coinage was from around 120 B.C. until the Roman conquest. All of the major oppida have yielded ceramic molds in which coin blanks were cast, and a number of smaller settlements have as well. Coins became an important medium for storing wealth, just as bronze ingots and objects had been during the Bronze Age. Central European coinage was almost exclusively gold and silver; bronze coins were minted only in small numbers. Thus there was little small change circulating in Europe which would have been necessary for everyday transactions in a true money economy.

That most central European coins have been recovered in hoards supports the interpretation that they mostly represented bullion. Many hoards contained only coins, while others contained coins and other forms of precious metal. At Irsching, 6 kilometers northeast of Manching, a hoard of more than one thousand gold coins was found, contemporaneous with the occupation of the oppidum, and within the settlement a hoard of silver coins was recovered in a pot buried in the ground. A hoard containing both local and Roman coins along with silver jewelry was found at Lauterach near Bregenz in Vorarlberg, Austria. It contained twenty-four Roman silver coins dating between 150 and 106 B.C., three central European silver coins, two silver fibulae connected by a silver chain, a silver neckring, a small silver ring, and a small bronze ring. A recently discovered hoard from a settlement pit at Niederzier near Düren in northwestern Germany contained three sheet-gold rings and forty-six gold coins, twenty-six European and twenty Roman. All of the coins together weighed 321.84 grams, close to the Roman pound of 327.45 grams.

These media for the storage and display of wealth at the end of the prehistoric Iron Age were similar to those of preceding centuries. The hoards of precious metals, iron tools, and iron ingots, like hoards in the late Bronze Age, constituted supplies of usable wealth stored in safe places. The rich burials, such as those at Goeblingen-Nospelt, and the gold and silver ring jewelry were means of displaying luxury wealth in ways very similar to those at early Iron Age commercial centers. In the final century before

Christ, as in earlier periods, the connection between accumulation of wealth, growth of commerce, and development of towns is apparent. At the end of the Iron Age the new tools for work in agriculture, metallurgy, and other crafts made production much more efficient so that larger communities could be sustained. The patterns of town formation in Iron Age Europe were, however, interrupted by the arrival of armies from the land that had been the principal source of imported luxuries.

7 Roman Interlude and the Formation of Medieval Towns

The Roman conquest of western and southern central Europe broke the continuity of European development. The Romans introduced a new, Mediterranean culture with true cities, a written language, and a centralized economic and political hierarchy. European communities within the imperial boundaries became subservient to Roman administration for about four hundred years after the conquest just before the birth of Christ.

ROME NORTH OF THE ALPS

In 121 B.C. Roman armies crossed the western Alps to establish the new province of Gallia Narbonensis. The Gallic Wars fought by Julius Caesar between 58 and 50 B.C. ended with the conquest of the rest of Gaul—lands that are now France, Belgium, part of the Netherlands, Germany west of the Rhine, and Switzerland north of the Alps. In 15 B.C. Roman armies under Tiberius and Drusus, the adopted sons of the Emperor Augustus, crossed the central Alps and conquered the territory south of the Danube. By the birth of Christ all of southern and western Europe and much of the central portion had been annexed into the Roman Empire. The only later addition to the Empire in Europe was the land between the Rhine and Danube, the *Agri decumates*, conquered in A.D. 81–96.

The Roman conquest put an end to the indigenous European economic and political organization and replaced it with the centrally directed Roman policies. The Roman Empire was a civilization with urban populations much larger than those of prehistoric

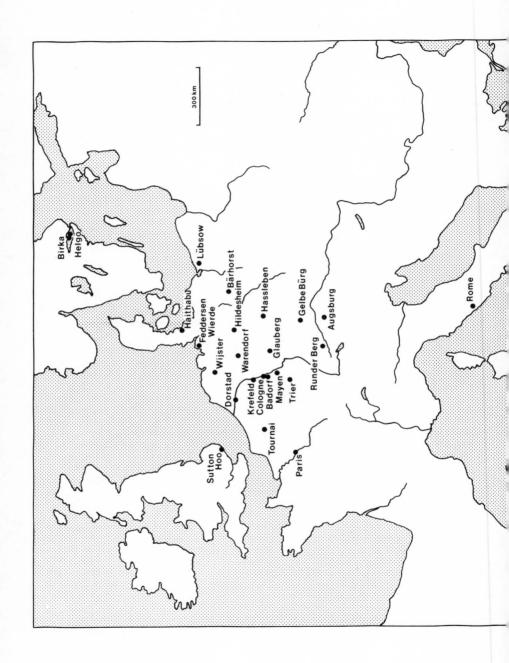

300 km

Birka
Helgö
Lübsow
Bärhorst
Haithabu
Feddersen
Wierde
Hildesheim
Hassleben
Wijster
Warendorf
Glauberg
Gelbe Bürg
Augsburg
Dorstad
Krefeld
Cologne
Badorf
Mayen
Trier
Runder Berg
Tournai
Sutton
Hoo
Paris
Rome

European communities (the city of Rome had about a million inhabitants at the birth of Christ), trade and industry directed from an imperial capital, and an economy based on slavery. Immediately after the conquest the Romans began building Mediterranean-style cities north of the Alps, which differed from the preceding settlements in size, their function as administrative centers, and the use of stone for construction. Cities such as Trier, Cologne, Mainz, and Augsburg were Mediterranean metropolises transplanted into the environment of temperate Europe.

With the establishment of imperial boundaries through central Europe (Figure 61) a new cultural and economic frontier was formed along the Rhine and Danube, with Romans and their subjects to the west and south and indigenous Europeans, principally Germans and Celts, to the east and north. During the final centuries before Christ, some Germanic groups moved southward from northern Europe into central and southern parts of the continent, and by the end of the last century B.C. the archaeological evidence from much of the middle part of Europe, particularly Bohemia and southern Germany, suggests that the cultural traditions, such as settlement patterns, burial practices, pottery styles, and jewelry types, of the late Iron Age Celtic populations were replaced by those of immigrant Germanic peoples. Changes in settlement patterns, burial practices, and material culture reflect the dominance of the immigrants. The indigenous Celtic peoples were not driven out or killed off. The Germanic newcomers simply moved in and forcibly established themselves as the dominant group.

After the middle of the second century of the Christian era, the peace of Roman Europe was disturbed by ever-increasing border attacks by Germanic bands. The Marcommani, Quadi, and Naristi in the east Alpine region attacked across the Danube frontier in A.D. 167 and again in 170. In 170 they uprooted the Roman defenders of the border, pillaged lands within the empire, and went on to northern Italy where they attacked the port city of Aquileia and other urban centers. They were finally defeated by Roman armies, but after the end of the second century of the Christian era the danger of raids by Germanic war parties from north of the Alps was always present.

Early in the third century the Germanic Alamanni launched a series of attacks against the Limes frontier between the Rhine and the Danube, and in 259–260 they crossed the border and sacked much of southern Germany. These bands were finally defeated

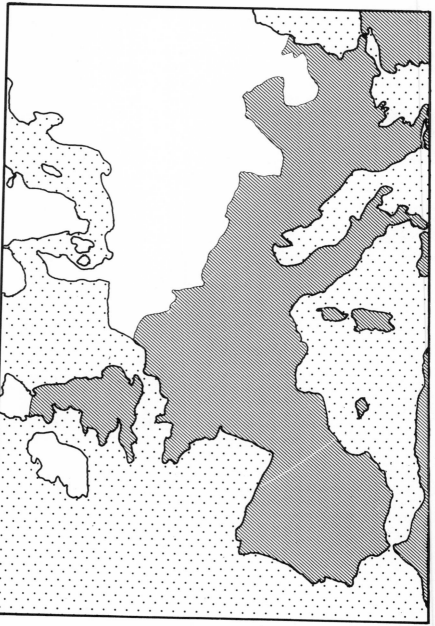

61. The Roman Empire (shaded area) in Europe during the first and second centuries of the Christian era

near Milan in 261, but as a result of their attacks the Romans abandoned the *Agri decumates* and retracted the boundary of the empire southward to the Danube and Lake Constance. The attacks continued throughout the third and fourth centuries. Along the central and northern Rhine, Frankish warrior bands invaded across the river and sometimes drove deep into Roman territory. At the beginning of the fifth century the Roman forces could no longer hold back the growing pressure of the attacking groups and relinquished their hold on Europe.

ECONOMY AND SOCIETY IN THE ROMAN PERIOD (A.D. 1–400)

Within the Empire

Roman administrators, engineers, and merchants were quick to exploit the rich resources of central Europe. Roman capital was invested in mining, manufacturing, and commerce in the newly acquired lands. Large pottery production centers were established in Gaul and in the Rhineland. Brass industries were begun in the Rhineland and in Belgium. Cologne became a center of Roman glass manufacture. Mayen and its environs in the middle Rhineland was a major source for basalt for grindstones. Iron was mined and processed on a large scale in regions where the ores were especially rich and accessible, as in Noricum in the southeastern Alps. Vineyards were planted along the Rhine and the Mosel as well as in Gaul, and wine was produced and traded.

In the cities great public buildings of local stone were constructed (Figure 62). Paved roads were laid out to connect all points of the empire, especially to assure the rapid movement of troops in case of rebellion or border attack, but also for the passage of trade goods, travelers, and messengers. Bridges were built over the rivers.

Roman troops were stationed all along the boundary of the empire. These soldiers, along with the many full-time workers in construction, metalsmithing, pottery manufacture, and other industries, required substantial quantities of food. This demand stimulated high levels of production by the farming population of indigenous Europeans and Roman slaves and encouraged circulation of other items such as Roman coins and local craft products.

Besides establishing cities and military camps, Romans also settled the countryside, building villas of Mediterranean style. The

[187]

62. The Porta Nigra, the gate to the walled Roman city in Trier, West Germany.

country villas (*villae rusticae*) were organized around agricultural production and were usually owned and managed by wealthy Romans, many of whom lived in the cities most of the time, and by army veterans. Agricultural laborers were both native Europeans and slaves brought in from other parts of the empire. The estates centered on the Roman villas were to a large extent self-sufficient and included crafts industries such as iron smithies, pottery manufacture, and workshops for leather and textiles.

Industry and trade were much more centrally organized in the Roman world than in prehistoric Europe and were carried out on a larger scale. The integration of all the provinces into the empire with its economic and political center at Rome fostered development of long-distance trade and the growth of industries producing goods specifically for trade. By contrast, the pattern of economic organization during the late Bronze Age and the Iron Age had been determined by the existence of small communities without a well-developed political or economic hierarchy, and fighting over the available wealth had limited the development of large-scale commercial enterprise.

Status and authority now depended largely on the individual's position in the hierarchy based in Rome. Some higher-status individuals of the indigenous societies in Europe were accorded honors by the new Roman overlords, as we know from both written documents and rich natives' graves, such as those at Goeblingen-Nospelt in Luxembourg, which date from between 50 and 10 B.C. In general, however, the indigenous population was forced to occupy the lower ranks of the new Roman society. They served as tenant farmers on the estates of wealthy Romans and as workers in the industries and on construction projects.

Outside the Empire

Economic and social conditions in the lands north and east of the Roman Empire in Europe were different and resembled those of prehistoric Europe. Although Roman merchants and other travelers regularly crossed the frontier into Free Germany and trade took place along the border, the influence of the Romans outside of the empire was minimal.

After the birth of Christ the lands beyond the empire were dominated by Germanic groups. There were no settlements as large as the major oppida of the late Iron Age, and no sites suggest communities larger than one hundred or at most two hundred individuals. Central Europe outside of the empire maintained industry and trade on a very small scale. Many settlements in northern Europe have been well excavated and studied, such as Feddersen Wierde in Lower Saxony and Ezinge and Wijster in the Netherlands, and they provide a good view into the economic patterns of the time.

Feddersen Wierde, situated on an artificial mound in the marshland of Lower Saxony close to the North Sea, was occupied between the end of the final century B.C. and the fourth or fifth century of the Christian era. The houses were tripartite in structure, with an entrance and hall, living quarters for the human occupants, and stalls for cattle, a form of farmhouse characteristic of the North Sea coastal regions from the late Bronze Age into modern times. During the earliest phase of occupation the settlement consisted of five houses; it later grew to twenty-five houses (Figure 63). Variation in house size, and particularly in the number of stalls for livestock, probably reflects differences in wealth between households. Pottery was manufactured at Feddersen Wierde, and iron was smelted. Trade is attested by the presence of Roman terra sigillata pottery, glass vessels and beads, coins, and fibulae, as well as basalt grindstones from Mayen. Other excavated settlements show similar characteristics, for example, Wijster, Ezinge, Zeijen, and Fochteloo in the Netherlands, Tofting in northern Germany, and Gröntoft and Nørre Fjand in Denmark. All were farmsteads and small villages with agricultural and pastoral economies. The livestock stalls in the longhouses and the large proportion of cattle bones on the settlements suggest that cattle raising was the main occupation. There was also some local manufacturing and limited trade. The ever-present Roman luxury imports were probably obtained in exchange for leather goods, preserved meats, live cattle, and other pastoral products. Woolen textiles may have played a part as well. Less research has been carried out on settlements in the interior regions of the continent, but the sites that have been studied, such as Bärhorst, Glauberg, and Gelbe Bürg, indicate community sizes and economic patterns similar to those on the coast.

The subsistence base of the lands beyond the Roman empire was similar to that of late prehistoric times, with reliance on the same assemblage of grains, garden crops, and domestic animals, supplemented by wild plants and animals. The plow with moldboard was now regularly employed. Plow furrows under the settlement at Feddersen Wierde attest to its use by the final century before Christ. The use of stalls on the North Sea coastal sites shows that many cattle were being tended indoors through the winter months.

There is little indication of manufacturing beyond local needs, except for evidence of intensive iron production in some areas, particularly in Schleswig-Holstein in Germany and in Poland. Sites in these regions show extensive smelting and forging. Iron was traded both within Free Germany and across the frontier with the Roman Empire.

Latin authors refer to Roman merchants crossing the border and trading to Free Germany and to Germans entering the imperial lands to carry on commerce. Trade goods mentioned include Roman silver vessels, coins, and wine in exchange for German amber, slaves, leather, and cattle. The archaeological evidence shows that Roman pottery, grindstones, wine amphorae, bronze and glass

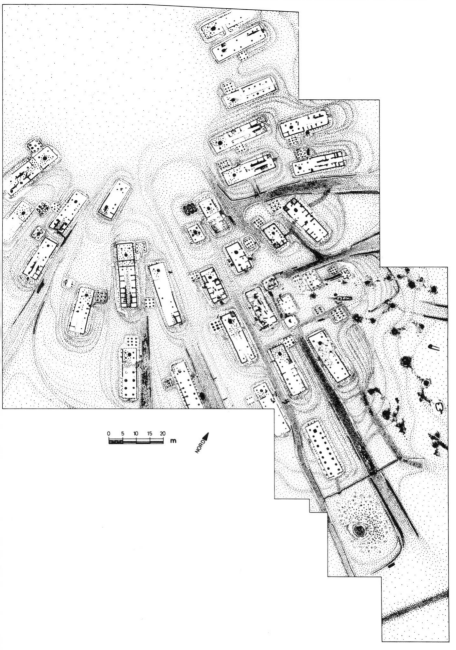

63. Plan of Feddersen Wierde during its most populous phase (around 300 A.D.).

vessels, and jewelry were extensively traded into Free Germany. As in the Iron Age sites discussed in chapters 4 and 6, Europeans were supplying basic raw materials for trade with urban Mediterranean societies, which were in turn exchanging luxury goods including wine and the vessels in which to carry and serve it.

Wealth in Europe outside the empire is apparent in the form of precious metal objects found in graves and hoards, especially Roman silver and bronze vessels, Roman gold and silver coins, and jewelry of both Roman and Germanic origin. Most of the richest graves and hoards contained Roman materials, either alone or together with Germanic objects, a fact that emphasizes the close connection between interactions with the Roman world and the accumulation of wealth. A spectacular hoard of Roman silver was found by soldiers digging in Hildesheim, Germany, in 1868. The hoard was buried sometime during the first or second century of the Christian era and contained twenty-six silver vessels and a silver folding table. Among the vessels were plates, bowls, beakers, and a large cauldron, most of them highly ornate and of exceptionally fine workmanship. A hoard of the second or third century of the Christian era from Bad Pyrmont, Westphalia, Germany, contained a Roman bronze pan, about 250 Roman and Germanic fibulae, and Roman silver coins. One dating to the late fourth century after the birth of Christ, from Lengerich, East Frisia, had in it a gold fibula, two gold bracelets, three gold finger rings, four gold buttons, and a Roman gold coin.

Many richly outfitted graves similarly attest to the accumulation of wealth. Twenty-five rich burials, mostly inhumations, known as the Lübsow group are scattered throughout Free Germany as far east as Poland and as far south as Bohemia, all with similar grave structures and contents. The first of five such graves discovered at Lübsow in northern Poland was situated under a stone cairn. The burial contained a coffin cut from a tree trunk and the following objects of Roman origin: two silver beakers, a bronze bucket, a bronze basin, a bronze jug, two bronze pans, two blue glass bowls, a silver-coated bronze mirror, and a gold fibula. Local objects included three silver fibulae, two silver pins, a silver belt hook, two silver-covered drinking horns, a pair of bronze shears, and a ceramic vessel. The Lübsow graves belong to the first century of the Christian era, but rich burials of the later centuries of the Roman period, such as those at Leuna and Hassleben in East Germany, contained similar assemblages of Roman and Germanic luxury objects.

[192]

During the four centuries of the Roman period the sources of wealth in Free Germany were manifold, but three mechanisms probably account for most of the wealth in the hoards and graves. Tacitus notes that silver vessels were often presented by Romans to Germanic chiefs as gifts, presumably to buy peace and discourage attacks on the frontier, perhaps also to establish friendly relations for organized trade. Much of the wealth in Roman luxuries was probably obtained through such trade. During the third and fourth centuries, especially, luxury goods were seized by Germanic raiding parties crossing the frontier stations to plunder the villages and estates of the imperial lands. It is not always easy to distinguish between peaceful trading and violent plundering, and, as Philip Grierson (1959) has shown, the difference was not always as great as we might think.

EARLY MEDIEVAL PERIOD (A.D. 400–900)

After the middle of the third century of the Christian era, Germanic raids across the frontier into the empire increased in frequency and effectiveness. Friendly Germanic groups were invited by the Roman administration to settle in Roman territory to act as buffers against unfriendly ones. The leaders of some of these tribes rose in status and wealth in late Roman provincial society. For example, Childeric, a Frankish king, lived in northern France and Belgium and helped defend the empire against Saxons, West Goths, and Alans. He was buried in A.D. 482, and his grave at Tournai, discovered during the sixteenth century, showed him to have been both rich and esteemed. Germanic leaders in alliance with the Romans, knowledgeable in the ways of their Germanic followers and of the Roman administrators they served, played an essential role in the formation of the Merovingian Empire at the end of the fifth century.

After the departure of the Romans from Europe north of the Alps, around the middle of the fifth century, Romanized Germans west of the Rhine and south of the Danube maintained some of the Roman industries and commerical networks. Specialized glass production was continued at Cologne, and jewelry was still manufactured and coins minted at other former Roman centers. Trade never broke down completely, either within central Europe or between Europe and the Mediterranean world. Yet the populations of the provincial cities declined during the fifth and sixth centuries, and

[193]

Roman industries were gradually taken over by central Europeans and began producing goods distinctively Germanic in character. The patterns of change are especially well documented at sites that were continuously occupied from the Roman period into medieval times. At Krefeld-Gellep on the lower Rhine four thousand graves spanning the period from the first century to about A.D. 700 reflect changes in burial customs and in material culture. A few graves outfitted with weapons dating to the third century of the Christian era are the first indication of the arrival of Germanic groups on the site. The proportion of graves with weapons grew in the fifth century, suggesting a substantial increase in the Germanic component of the community. Around A.D. 500 the graves show evidence for the arrival of a large contingent of Franks, who buried their dead with more goods than their predecessors.

In some locations, as at Krefeld-Gellep, Cologne, Augsburg, and Regensburg, the Germanic newcomers settled directly on the old Roman sites, while in others they chose new locations for their settlements, as Kurt Böhner has demonstrated in his study of settlement topography in the region around Trier. In some instances, as at the Lorenzberg in Bavaria, Germanic groups used abandoned and deteriorating Roman stone structures for their cemeteries.

Settlements

Although some of the Roman cities survived as Germanic settlements, they declined in population, area, and economic activity, and many were abandoned by the Germans a century or two after the departure of the Romans. The characteristic settlements of the early medieval period were hamlets, similar to Feddersen Wierde and Wijster. Like them, they were agricultural and pastoral communities with at most a couple of hundred members, and they carried on limited manufacturing and trade for a small range of luxury goods. The settlement at Warendorf on the Ems River near Münster, occupied from about 650 to 800, is a well-studied example. One hundred eighty-six buildings were excavated on the site, including large structures with double rows of posts and with hearths, smaller post-build structures with and without hearths, sunken huts, and small structures such as sheds and drying racks (Figure 64). The settlement consisted of four or five farmsteads and had a population of twenty-five to fifty. Most of the pottery found was plain, but some sherds were of ceramics imported from Rhine-

[194]

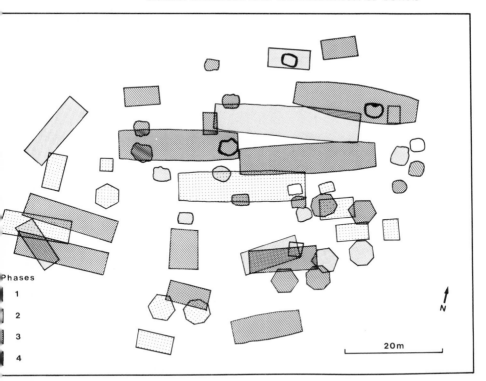

...n of part of the excavated settlement of Warendorf, showing the long house-and barn structures and
...buildings during the different phases of occupation. Four successive phases over 150 years of
...ion were identified. Based on Winkelmann 1958, insert 2.

land potteries. A range of iron tools and ornaments was recovered,
and slag attests to local production of the metal. Loom weights and
spindle whorls are evidence of textile manufacture. Glass vessels
and beads from the Rhineland and basalt grindstones from Mayen
were also found. Similar settlements have been excavated throughout Europe, such as Gladbach on the middle Rhine and Burgheim
in Upper Bavaria.

The only communities that were considerably larger in population were trading sites on the coasts of the North and Baltic seas,
such as Helgö and Birka in Sweden, Dorstad in the Netherlands,
and Haithabu in Schleswig-Holstein. These were among the first
indigenous commercial towns north of the Alps since the late Iron
Age oppida.

[195]

Commerce

Local manufacturing is well attested on settlements such as Warendorf. The development of industries aimed specifically at trade was important in the formation of the medieval towns. Pottery production in the Rhineland is the clearest example. At the beginning of the eighth century, large-scale potteries began production around the town of Badorf between Bonn and Cologne on the Rhine. Thin-section studies of Badorf pottery show that this ware was produced in the one locale and traded from there all along the lower Rhine valley and the southern North Sea coast, as far north as Birka in Sweden, and as far south as Strasbourg on the upper Rhine. Badorf pottery was made between 720 and 860, and it was replaced by another variety, Pingsdorf ware, also produced for trade. Other industries produced decorated metalwork, swords, raw iron, metal vessels, leather goods, glass vessels and beads, and grindstones for commerce. These new industries of the early medieval period were concentrated in the Rhineland, along the North Sea coasts, and in Sweden. Growth of these industries was closely tied to the formation of the new towns.

Although the demise of the Roman Empire in Europe resulted in the disruption of the commerce based in the urban centers, local trade in Free Germany was little affected. Commerce between central Europe and Italy resumed about A.D. 500 and is well represented by Italic coins, Coptic bronze bowls and other vessels, and Ostrogothic helmets in rich men's graves. The expansion of this trade in Italic luxury goods coincided with the appearance of the first series of post-Roman rich graves, such as Krefeld-Gellep Grave 1782, the woman's and boy's graves under the Cologne Cathedral, and the women's graves at St. Severin in Cologne and at St. Denis in Paris. All of these exceptional burials date to the sixth century. Like the rich graves of the Iron Age, these are characterized by both local elite objects (particularly gold jewelry and iron weapons) and exotic Mediterranean luxuries (gilded helmets, silk, garnet ornaments). Yet in the early medieval period the growing industries in central Europe supplied goods for trade not with Mediterranean societies, but with northern Europe. The commercial focus shifted from the Mediterranean Sea to the North Sea.

Distribution of Wealth

Accumulated wealth is present in the rich graves of the early medieval period, from the sixth century on. Grave 1782 at Krefeld-

Gellep, dating from about 525, was larger than most in the cemetery and had an unusual stone covering. It contained an extraordinary assemblage of special objects including a gold coin, a gold finger ring with a chalcedony mount, two gold attachments with garnet and green glass inlay, an iron bit and cheek pieces with gold foil covering, a gold rein divider with silver and garnet trim, a silver belt buckle, an iron long sword with gold and garnet pommel and pendant with meerschaum knob and gold button, an iron throwing spear, an iron hunting spear, a third iron spear, an iron throwing axe and short sword, an iron helmet with gilded bronze ornament, a gilded shield, two iron knives with gilded handles in sheaths with gold chapes, an iron roasting spit, a silver spoon, a pouch hinge of silver and garnet, a silver pin, an iron awl, and a flint-and-steel set. Vessels in the grave included three silver pails, two bronze pails, one gold pail, a glass bowl and jug, a bronze cauldron, a hanging basin, and a wooden bucket. The weapons and bronze vessels were of local Frankish origin, as were the gold ornaments. The helmet and silver spoon were of Ostrogothic manufacture, from Italy. The two glass vessels were products of the late Roman glass industry, probably in Cologne.

The objects in this grave are characteristic of a series of rich burials of the sixth and seventh centuries in continental Europe. As in the Iron Age, this wealth derived ultimately from surplus agricultural production and secondarily from the commerce that the surplus made possible (and that stimulated generation of such surplus). These rich graves are concentrated along the main rivers in particularly fertile lands, not at deposits of extractable resources such as salt or iron. Regions in which rich graves are particularly numerous are the Cologne-Bonn area, the Mosel-Rhine-Lahn confluence, the Rhine-Nahe-Main area, the middle Neckar valley, and along the upper Danube.

General conditions of life in Europe had changed in a number of ways since the prehistoric Iron Age. The population was substantially greater than before the Roman conquest, and communities were often larger than all but the biggest pre-Roman settlements. Agricultural production was probably more efficient, since the Romans introduced new breeds of plants and animals and new techniques of planting, harvesting, and maintaining soil fertility, improvements that spread during the medieval period to the east and north of the formerly imperial lands.

As during the Iron Age, surpluses were used to support specialist crafts workers and to exchange for luxury goods. Imports

[197]

such as glass vessels and basalt grindstones at small agricultural settlements show that the farming communities were participating in a complex exchange system involving trade of agricultural products. The persons buried in the rich graves can be interpreted principally as those who played the entrepreneurial roles in coordinating trade and reaped the benefits from that trade. The status of such persons has been much discussed in the medieval historical literature. Georges Duby (1974:43–44) notes that during the seventh and eighth centuries, in the economically most developed regions of central Europe, magnates for the first time gained economic control over peasants in their territories. Before that time the largely nonhierarchical and noncentralized farming communities were relatively independent and could use their resources as they chose.

During the sixth century the intensified production of agricultural surpluses and accompanying growth in trade led to the emergence of groups of professional merchants who played an important role in the development of long-distance and regional trade during the seventh and eighth centuries. Villages and estates supplied the basic capital in the form of surplus agricultural produce. The growing ranks of merchants were able to stimulate such surplus production and at the same time to encourage growth of commerce and specialized industries. Many parties benefited from the stepped-up pace of commerce and hence willingly participated in the intensification of production in their different spheres.

Formation of Medieval Towns

The same kind of interplay of mutually reinforcing processes can be identified in the early medieval period as was discussed in connection with the Iron Age towns. Some of the surpluses generated by peasant communities were traded directly for desired goods, others were invested by regional entrepreneurs to support specialist potters, metalworkers, and glass makers. The products of these industries were traded locally and to distant lands, as the distributions of Badorf pottery, Rhineland glassware, Mayen basalt grindstones, and decorative metalwork demonstrate. Some of these were distributed among the agricultural communities, thereby further stimulating production of tradable agricultural goods. The middlemen who coordinated these production and distribution systems were largely responsible for the commercial growth of the period. The trading towns of the sixth, seventh, and eighth centuries were established to improve the efficiency of commerce. Merchants from different regions could bring their wares to common points to meet with other merchants and exchange goods. Most of these towns were originally founded for trade but soon became centers of manufacturing as well. The pattern of commercial growth and town formation is well illustrated in central Sweden, where the sites of Helgö and Birka, both on islands in Lake Mälaren just west of Stockholm, have been extensively excavated. Helgö was active in the period 400–800. Its role in long-distance trade has been made apparent by the discovery of such foreign items as a Buddha figurine from India, a bishop's crosier from Ireland, a Coptic ladle from Egypt, and Badorf pottery from the Rhineland. The community also produced goods for export. Molds for casting jewelry and sword hilts have been recovered, as well as gold foil used in jewelry manufacture. Iron slag and hearths for forging attest to metalworking, and bronze, gold, and silver were cast. Wilhelm Holmqvist, the excavator, thinks (1976) that Helgö's industries were supplying manufactured goods to much of Scandinavia and that Helgö was a center of trade in raw iron with continental Europe. Local natural products, such as furs, skins, honey, wax, and tar, may also have been traded southward, though, of course, none of them survives in the archaeological record.

Birka, six kilometers northwest of Helgö, supplanted Helgö as the trade center of the region and flourished between 800 and 1000. Industries similar to those at Helgö are evident at Birka, and trade goods indicate similar commercial relations. The graves at Birka contained Arabic, Frankish, and Anglo-Saxon coins, Frankish and Slavic pottery, Chinese silks, and weights and balances used by merchants. To judge from the three thousand graves known at Birka, the average population may have been around five hundred, similar to that of the largest towns of the early Iron Age and the small late Iron Age oppida.

Other trade centers on the Baltic and North Sea coasts of Scandinavia provide a similar picture. Kaupang in southeastern Norway, Ribe on the west coast of Jutland, and Löddeköpinge in southern Sweden have yielded pottery from the Rhineland and from eastern Europe, coins of diverse origins, and workshops for glass beads, soapstone vessels, and metalwork.

On the continent similar towns developed at Dorstad at the

[199]

mouth of the Rhine and at Haithabu near Schleswig at the southeastern edge of the Jutland peninsula. The pottery at Dorstad, most of which was manufactured in the Rhineland, dates the settlement to about 700 to 900. Other foreign goods include glass vessels and beads and basalt grindstones. Industries in iron and bronze, textile production, bone carving, and amber cutting were also active at Dorstad.

Haithabu was settled during the seventh century (Figure 65). In contrast to the other sites, it had no hinterland population. Haithabu's situation on the Schlei, an inland bay of the Baltic Sea, linked trade networks of the Baltic and North seas, and an overland portage of 17 kilometers from Haithabu to the river Treene enabled the rapid transportation of cargo across the southern end of Jutland. Even though the land around Haithabu lacked tradable resources, the site became a major commercial center of early medieval Europe and, at least after 900, an industrial center as well. Pottery from the Rhineland and from Slavic eastern Europe is well represented. Basalt grindstones from Mayen were brought to Haithabu in rough form and there cut and ground into the final products. Ironworking was done, and jewelry, glass objects, textiles, and bone implements were manufactured.

In Britain the principal trade port during the eighth and ninth centuries was Hamwih, modern Southampton. Extensive imported pottery, glassware, metal objects, and bone artifacts attest to the intensity of trade with the continent, particularly with areas in northern France and the Rhineland. Local manufacturing was done in iron, bronze, lead, silver, pottery, textiles, and bone.

With the exception of Dorstad on the lower Rhine and Hamwih in Britain, all of these eighth- and ninth-century trading towns were located in regions never conquered by the Romans. The Romans had nothing directly to do with the origins of these medieval towns. None were in territories ruled by state forms of government, though as Randsborg (1980) has recently argued, a state organization may have developed in Denmark during the tenth century. These early medieval trading towns were not administrative or political centers. In this respect they were similar to the commercial towns of the early and late Iron Ages.

The separation of political and administrative functions from the commercial centers is particularly well demonstrated in the case of Hamwih. The political center of Winchester was only 18 kilometers away up the Itchen River. Martin Biddle characterizes early medieval Winchester as "royal, ecclesiastical, ceremonial, heir of an

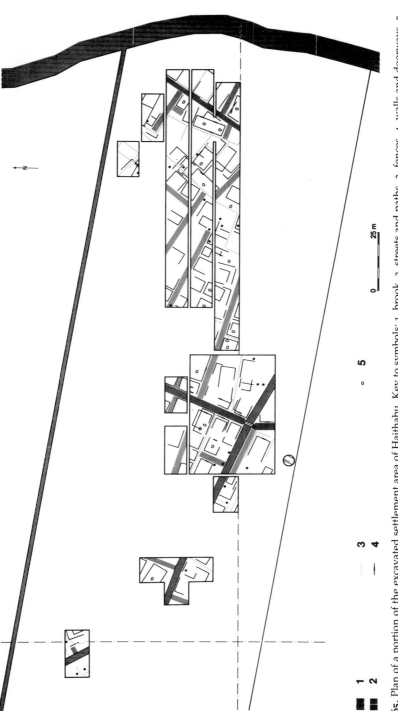

65. Plan of a portion of the excavated settlement area of Haithabu. Key to symbols: 1, brook. 2, streets and paths. 3, fences. 4, walls and doorways. 5, hearths.

ancient and still lively dignity," and Hamwih as "bustling, crowded, commercial, outward-looking." The two communities were closely connected, one as the political and religious capital of Wessex, the other as its commercial center. It was the latter that became the early town.

These towns of northern Europe represent an early stage in the urban development of Europe, a process documented by Pirenne (1925) and others from a principally historical perspective. From the eighth and ninth centuries on, intensified agricultural production, expanding manufacturing activity, and growing trade continued to reinforce one another, and resulted in the growth of commercial centers, a process that culminated in the appearance of the great cities of Renaissance and early modern Europe.

Summary

The formation of complex societies—how cities and states evolved and, more generally, how the modern world developed from its prehistoric roots—has been a popular theme of anthropological research in the past two decades. Most investigations into the origins of urbanism and states have focused on two parts of the world, the Near East and Mesoamerica, in which "pristine" urban developments took place (that is, where neighboring urban societies could not have played a part in the change to urbanism). In recent studies, Klaus Randsborg (1980) and Richard Hodges (1982) have applied theoretical models generated for those regions to early urban formation in medieval Europe, but little systematic research has been devoted to the emergence of the commercial centers of prehistoric temperate Europe.

Urban centers of the scale of those in the Near East and Mesoamerica never developed in prehistoric central or northern Europe, but commercial settlements that can justifiably be called towns, that share important similarities with later European cities and with the early urban centers of other parts of the world, emerged during the final centuries before the birth of Christ, as outlined in this book. The study of the growth of cultural complexity in Europe is necessarily different from that in the Near East and Mesoamerica, largely because of the different environmental and cultural possibilities and constraints.

Most of the explanations offered for the origins of cities and of state organization in the Near East and Mesoamerica do not apply to temperate Europe. For example, irrigation, important for the intensification of agriculture in the Near East, involved enormous outlays of capital and a complex labor organization, which Karl Wittfogel (1957) and others have viewed as motivating factors in

[203]

the development of urbanism. But in the wet and fertile environment of temperate Europe irrigation was unnecessary. Environmental diversity and the organization of trade systems to bring different goods to locations where they were not naturally available figure in some explanations of urban origins in Mesoamerica and to some extent in the Near East. But these factors were less significant in temperate Europe, where the environment was much more homogeneous. There is no evidence that theocratic institutions played major roles in town formation in Europe, as they may have in the other areas; the early towns in Europe were established as commercial centers.

For the European case, some investigators have argued that the formation of the trading towns between 600 and 500 B.C. (chapter 4) resulted specifically from interactions with urban Mediterranean societies, in particular from the importation of luxury materials manufactured in those state societies. But as I have demonstrated, it was not the arrival of the Mediterranean luxury goods and their distribution in Europe that led to the formation of the commercial centers; it was rather the organizational efforts to produce goods to exchange for those desired luxuries. This was the essential process behind town and city development in the early and late Iron Ages and, after the Roman period, in the early Middle Ages. The two processes—arrival and distribution of luxury goods on the one hand, organization of production for exchange on the other—were certainly closely related, but the distinction is important. At Hallstatt, a center of salt mining and trade (chapter 3), there is no indication of any connection with urban societies. The formation of the towns of Slovenia in the eighth and seventh centuries B.C. similarly can be understood in terms of the growth of commerce and of production for commerce between prehistoric European societies, without any strong contacts with urban Mediterranean peoples.

In the model proposed here, the critical factors in the development of temperate Europe's first towns were the growing commerce at the end of the Bronze Age, individual initiative and motivation to acquire specific luxury goods, and the mobilization of communities to produce materials that could be exchanged for desired luxuries. A threshold in the intensification of production was reached during the late Bronze Age. The larger quantities of bronze made possible greater amassing of personal wealth, as well as more efficient production of agricultural goods, tools, and weapons, all of which contributed to the generation of greater surpluses for the support of trade and manufacturing. After about 1000 B.C., the subsistence economy, commercial systems, and manufacturing techniques permitted the agglomeration of larger numbers of individuals in production centers that generated goods for exchange for desired luxuries. The ability to accumulate these luxuries motivated individuals to produce more.

This same process occurred at various times and places in Europe during the final millennium B.C. and again several centuries after the departure of the Romans. Not until the formation of some of the ninth- and tenth-century towns in central and northern Europe did some of these communities become permanent. They continued to grow throughout the Middle Ages, and some survive as cities in today's world.

Bibliographic Essay

Preface

On possible alternative approaches to the study of growing complexity in late European prehistory; see Redman 1978 on the Near East. He reviews a series of models that have been applied to the development of urbanism and civilization in that part of the world, including those focusing on irrigation systems, craft specialization, population pressure, local and long-distance trade, and ecological systems. Because of the great differences between natural environments in the Near East and Europe, only the craft specialization and trade approaches could apply equally well to late prehistoric Europe, and elements of each have been adopted in this book.

In reference to Europe, Alexander (1972) distinguishes a number of functions of early towns and cities which could serve as approaches to study of their origins. These include political, commercial, industrial, cultural, and sociological factors. Of these, Alexander emphasizes the commercial and industrial as particularly important for European developments.

On use of analogy in archaeological interpretation, see Leach (1977) and Leone (1982), who discuss possibilities of reconstructing past cognitive patterns from archaeological evidence. The literature on the use of ethnographic analogy in archaeology is now voluminous; see, for example, Orme 1981 and Hodder 1982. The direct historical approach has been applied relatively little to late prehistoric Europe by investigators concerned with behavior and cultural change, although scholars working along more traditional lines have demonstrated the validity of the approach. See, for example, Jackson 1964, an important attempt to connect early medieval Irish literature with the prehistoric Iron Age of continental Europe, and Ross 1967 on continuities in art and ritual. Much work in

[206]

central and northern Europe has shown strong continuities in settlement patterns and economy; see Jankuhn 1969; Müller-Wille 1977a; Pauli 1972, 1974, 1978, 1980a. Kahrstedt (1938) applies a model of social and political revolution to changes during the early Iron Age; Werner (1961) draws on medieval data pertaining to long-distance trade to interpret Iron Age patterns.

Chapter 1. The First Towns in Prehistoric Europe

See Childe 1950 on ten criteria for cities in the Near East and Meso-america. Adams (1960) discusses Childe's criteria. On urbanization in the Near East and Mesoamerica see Adams 1966; Rathje 1971, 1972; Redman 1978. Important treatments of towns and cities in late prehistoric and early medieval Europe are in Werner 1939; Christ 1957; Hrubý 1965; Neustupný 1969, 1970; Alexander 1972; Denecke 1973; Biddle 1976; Collis 1976, 1979; Nash 1976; Milisauskas 1978; Hodges 1982. On the relatively small size of European cities before modern times see Braudel 1981. A good general geography of Europe is Malmström 1971.

Excavations of specific sites are described in the following works. Buchau: Reinerth 1928, 1936. Goldberg: Schröter 1975. Little Woodbury: Bersu 1940. Heuneburg: Kimmig 1975a, 1975b. Manching, Krämer 1975. Třísov: Břeň 1966. Závist: Motyková, Drda, and Rybová 1978. Hrazany: Jansová 1965. Staré Hradisko: Meduna 1970. Steinsburg: Spehr 1971. Danebury: Cunliffe 1976. Studies incorporating anthropological approaches to later European prehistory include Jankuhn 1977; Jankuhn, Schützeichel, and Schwind, eds. 1977; Wahle 1964; Moberg 1977, 1981; Stjernqvist 1972, 1981; Randsborg 1973, 1974, 1980; Neustupný 1969; Otto 1955; Otto and Herrmann, eds. 1969; Child 1930, 1951, 1958. On the organization of metallurgy see Rowlands 1972. Filip's arguments about the origins of the early Iron Age centers: 1962, 1978. See also Frankenstein and Rowlands 1978. On the late Iron Age oppida see Crumley 1974a, 1974b; Nash 1976, 1978a, 1981; Alexander 1972. On the distinction between the two principal kinds of trade, elite luxury gift exchange and value-based trade, see Hawkes 1940:380 and Rowlands 1973:596. For a similar idea in another context see Tourtellot and Sabloff 1972. Clark and Piggott (1965:308) suggest that a "merchant class" may have been forming during the latter part of the Bronze Age. On exercise of free will and individuals' working in their own self-interest see Glassie 1977.

ACCUMULATION OF WEALTH IN LATER PREHISTORY

On Neolithic trade see the summary in Wyss 1969. On the Bell Beaker graves see Harrison 1980. On Varna see Ivanov 1978 and summarized by Renfrew 1978. The cemetery at Straubing is published by Hundt 1958, that at Brančby Vladár 1973 and Shennan 1975. For distribution maps of copper and bronze ingots see Kleemann 1954 and Hundt 1974. On the Leubingen group of rich graves see Grössler 1907 and Otto 1955. For an overview of middle Bronze Age objects see Pirling 1980 and Stary 1980. On the Wessex culture in Britain see Megaw and Simpson, eds. 1979:207–230. On hoards of the period see Primas 1977a.

THE ECONOMIC BASE

For descriptions of conditions of life and daily activities of European peasants which probably give a fair view of what life was like in later prehistory see Homans 1942 and Duby 1968 for the medieval period and Fél and Hofer 1972 and Hartley 1979 for modern times. Percival 1980 describes an experiment in Iron Age living which nicely points up the contrasts between modern urban life and prehistoric existence. The Butser Farm experiments are described in Reynolds 1979. On the supposed low agricultural productivity of medieval Europe see Duby 1974. See also Sahlins 1972:137–138, according to whom peasant communities tend not to produce surpluses unless specially motivated to do so.

EXCHANGE

On exchange mechanisms in traditional societies see Polanyi 1944, 1959; Finley 1973; Sahlins 1972; Dalton 1977. For discussions of the complexity of different mechanisms in early Europe see Grierson 1959; Bloch 1961; Herlihy 1971. On the early texts, which deal mainly with exchanges among elite persons, see Finley 1965a; Mauss 1967; Charles-Edwards 1976. For examples of trade in traditional societies lacking markets but where the trade operates according to value of goods rather than social obligations, see Spicer, ed. 1952. For examples of part-time crafts workers who produce food most of the year and also engage in seasonal manufacturing for trade see Rowlands 1972; Fél and Hofer 1972; Papousek 1981.

ENTREPRENEURS

On entrepreneurs in general see Greenfield, Strickon, and Aubey, eds. 1979, especially articles by Greenfield and Strickon; Scudder and Colson 1972. On non-Western entrepreneurs see Firth and Yamey, eds. 1964, especially introductory essay by Firth; Firth 1965. Entrepreneurs in the ancient Near East: Adams 1974. Entrepreneurs in the ancient Mediterranean world: Knorringa 1926; Finley 1973. On raiding as a regular source of income in early medieval Europe see Bloch 1961; Grierson 1959.

Herskovits's survey of primitive economics provides numerous examples of entrepreneurial behavior. According to Herskovits, the goal of profit making is not uncommon among modern non-Western peoples, and such concepts as credit and interest on loans are well documented in traditional, nonmonetary societies (1940:225–230). Standards of value, such as bars of salt in Africa and cacao kernels in pre-Spanish Mexico are frequent in exchange transactions (214–215), and regular exchange rates are usual between parties involved in regular trade (206–216). See also Dalton 1977:199 on standard value items, which he calls "primitive money." Middlemen are common in trading systems, and they are often able to generate profits through their efforts (Herskovits 1940:216–225). Exchange of labor for goods is also well documented in traditional contexts (Herskovits 1940).

DISTRIBUTION OF WEALTH

On differences between categories of interpretation of ethnological and archaeological data, see Deetz 1977a, 1977b; Ferguson 1977. On attempts to interpret early medieval burials in terms of textual evidence on social structure see Böhner 1958; Christlein 1973, 1979. See also Steuer 1979 on the archaeological evidence; Bloch 1961 and Duby 1974 on the documentary. On the usefulness of material wealth as a criterion for assessing relative status in society see Demos 1970:37–38; Christlein 1973; Dethlefsen 1981:137. On the connection between material wealth in graves and social status and power in society see especially Böhner 1958; Steuer 1979. The grave of Childeric, a Frankish king buried in A.D. 482, provides valuable insight into the connection between material wealth and social position (Böhner 1970:84–88). For general discussion of wealth and status in traditional societies see Sahlins 1963, 1972; Oberg 1973.

On interpreting wealth in burials see the essays in Chapman, Kinnes, and Randsborg, eds. 1981, especially the summary by Chapman and Randsborg and the paper by Brown. See also Ucko 1969; Binford 1971;

Christlein 1973; Steuer 1979. On the criteria that determine what burial goods are put in a grave, see Bruck 1926; Binford 1971; Kurtz and Boardman 1971; Brown 1981. Attempts to compare values of prehistoric burial goods have been made by Winters 1968 and Rathje 1970. Coles (1973, 1977, 1979) has studied the time and effort required to produce objects. Attempts to measure and compare burial wealth in prehistoric Europe have been made by Randsborg (1973, 1974, 1980). On counting grave goods to assess relative wealth, see Kilian-Dirlmeier 1970, 1974, Čižmář 1972; Waldhauser, ed. 1978; Randsborg 1980. On differential distribution of wealth in men's and women's graves see Arnold 1980. On wealth as a function of the household rather than of the individual see Tax 1953:189. For wealth and its distribution among families and individuals in early modern Europe see Laslett 1973; Mittauer 1979.

POLITICAL INTEGRATION

On the scheme of bands, tribes, chiefdoms, and states see Service 1962, and on applications to prehistoric Europe see Renfrew and Shennan, eds. 1982. On the early medieval political-ritual centers, as distinct from commercial towns, see Macalister 1931, and see O'Riordain 1964 on Tara, Biddle 1973 on Winchester, and Lindqvist 1936 on Uppsala. Biddle's discussion of Winchester is particularly enlightening on the separation of commercial and political-ritual centers.

CHANGE

On culture change in general see Barnett 1953; Rogers and Shoemaker 1971. A particularly lucid and thorough discussion of economic and social change in an archaeological context is found in Renfrew 1972. (The Aegean world of the third millennium B.C. was very different environmentally and culturally from that of late prehistoric Europe, however, and so the specifics are not fully comparable.) On the connection between entrepreneurial behavior and change see especially Barth 1963 and essays in Greenfield, Strickon, and Aubey, eds. 1979. On the desire for wealth and prestige as universal human drives see Herskovits 1940.

Chapter 2. Europe in 1000 B.C.

On the major cultural changes of the late Bronze Age see Otto 1978, Peroni 1979, and Coles and Harding 1979.

LANDSCAPE, POPULATION, AND SETTLEMENTS, 1000–800 B.C.

General discussion of the prehistoric European landscape are found in Clark 1952; Jankuhn 1969; Piggott, ed. 1981. For good educated guesses of regional populations see McEvedy and Jones 1978. Also on prehistoric populations, see Russell 1958; Acsádi and Nemeskéri 1970; Donat and Ullrich 1976. On the settlement of Elp see Waterbolk 1964. On life expectancy in prehistoric Europe see Acsádi and Nemeskéri 1970:211; Pauli 1980a:135, 314 n. 19. For early modern village demography in central Europe see Schönberger 1926. On cemeteries see Eibner 1974 on St. Andrä; Müller-Karpe 1957 on Grünwald, Unterhaching, and Gernlinden; Müller-Karpe 1952 on Kelheim. In many regions no cemeteries of more than ten graves are known, as, for example, in north Württemberg (Dehn 1972:39). On the regularity of small-scale settlements throughout Europe see Bouzek, Koutecký, and Neustupný 1966:111.

Examples of flatland settlements are Künzing (Herrmann 1974–1975), Hascherkeller (Wells 1983), Aulnay-aux-Planches (Brisson and Hatt 1967), and Lovčičky (Říhovský 1972). For a general discussion of such settlements see Šaldová 1981. Lakeshore settlements include Wasserburg Buchau (Reinerth 1928, 1936), Zug-Sumpf (Speck 1955), and Auvernier (Rychner 1979). Hillforts include Wittnauer Horn (Bersu 1945, 1946), Kastenberg (Laur-Belart 1955), Lochenstein (Bersu and Goessler 1924), and Hohlandsberg (Jehl and Bonnet 1968, 1971; Bonnet 1974). On hill forts of this period in general see Coblenz 1967; Herrmann 1969; Šaldová 1977; Jockenhövel 1974. Most of the site reports referred to here include discussions of houses; see especially Herrmann 1974–1975. On round houses in Britain: Bradley 1978. On the economies of the various communities see syntheses in Wyss 1971b and Coles and Harding 1979. Destruction levels on settlements are described in Bersu 1945:81; Härke 1979:26. Hours of labor required to construct large earthworks are given by Coles 1973, 1979; Burl 1979.

SUBSISTENCE ECONOMY

General discussions of subsistence are found in Clark 1952; Jankuhn 1969.

Plant Foods. Renfrew 1973 provides an overview of the plants used. A bibliography on plant remains from prehistoric central and north central Europe is in Körber-Grohne 1981; see also Lüdi 1955. For recent European ethnographic data on agricultural scheduling and technology see Fél and

Hofer 1972; Hartley 1979; Piggott, ed. 1981. On prehistoric agricultural tools see Rees 1979, 1981. On distribution map of finds of prehistoric plows see Glob 1951:13, fig. 5. On rock carvings of plowing scenes see Anati 1961; Glob 1954.

Technology of Agriculture. Excellent illustrations of the different types of plows are presented in Steensberg 1936 and Glob 1951. On the possible use of the plow in Neolithic times see Glob 1951:124–125; Kjaerum 1954. For descriptions of specific implements see the following. History of the sickle: Steensberg 1943. Earliest metal sickles in central Europe, at beginning of middle Bronze Age: Filip 1969:1289; Courtin et al. 1976:175; Primas 1977a:164. Frankleben hoard: von Brunn 1968:319. Other hoards containing sickles: Müller-Karpe 1959; von Brunn 1968; Herrmann 1966. Examples of sickles in settlement deposits: at Buchau, Reinerth 1936:pl. 39, 2); at Zürich-Haumesser, Wyss 1971b:137, fig. 21, 2). Wooden handles for sickles preserved at Swiss lakeshore settlements: Ruoff 1971:81; Wyss 1971b:137, fig. 21, 1–2. Molds for sickles in settlement deposits: von Brunn 1968:240 n. 1. Von Brunn makes the suggestion that sickles were being cast in numerous small settlements throughout Europe (1968:240–241).

See Bradley 1978 for a general discussion of field systems. Wailes (1970:282, fig. 2) provides a distribution map of prehistoric field systems in Europe. For further discussion of fields see Clark 1952:98–99, 106–107; Piggott 1965:250; Peroni 1979:9.

Domestic Animals. On domestic animals in prehistoric Europe see especially Boessneck et al. 1971; Bökönyi 1974; Jankuhn 1969. On uses for cattle see Sherratt 1981, and on stalls for livestock, Müller-Wille 1977a; Waterbolk 1964.

MANUFACTURING

Material Culture in the Late Bronze Age. Many studies deal with pottery; see, for example, Unz 1973. For bronze objects, see the series *Prähistorische Bronzefunde* published by C. H. Beck, Munich. See Herrmann 1966 on stone used in this period. On wood see Coles, Heal, and Orme 1978; Schweingruber 1976. The Swiss lakeshore settlements yield abundant wood materials—see Speck 1955; Wyss 1971a; Primas and Ruoff 1981. On early iron in the period see Vogt 1949–1950; Kimmig 1964; Pleiner 1980; Šramko 1981. On glass: Haevernick 1978. On textiles: Hald 1950; Hundt 1970. On gold: Eogan 1981 (with catalogue and bibliography).

Organization of Manufacturing. The finds of kilns in specific sites are discussed as follows. Elchinger Kreuz: Pressmar 1979. Hohlandsberg: Jehl and Bonnet 1968. Sévrier: Bocquet and Couren 1974. Breisach-Münsterberg: Bender, Dehn, and Stork 1976: 217–220. Buchau: Pressmar 1979:31. Hascherkeller: Wells 1983. Sites in Saône valley: Bonnamour 1976. On potters in traditional societies see David 1972; David and David-Hennig 1971; Papousek 1981. On graphite deposits and graphite trade see Kappel 1969.

The distribution of copper ores in Europe is discussed in Gimbutas 1965:21, fig. 2; Muhly 1973. On the evidence from the copper mines in the Tirol and Land Salzburg see Pittioni 1951, 1976; Neuninger, Pittioni, and Preuschen 1969. On the Lebenberg cemetery see Pittioni 1952; Eibner, Plank, and Pittioni 1966. Copper ingots in hoards are illustrated in Müller-Karpe 1959: pls. 139, A28; 164, 37; 175, B2; 177, C1–2; von Brunn 1968: pl. 194, 15–20. Ingots at Zürich-Wollishofen are illustrated in Wyss 1967a:pl. 16, 7, 8. Ingots in graves are discussed in Jockenhövel 1973. The Pfeffingen hoard is illustrated in Müller-Karpe 1959:pls. 164, 165A and the Winklsass hoard in Müller-Karpe 1959:pl. 149. On the idea of fixed values for bronze metal see Primas 1977a, 1977b.

On bronze casting at various sites see the following Swiss lakeshore settlements: Wyss 1967a:4. Hohlandsberg: Bonnet 1974. Runder Berg: Stadelmann 1980:38. Swiss hilltop sites: Wyss 1971b:123. Settlements in the Saône valley: Bonnamour 1976. Hascherkeller: Wells 1980a, 1983. Velemszentvid: Von Miske 1929; Foltiny 1958:20–32. Hallunda: Jaanusson 1971. Aldermaston Wharf: Bradley at al. 1980. Actual remains of a furnace at St. Germain-du-Plain are illustrated in Bonnamour 1976:pl. 34. See Rowlands 1972 on the question of degree of specialization. On the lack of evidence for slavery before the end of the Iron Age see Peschel 1971a. The whole issue of social and political status of craft workers in traditional central Europe is discussed in Pauli 1978. On casting molds found on settlements see Herrmann 1966, and on molds, casting techniques, and hammering see Drescher 1958, 1980; Hodges 1964. Upper Tisza and Carpathians as possible centers of bronze-working are discussed in von Merhart 1952; Gimbutas 1965:152–153. On distribution of sheet-bronze objects see Sprockhoff 1930; von Merhart 1952, and on experiments with sheet bronze, Coles 1977. Graves of bronzesmiths are discussed in Müller-Karpe 1969; Jockenhövel 1973. On hoards containing objects from many different areas see Brongers and Woltering 1973:26, and on the Villethierry hoard, Mordant and Prampart 1976. On movement of bronzesmiths see Pauli 1978:444.

On distribution of small jewelry items see studies by Betzler (1974), Kubach (1977), and Beck (1980) and the maps included therein. The evidence of the gold objects also suggests that smiths were producing for local taste as they traveled; see Kimmig 1948–1950. For distribution of swords see maps in Cowen 1955; Schauer 1971. On the Hajdúböszörmény hoard see Hampel 1887; on Unterglauheim, Müller-Karpe 1959: 293, pl. 269; Dresden-Dobritz, Coblenz 1951. For a discussion of bronze in graves of this period see Wells 1981:110. On votive deposits of bronze see Torbrügge 1970–1971.

TRADE

For a discussion and illustrations of the tools of this period, see the hoards published in Müller-Karpe 1959 and von Brunn 1968. On amber trade see Bohnsack 1976. Mediterranean shells: Wyss 1971b:140, fig. 25. Salt mining for trade at Hallstatt: Barth, Felber, and Schauberger 1975. Trade in cattle and hides from the Northern European Plain southward: Brongers and Woltering 1973:13. Possibility of wine trade from the Mediterranean: Piggott 1959. On vehicles of transport and packhorses see Pauli 1980a:220–231.

DISTRIBUTION OF WEALTH

On the increasing accumulation of personal wealth over time see the discussion and illustration of hoards in Müller-Karpe 1959 and graves in Stary 1980. On luxury weaponry, helmets are discussed in Hencken 1971, shields in Coles 1962, and cuirasses in Gabrovec 1960. On bronze vessels of this period see von Merhart 1952. Gold objects: Eogan 1981. New types of swords: Cowen 1955; Müller-Karpe 1961; Schauer 1971. Appearance of metal keys: Pauli 1978:262–264. Herrmann (1969) discusses construction of hill forts.

A general discussion of burial patterns is found in Coles and Harding 1979. Burial patterns at Hart an der Alz are discussed in Müller-Karpe 1955, and other exceptionally rich graves in Říhovský 1978; Stary 1980.

Chapter 3. Emergence of Centers of Production and Trade (800–600 B.C.)

HALLSTATT

On the environment of Hallstatt see Morton 1954, 1956. The early finds from the Hallstatt area are summarized in Reitinger 1968. On the late Bronze Age hoard see Reinecke 1934; Reitinger 1968:128–129.

The Mines. The mines and their contents are discussed by Schauberger (1960, 1976) and by Barth (1970a, 1970b, 1971, 1973, 1980a, 1980b). Absolute dates from the mines are given in Barth, Felber, and Schauberger 1975.

The Cemetery. See Kromer 1959 and Wells 1981 on the graves. The chronology of the graves is treated in Kromer 1959 and Peroni 1973.

Emergence as a Commercial Center. On early salt production in Europe see Riehm 1954; Nenquin 1961; Alexander 1982. Early Iron Age salt production elsewhere: Bertaux 1977. The historical importance of salt and the body's need for salt: Bloch 1963; Multhauf 1978. Salt in later prehistory: Pauli 1974. For trade indicated by the grave goods see Kromer 1963; Wells 1978. On the copper mines at Bischofshofen see Neuninger, Pittioni, and Preuschen 1969.

Kromer (1958) suggests that the mining community at Hallstatt consisted mainly of able-bodied men, but Häusler's important analysis (1968) shows that the community was made up of men, women, and children. See also Kilian-Dirlmeier 1971. Compare Pauli 1978 on the salt miners at the Dürrnberg.

STIČNA

On the environment of Slovenia see Winner 1971, and on the late Bronze Age settlements of the region see *Arheološka Najdišča Slovenije.* On the establishment of the new hill forts during the eighth century B.C. see Gabrovec 1973, 1976. The early Iron Age in Slovenia is summarized in Gabrovec 1966, 1974. On the excavations at the Stična settlement see Gabrovec, Frey, and Foltiny 1970.

The Cemetery. Excavations by the Duchess of Mecklenburg are described in Wells 1981. The recent excavations in the cemetery by the National Museum in Ljubljana are discussed in Gabrovec 1974.

Emergence as a Commercial Center. The importance of iron is discussed as follows. Iron in late Bronze Age contexts: Vogt 1949–1950; Kimmig 1964; Pleiner 1980. Iron ores in Slovenia: Müllner 1908; Davies 1935:182–184; Rieth 1942; Gabrovec 1966. Slag on settlements: Müllner 1908:39–88. Slag in graves at Magdalenska gora: Rieth 1942:81–82; at Vače: Müllner 1908:63; at Teplice: Müllner 1908:64. The iron workshop at the Waschenberg in Austria: Pertlwieser 1970; Pleiner 1980:386–387. Iron objects at Este cemetery: Frey 1969. Later, Roman-period exploitation of the iron ores in Slovenia: Davies 1935; Alföldy 1974:113–114. Modern iron production: Mutton 1961:145–146; Pounds 1969:706, 710.

On amber trade see Bohnsack 1976. Italic imports in Slovenia: Wells 1981:114. Contacts generally between Slovenia and northeast Italy: Frey 1966, 1969; Frey and Gabrovec 1971; Kimmig 1974. Objects from Slovenia in graves at Hallstatt see Egg 1978.

Specialized Production and the Formation of Towns

For examples of enterprising individuals organizing productive ventures to gain profits, see Tax 1953; Barth 1963; Greenfield, Strickon, and Aubey, eds. 1979. Examples of people willingly quitting agricultural life to move to production centers appear in Landes 1969; Hareven and Langenbach 1978. On the concept of capital as goods and services invested in production for further profits, see Firth 1964. In the late Bronze Age one (but not necessarily the only) source of capital was the accumulated bronze objects so evident in the hoards.

In contrast to the Mediterranean world, where there is abundant evidence for the use of slave labor at this time (see, e.g., Lauffer 1955–1956; Burford 1972:73, 171), there is no indication of slavery in central Europe (Peschel 1971a).

The Rest of Europe

Härke 1979 gives a good summary of settlement evidence for central Europe. Kossack 1959 is an exceptionally detailed regional study. On Kleinklein see Schmid 1933; Dobiat 1980 discusses the iron ores in the vicinity as well as the cemeteries. On the Bylaný burials see Dvořák 1938; Koutecký 1968; Pleinerová 1973. On burials in other sites see the following. Grosseibstadt: Kossack 1970. Nové Košariská: Pichlerová 1969. Uttendorf: Moosleitner 1977. The Netherlands: Kooi 1979. Eastern France: Schaeffer 1930; Millotte 1963. Zainingen: Zürn 1957. Gomadingen: von Föhr 1892. Bologna: Mansuelli and Scarani 1961. Este: Frey 1969. On burials in France see the summary articles in Guilaine, ed. 1976, in Switzerland see Drack, ed. 1974.

Many European archaeologists attribute major cultural changes to the immigration of horse-riding, nomadic groups from the East into central Europe at this time. For discussion of these groups, generally known as Cimmerians, see Kossack 1954; Powell 1971; Gabrovec 1980; Terenožkin

1980. The question of the size and significance of these groups is not critical for the present discussion.

Chapter 4. Growth of Commercial Centers (600–400 B.C.)

TRADE WITH THE GREEKS

On the Greek colonization of 800–500 B.C.: Dunbabin 1948; Roebuck 1959: Boardman 1973. Foundation of Massalia around 600 B.C.: Wackernagel 1930: Clavel-Lévêque 1974. Early Greek and Etruscan imports in central Europe: Dehn and Frey 1979; Wells 1980b. Wine as a trade good: Seltman 1957. Commerce in Attic pottery: Boardman 1979. The character of Greek commerce: Hasebroek 1933; Casson 1979. Massalia's trade in the sixth and fifth centuries B.C.: Villard 1960; Benoit 1965. Heuneburg claybrick wall: Dehn 1957. Hirschlanden stele: Zürn 1970. Potter's wheel introduced into central Europe: Dehn 1962–1963; Lang 1974, 1976. Literary evidence pertaining to Greek commerce: Knorringa 1926; Will 1958. Products probably traded with central Europe: Minns 1913:438–441; Semple 1931; Finley 1959, 1965b; Wells 1980b:67–70.

THE HEUNEBURG AND OTHER TOWNS

General discussion of the Heuneburg is in Kimmig 1968, 1975a, 1975b; Gersbach 1975, 1978, 1981. Special studies include Mansfeld 1973; Lang 1974; Dämmer 1978. Graves around the Heuneburg: Riek 1962; Schiek 1959. Discussion of the chronology of occupation: Kimmig 1975a: 196; Spindler 1975; Dämmer 1978:67, fig. 11. Outer settlement: Schiek 1959; Gersbach 1969; Sperber 1980, 1981; Kurz 1982.

On the concept of "town" in relation to the Heuneburg and other contemporaneous sites see Neustupný 1969, 1970, 1977; Hensel 1970. On Heuneburg and other settlements as political centers see Zürn 1970:118–128; Frankenstein and Rowlands 1978.

LUXURY TRADE, SURPLUS PRODUCTION, AND THE EMERGENCE OF TOWNS

Pre-600 B.C. Greek trading activity around the mouth of the Rhône: Rolland 1951; Villard 1960; Benoit 1965. Gift exchange between Greeks and other peoples: Fischer 1973. Motivation for surplus production: Sahlins

1972:136–137. Distribution map of Mediterranean imports in central Europe: Schaaff and Taylor 1975a. Attic pottery at Vulci: Hus 1971:87–88 n. 1. Distribution of gold objects: Paret 1942; Drack 1980. Decline of trade at Massalia and end of relations between Mediterranean and central Europe: Villard 1960; Benoit 1965; Wells and Bonfante 1979. Patterns in the archaeological evidence following the decline of trade: Bittel 1934; Liepschwager 1972. Discussion of Mycenaean centers in Greece: Vermeule 1964.

CHANGING PATTERNS THROUGHOUT EUROPE

Settlements. For a general discussion of settlements see Härke 1979; Dušek 1974a. Although settlement evidence is not abundant, some excellent studies make clear the general small scale and rural character, for example, at Těšětice in Moravia (Podborský 1965) and at Kornwestheim in north Württemberg (Joachim and Biel 1977). See also regional surveys in Millotte 1963; Haffner 1976. Copper miners' cemetery at Welzelach: Lippert 1972. Specific settlements are discussed as follows. Hellbrunnerberg: Moosleitner 1979. Biskupin: Rajewski 1959; Niesiołowska-Wędzka 1974. Large sites of Kalenderberg culture: Patek 1976; Kaus 1981. Smolenice: Dušek 1974b, 1980. Závist: Motyková, Drda, and Rybová 1978; Motyková, Rybová, and Drda 1981. Lausitz settlements: Herrmann 1969.

On the point that less differentiation in wealth is apparent in eastern Europe than in west central Europe: Rajewski 1974:431; Dušek 1977a, 1977b. Sopron: Patek 1976, 1981. Nové Košariská: Pichlerová 1969. Szentes-Vekerzug: Párducz 1952, 1954, 1956. Tápiószele: Párducz 1966. Chotín: Dušek 1966. Bologna: Mansuelli and Scarani 1961; Chevallier 1962a. Spina: Alfieri and Arias 1958; Aurigemma 1960.

Economy. Waschenberg: Pertlwieser 1969, 1970, 1971. Hillesheim: Haffner 1971a. Býčí Skála: Nekvasil 1980, 1981. Iron coming into general use at this time: Šramko 1974; Nebehay 1977:55; Pleiner 1962.

Distribution of Wealth. Hohmichele: Riek 1962. Magdalenenberg: Spindler 1971–1977. Hochdorf: Biel 1980, 1982. Grafenbühl: Zürn 1970. Vix: Joffroy 1954, 1962. Distribution of gold rings: Drack 1980. Rich graves of the fifth century B.C.: summary in Wells 1980b:104–142.

Chapter 5. Raids and Migrations into Southern Europe (400–200 B.C.)

On the disappearance of the larger communities that had maintained strong trading relations with Mediterranean societies see Wells and Bonfante 1979. Papers in Guštin, ed. 1977 treat the decline in manufacturing and commerce evident in the east Alpine region.

EXPEDITIONS INTO ITALY AND EASTERN EUROPE

An excellent summary of the issues is Dehn 1979, with full bibliography. Classical sources on the invasions and migrations: Contzen 1861. Literary evidence for the invasions in Greece: Maier 1973. Celtic mercenaries in Mediterranean armies: Scheers 1981:23 n. 8. *I Galli e l'Italia* (1978) contains a full survey of the archaeological evidence in Italy. Cemeteries at Bologna: Zannoni 1876–1884. General discussions of the archaeological evidence in northern Italy: Chevallier 1962a, 1962b; de Marinis 1977. Greece: Maier 1973. Hungary: Szabó 1971. Yugoslavia: Todorović 1968. Romania: Zirra 1979.

PLUNDERING FOR WEALTH

For the names of the central European tribes that migrated into Italy see Contzen 1861. For an impression of the great wealth available for plunder in the towns of northern and central Italy see Scullard 1967; Pallottino 1971; Boitani, Cataldi, and Pasquinucci 1973. Graves of central European character in northern Italy: *I Galli e l'Italia*. Benacci Grave 953: Sassatelli 1978. Rich grave at Ciumeşti: Rusu 1969.

THE FOURTH AND THIRD CENTURIES B.C.IN CENTRAL EUROPE

Settlements. Nebringen: Krämer 1964. Vevey: Martin-Kilcher 1981. Au an der Leitha: Nebehay 1971. Jenišův Újezd: Waldhauser, ed. 1978. Münsingen-Rain: Hodson 1968. Radovesice: Waldhauser 1977, 1979, 1981.

Economy. Quantities of weapons in graves: Sankot 1978. Smith's grave at St. Georgen: Taus 1963. For general comparisons of quantities of iron and bronze objects and of material culture forms see also, e.g., Bretz-Mahler 1971 for France; Nebehay 1973 for Austria. Pleiner 1962 is the best general summary of the progress of iron working. Waldalgesheim: Driehaus 1971; Zahlhaas 1971. Mannersdorf: Mossler and Pauli 1980.

The Dürrnberg. The most important studies are Penninger 1972, 1980; Maier 1974; Moosleitner, Pauli, and Penninger 1974; Pauli 1978; Zeller 1980.

Distribution of Wealth. Dürrnberg Grave 44/2: Penninger 1972. Duchov hoard: Megaw 1970:99; Kruta 1971.

THE NEW ART STYLE

On Iron Age art in general see Megaw 1970. Jacobsthal 1944 focuses on the La Tène style, from about 500 B.C. on. Von Hase 1973 examines Mediterranean models for European motifs.

**Chapter 6. Emergence of Urbanism in Late
Prehistoric Europe (200–1 B.C.)**

INTENSIFICATION OF IRON PRODUCTION

Jacobi 1974 presents results of the analysis of iron tools from Manching, where they have been most thoroughly studied. On iron at other major settlements of the period see the following. Stradonice: Pič 1906. Velemszentvid: Foltiny 1958. Třísov: Břeň 1966. Steinsburg: Spehr 1971. Dünsberg: Jacobi 1977. Heidetränk: Müller-Karpe and Müller-Karpe 1977. Vienne: Chapotat 1970. Bibracte: Bulliot 1895; Déchelette 1904. Titelberg: Rowlett, Thomas, and Rowlett 1982. Glastonbury: Bulleid and Gray 1911, 1917. Meare: Gray and Bulleid 1953. The striking similarity of late Iron Age tools and early modern ones is evident if one compares these prehistoric implements with those illustrated in Fél and Hofer 1972 and Hartley 1979. A good map of major ore deposits in central and north central Europe is in Pleiner 1964, suppl. 1. Techniques of exploitation of ores: Davies 1935. Technical development and scale of iron production at this time: Pleiner 1964, 1977a. Techniques of smelting used: Pleiner 1962, 1976, 1977a, 1977b, 1981; Bielenin 1977; Coghlan 1977.

On the small sites see the following studies. Steinebach: Krämer 1951–1952. Uttenkofen: Neubauer 1956. Gussage All Saints: Wainwright 1979. Glastonbury: Bulleid and Gray 1911, 1917. Msec: Pleiner 1977b:107–109. Burgenland smelting sites: Bielenin 1977; Kaus 1977. On the dispersed organization of iron production because of intense exploitation of forests see Davies 1935:6.

On tools and techniques of blacksmiths, see especially Pleiner 1962;

Jacobi 1974. Kappel hoard: Fischer 1959. Wauwilermoos hoard: Wyss 1974a:187, fig. 17. Celles grave: Pagès-Allay et al. 1903. St. Georgen grave: Taus 1963. Specialization by smiths: Jacobi 1974:260–261; Reim 1981:209–210. Analysis of iron swords: Guyan 1977. Makers' marks on swords: Wyss 1954, 1956. Körner hoard: Goetze 1900. Status of smiths in early medieval Scandinavia and continental Europe: Müller-Wille 1977b. Idrija graves: Szombathy 1903. Cross-cultural status of smiths: Forbes 1964. Smiths' status in Irish epics: Wainwright 1979. Aubstadt hoard: Pauli 1980b:300.

Growing Commerce with Urban Italy

History of Roman expansion into northern Italy and beyond: Toynbee 1965; summary in Pauli 1980a:45–55. Chronology of trade between Roman Italy and lands north of the Alps: Stöckli 1979a; Werner 1978; Meduna 1982. On imported wine amphorae north of the Alps: Nash 1978b:app. 3; Stöckli 1979a. Amphorae in the Saône at Chalon: Bohn 1925:79. Amphorae in Britain: Peacock 1971. Wine in skin and wooden containers traded over the Alps: Werner 1961. Roman bronze vessels north of the Alps: Werner 1954, 1978; Christlein 1963–1964. Foods imported from Italy just after the conquest: Staehelin 1948:430–440.

On the Magdalensberg and the evidence there for iron trade with Italy see Egger 1961; Obermayr 1971; Alföldy 1974. Aquileia: Panciera 1957. Iron ingot from the Burgkogel near Zell am See: Moosleitner 1980. For an impression of the quantities of iron required by the Romans see Dietz et al. 1979:289–307: Kellner 1972:92–96. Roman military need for leather: Dietz et al. 1979:291–293, 301, 305. Roman trade for leather and cattle between the central European provinces and Free Germany: Sawyer 1977:142–143. Prehistoric trade in leather and cattle from the Northern European Plain southward: Brongers and Woltering 1973. Abundance of cattle at central European settlements: Boessneck, et al. 1971:32–59. Tools for leather working: Jacobi 1974:51–57. On the Roman need for slaves and on the slave trade see Hopkins 1978. Romans trading for slaves in the middle Danube region: Harris 1980. Manacle from La Tène: Wyss 1974b:129, fig. 25, 3. Organic materials traded from central Europe to Italy after the conquest: Staehelin 1948:440–442.

Transport in ships: Casson 1971. Packhorses as principal means of transport over the Alps: Werner 1961. Donkey teeth at Závist in Bohemia: Jansová 1971:280. Wooden frame for saddlebags from La Tène: Vouga 1923:pl. 35, 3–8; Wyss 1974:126, fig. 22, 21.

[221]

BIBLIOGRAPHIC ESSAY

URBAN CENTERS OF THE LATE IRON AGE:
MANCHING AND OTHER OPPIDA

On uses and meanings of the word *oppidum* see Kornemann 1939. The literature on oppida is voluminous; the recent studies cited here include bibliographies of earlier works. Collis 1975 provides a catalogue of the sites. Crumley 1974a and 1974b and Nash 1976 and 1978b focus on the French sites. See *Archeologické rozhledy* 23 (1971) for short studies of many specific sites. A recent distribution map of the sites appears in Schaaff and Taylor 1975b. Dehn 1951 discusses the oppida in relation to Caesar's statements. On topography of the sites see Dehn 1965. The British oppida, concentrated in southern Britain, are usually treated separately from the continental sites; principal British ones are Maiden Castle (Wheeler 1943), Danebury (Cunliffe 1976), and Hengistbury Head (Cunliffe 1978). Chronology of the oppida: Stöckli 1979a. Chronology of specific sites: Břeň 1971; Fischer 1971; Peschel 1971b; Crumley 1974a:35; Nash 1978b; Waldhauser 1979; Meduna 1980. Occupation of some into Roman period: Dehn 1971:401–402; Crumley 1974a:35.

For settlement plans of oppida see the following. Manching: Krämer and Schubert 1970; Schubert 1972. Hrazany: Jansová 1965. Třísov: Břeň 1966, 1971. Staré Hradisko: Meduna 1970, 1971. Stradonice: Pič 1906. Velemszentvid: Foltiny 1958. Bibracte: Bulliot 1895; Déchelette 1904.

Relations between oppida and smaller surrounding communities: Spehr 1971; Stöckli 1979a, 1979b; Collis 1980. For Závist: Motyková, Drda, and Rybová 1978; Motyková, Rybová, and Drda 1981.

Krämer and Schubert 1970 provides a full introduction to the site of Manching. Krämer 1975 is a more recent synthesis. Krämer 1960 is a good early summary in English. Iron production at the site: Jacobi 1974. Trade with the Roman world: Stöckli 1979a. Coin hoards: Krämer 1958. Graphite trade: Kappel 1969. Pottery production: Maier 1970; Pingel 1971; Stöckli 1979a. Defoe's remarks on the Sturbridge Fair: Muncey 1936. Fairs in medieval Europe: Walford 1883; Duby 1968; Braudel 1972. Barthelmarkt at Oberstimm: Krämer 1958:197.

ECONOMY AND SOCIETY IN THE LATE IRON AGE

Population: Russell 1958; McEvedy and Jones 1978. Discussion of figures given by Caesar and other classical writers: Staehelin 1948; Rieckhoff-Pauli 1980:43. Waldhauser on Bohemia: 1981:116.

Settlements. On important small settlements see the following. Steinebach: Krämer 1951–1952. Eschweiler-Laurenzberg: Joachim 1980. Haina: Donat 1968–1969. Záluží: Motyková-Šneiderová 1960. Mistřín: Ludikovský 1968. Feddersen Wierde: Haarnagel 1975, 1977, 1979. Hodde: Hvass 1975. Gussage All Saints: Wainwright 1979. Altendorf: Stöckli 1979b. Eschweiler-Lohn: Joachim 1980. Coins minted by small communities: Bónis 1971:523–524; Collis 1980. Houses in North Sea coast areas: Müller-Wille 1977a.

Economy. Discussion of classical authors' remarks about central European agriculture: Tierney 1960. Plows: Steensberg 1936; Glob 1951. Sites with good assemblages of iron plowshares include Manching (Jacobi 1974), Steinsburg (Spehr 1971), Heidetränk (Müller-Karpe and Müller-Karpe 1977), Dünsberg (Jacobi 1977), and Vienne (Chapotat 1970). Iron plowshares at small settlements—Záluží: Motyková-Šneiderova 1960; Gussage All Saints: Wainwright 1979. Plowshares in hoards: Amberger 1927; Goetze 1900. Hoard from Hainbach: Pauli 1980b:301. Coulters: Spehr 1966. General discussion of plows and their importance: Wailes 1972. Scythes: see reports cited for Manching, Steinsburg, Dünsberg, Körner, Kaiserbrunn, Kappel under "Intensification of Iron Production." Scythes with wooden handles preserved at La Tène: Vouga 1923:24–25, pls. 74–75. Use of the scythe: Steensberg 1943:239; Spehr 1971:488.

Salt at Reichenhall: Menke 1977. At Nauheim: Süss 1973. Production and trade of gold: Hartmann 1970, 1978.

Distribution of Wealth. Sinsheim-Dühren grave: Fischer 1981. Change in burial practice, with cremation replacing inhumation and decrease in quantities of goods: Krämer 1950:93, 1952; Waldhauser 1979:142–146. Grave at Markvartice: Waldhauser 1979:147. Examples of small cemeteries north of central Europe are Bad Nauheim (Schönberger 1952), Naumberg (Spehr 1968), and Dietzenbach (Polenz 1971). On other cemeteries see the following. Trier: Mahr 1967. Wederath: Haffner 1971b, 1974b, 1978. Hoppstädten-Weiersbach: Haffner 1969; Goeblingen-Nospelt: Thill 1967a, 1967b; Haffner 1974a. Trier-Olewig: Schindler 1971. Neuwied: Joachim 1973. Hannogne: Flouest and Stead 1977. Welwyn: Stead 1967. A few similar rich graves have been found in other parts of Europe, as for example in Slovenia at Novo mesto (Schaaff 1980). Trading and piracy in medieval times: Grierson 1959. Kappel hoard: Fischer 1959. Aubstadt hoard: Pauli 1980b:300. Hjortspring hoard: Rosenberg 1937; Becker 1948. Coins and coinage: Allen 1978a, 1978b; Nash 1978b, 1981; Scheers 1981; Oberbeck 1980; Kos 1980. Irsching hoard: Overbeck 1980:322. Lauterach: Pauli 1980a:288–290. Niederzier: Pauli 1980b:314–315.

Chapter 7. Roman Interlude and the Formation of Medieval Towns

ROME NORTH OF THE ALPS

On the Roman conquest of Europe see summaries in Toynbee 1965 and C. M. Wells 1972. Fischer 1976 discusses the regions directly north of the Alps. Problems of interaction between Celtic and Germanic groups, and the southward migrations of the latter, are treated in Hachmann, Kossack, and Kuhn 1962 and Todd 1975.

ECONOMY AND SOCIETY IN THE ROMAN PERIOD (A.D. 1–400)

Within the Empire. Some excellent regional syntheses provide a full picture of economy, society, and material culture in the provinces: Staehelin 1948; Wightman 1970; Kellner 1972; Alföldy 1974; Filtzinger, Planck, and Cämmerer, eds. 1976; Dietz et al. 1980. A more popular version: MacKendrick 1970.

Outside the Empire. Economy and society in Free Germany are discussed by Hachmann 1956–57; Jankuhn 1969; Todd 1975. See also more detailed studies by Donat 1977; Zimmermann 1978; Hedeager 1980. Settlements are summarized, with good bibliographies, by Böhner 1975a. Feddersen Wierde: Haarnagel 1975, 1977, 1979. Wijster: van Es 1965. Settlements in general: Müller-Wille 1979. Population sizes of communities: Donat and Ullrich 1976. Iron working in Free Germany: Pleiner 1964; Bielenin 1978; Hingst 1978. Trade between Free Germany and the Roman Empire: Eggers 1951; Nierhaus 1954; Sawyer 1977:142–143; Hedeager 1979a, 1979b; Kunow 1980. General treatment of trade: Todd 1975:35–38. Lübsow graves: Eggers 1949–1950; Oldenstein 1975. Problems of distinguishing between raiding and trading in the archaeological evidence are treated by Reinecke 1958 and Grierson 1959.

EARLY MEDIEVAL PERIOD (A.D. 400–800)

On continuity between Roman and medieval periods see summary with bibliography by Böhner 1975b. Childeric grave: Böhner 1970:84–88. Krefeld-Gellep: Pirling 1975.

Settlements. Good discussions of early medieval settlement patterns are in Böhner 1958; Janssen 1976, 1977; Donat 1978; Müller-Wille 1979. Britain: Rahtz 1976; Biddle 1976. Warendorf: Winkelmann 1958. Gladbach: Sage 1969. Burgheim: Christlein 1979.

Commerce. Growth of industries producing specifically for export trade: Tischler 1952; Böhner 1955–1956; Capelle 1968; Werner 1970; Christlein 1971; Hodges 1982. Medieval long-distance trade: Werner 1961. Krefeld-Gellep Grave 1782: Pirling 1964. Rich burials in Cologne: Doppelfeld and Pirling 1966. St. Denis grave: Werner 1964.

Wealth. In addition to the rich graves cited above, see Christlein 1973. Agricultural basis of wealth in early medieval period: Duby 1968, 1974; Hodges 1982.

Formation of Medieval Towns. Helgö: Holmqvist 1976. Birka: Ambrosiani 1973. Dorestad: van Es 1973. Haithabu: Schietzel 1975, 1981. These sites and others are reviewed in Hodges 1982. Role of commerce in formation of early medieval towns: Pirenne 1925, 1936; Ennen 1953; Schlesinger 1973; Barley, ed. 1977; van Regteren Altena and Heidinga 1977: Hodges 1982; Hodges and Whitehouse 1983. On towns in Britain see articles in Wilson, ed. 1976. Saxon Southampton: Addyman 1973; Hodges 1981. Winchester as the royal capital: Biddle 1973, 1976.

Summary

On general issues regarding the formation of cities and states see Braidwood and Willey, eds. 1962; Adams 1966; Rathje 1971, 1972; Renfrew 1972; Moore, ed. 1974; Redman 1978; Lamberg-Karlovsky and Sabloff 1979; Renfrew and Wagstaff, eds. 1982. The last work contains full bibliographic references. Childe (1958) and Orme (1981:276) discuss the special patterns of cultural development in Europe relative to other parts of the world.

Classical Sources Cited

Athenaeus Naucratita. *The Deipnosophists*. Trans. C. B. Gulick. Cambridge, Mass.: Harvard University Press, 1928–1957.

Caesar. *The Gallic War*. Trans. H. J. Edwards. Cambridge, Mass.: Harvard University Press, 1966.

Diodorus of Sicily. *Library of History*. Trans. C. H. Oldfather. Cambridge, Mass.: Harvard University Press, 1954.

Dionysius of Halicarnassus. *The Roman Antiquities*. Trans. E. Cary. Cambridge, Mass.: Harvard University Press, 1939.

Livy. *Roman History*. Trans. B. O. Foster. Cambridge, Mass.: Harvard University Press, 1967.

Pliny. *Natural History*. Trans. H. Rackham. Cambridge, Mass.: Harvard University Press, 1960.

Polybius. *The Histories*. Trans. W. R. Paton. Cambridge, Mass.: Harvard University Press, 1968.

Strabo. *Geography*. Trans. H. L. Jones. Cambridge, Mass.: Harvard University Press, 1917.

Tacitus. *The Complete Works*. Trans. A. J. Church and W. J. Brodribb. New York: Modern Library, 1942.

References Cited

For articles published in languages other than English, German, French, and Italian, having summaries in one of those languages, the main article title is listed first, followed by the title of the summary in parentheses.

Acsádi, G., and J. Nemeskéri. 1970. *History of Human Life Span and Mortality.* Budapest: Akadémiai Kiadó.

Adams, R. M. 1960. "Early Civilizations, Subsistence, and Environment." In C. H. Kraeling and R. M. Adams, eds., *City Invincible,* pp. 269–295. Chicago: University of Chicago Press.

————. 1966. *The Evolution of Urban Society.* Chicago: Aldine.

————. 1974. "Anthropological Perspectives on Ancient Trade." *Current Anthropology* 15:239–249.

Addyman, P. V. 1973. "Saxon Southampton: A Town and International Port of the 8th to the 10th Century." In H. Jankuhn, W. Schlesinger, and H. Steuer, eds., *Vor- und Frühformen der europäischen Stadt im Mittelalter,* pt. 1, pp. 218–228. Göttingen: Vandenhoeck and Ruprecht.

Alexander, J. 1972. "The Beginnings of Urban Life in Europe." In P. J. Ucko, R. Tringham, and G. W. Dimbleby, eds., *Man, Settlement and Urbanism,* pp. 843–850. London: Duckworth.

————. 1982. "The Prehistoric Salt Trade in Europe." *Nature* 300:577–578.

Alfieri, N., and P. E. Arias. 1958. *Spina: Die neuentdeckte Etruskerstadt und die griechischen Vasen ihrer Gräber.* Munich: Hirmer.

Alföldy, G. 1974. *Noricum.* Trans. A. Birley. London: Routledge and Kegan Paul.

Allen, D. F. 1978a. "The Coins from the Oppidum of Altenburg and the Bushel Series." *Germania* 56:190–229.

————. 1978b. *An Introduction to Celtic Coins.* London: British Museum.

Amberger, H. 1927. "Ein spätlatènezeitlicher Fund vom Attersee." *Mitteilungen der Anthropologischen Gesellschaft in Wien* 57:206–209.

REFERENCES CITED

Ambrosiani, B. 1973. "Neue Ausgrabungen in Birka." In H. Jankuhn, W. Schlesinger, and H. Steuer, eds., *Vor- und Frühformen der europäischen Stadt im Mittelalter*, pt. 2, pp. 58–63. Göttingen: Vandenhoeck and Ruprecht.

Anati, E. 1961. *Camonica Valley*. New York: Knopf.

Arheološka Najdišča Slovenije. 1975. Ljubljana: Izdala Slovenska Akademija Znanosti in Umetnosti, Inštitut za Arheologijo.

Arnold, C. J. 1980. "Wealth and Social Structure: A Matter of Life and Death." In P. Rahtz, T. Dickinson, and L. Watts, eds., *Anglo-Saxon Cemeteries*, pp. 81–142. British Archaeological Reports, vol. 82. Oxford: British Archaeological Reports.

Aurigemma, S. 1960. *La necropoli di Spina in Valle Trebba*. Rome: 'L'Erma' di Bretschneider.

Barley, M. W., ed. 1977. *European Towns: Their Archaeology and Early History*. London: Academic Press.

Barnett, H. G. 1953. *Innovation: The Basis of Cultural Change*. New York: McGraw-Hill.

Barth, F. 1963. *The Role of the Entrepreneur in Social Change in Northern Norway*. Bergen: Norwegian Universities Press.

Barth, F. E. 1970a. "Neuentdeckte Schrämspuren im Heidengebirge des Salzberges zu Hallstatt, Oö." *Mitteilungen der Anthropologischen Gesellschaft in Wien* 100:153–156.

———. 1970b. "Salzbergwerk und Gräberfeld von Hallstatt." In *Krieger und Salzherren: Hallstattkultur im Ostalpenraum*, pp. 40–52. Mainz: Römisch-Germanisches Zentralmuseum.

———. 1971. "Funde aus dem Ender-Werk des Salzberges zu Hallstatt." *Mitteilungen der Anthropologischen Gesellschaft in Wien* 101:37–40.

———. 1973. "Versuch einer typologischen Gliederung der prähistorischen Funde aus dem Hallstätter Salzberg." *Mitteilungen der Anthropologischen Gesellschaft in Wien* 102:26–30.

———. 1980a. "Das prähistorische Hallstatt." In D. Straub, ed., *Die Hallstattkultur: Frühform europäischer Einheit*, pp. 67–79. Linz: Oberösterreichischer Landesverlag.

———. 1980b. "Neue archäologische Forschungen im Salzbergwerk Hallstatt." *Oberösterreich* 30, no. 1, pp. 17–19.

Barth, F. E., H. Felber, and O. Schauberger. 1975. "Radiokohlenstoffdatierung der prähistorischen Baue in den Salzbergwerken Hallstatt und Dürrnberg-Hallein." *Mitteilungen der Anthropologischen Gesellschaft in Wien* 105:45–52.

Beck, A. 1980. *Beiträge zur frühen und älteren Urnenfelderkultur im nordwestlichen Alpenvorland*. Munich: Beck.

Becker, C. J. 1948. "Die zeitliche Stellung des Hjortspring-Fundes." *Acta Archaeologica* (Copenhagen) 19:145–187.

Bender, H., R. Dehn, and I. Stork. 1976. "Neuere Untersuchungen auf dem Münsterberg in Breisach (1966–1975). 1. Die vorrömische Zeit." *Archäologisches Korrespondenzblatt* 6:213–224.

Benoit, F. 1965. *Recherches sur l'hellénisation du Midi de la Gaule.* Annales de la Faculté des Lettres, Aix-en-Provence, n.s. 43. Aix-en-Provence: Ophrys.

Bersu, G. 1940. "Excavations at Little Woodbury, Wiltshire." *Proceedings of the Prehistoric Society* 6:30–111.

———. 1945. *Das Wittnauer Horn.* Basel: Birkhäuser.

———. 1946. "A Hill-Fort in Switzerland." *Antiquity* 20:4–8.

Bersu, G., and P. Goessler. 1924. "Der Lochenstein bei Balingen." *Fundberichte aus Schwaben,* n.s. 2:73–103.

Bertaux, J.-P. 1977. "Das Briquetage an der Seille in Lothringen." *Archäologisches Korrespondenzblatt* 7:261–272.

Betzler, P. 1974. *Die Fibeln in Süddeutschland, Österreich und der Schweiz I.* (*Urnenfelderzeitliche Typen*). Munich: Beck.

Biddle, M. 1973. "Winchester: The Development of an Early Capital." In H. Jankuhn, W. Schlesinger, and H. Steuer, eds., *Vor- und Frühformen der europäischen Stadt im Mittelalter,* pt. 1, pp. 229–261. Göttingen: Vandenhoeck and Ruprecht.

———. 1976. "Towns." In D. M. Wilson, ed., *The Archaeology of Anglo-Saxon England,* pp. 99–150. London: Methuen.

Biel, J. 1980. "Treasure from a Celtic Tomb." *National Geographic,* March 1980, pp. 428–438.

———. 1982. "Ein Fürstengrabhügel der späten Hallstattzeit bei Eberdingen-Hochdorf, Kr. Ludwigsburg (Baden-Württemberg)." *Germania* 60:61–104.

Bielenin, K. 1977. "Einige Bemerkungen über das altertümliche Eisenhüttenwesen im Burgenland." In A. Ohrenberger and K. Kaus, eds., *Archäologische Eisenforschung in Europa,* pp. 49–62. Eisenstadt: Burgenländisches Landesmuseum.

———. 1978. "Der frühgeschichtliche Eisenerzbergbau in Rudki im Świętokrzyskie(Heilig-Kreuz)-Gebirge." In W. Kroker, ed., *Eisen und Archäologie: Eisenerzbergbau und -verhüttung vor 2000 Jahren in der VR Polen,* pp. 8–23. Bochum: Deutsches Bergbau-Museum.

Binford, L. R. 1971. "Mortuary Practices: Their Study and Potential." *American Antiquity* 36, no. 3, pt. 2, pp. 6–29.

Bittel, K. 1934. *Die Kelten in Württemberg.* Berlin: Walter de Gruyter.

Bloch, M. 1961. *Feudal Society.* Trans. L. A. Manyon. Chicago: University of Chicago Press.

Bloch, M. R. 1963. "The Social Influence of Salt." *Scientific American,* July 1963, pp. 88–96.

Boardman, J. 1973. *The Greeks Overseas.* 2d ed. Harmondsworth: Penguin.

REFERENCES CITED

———. 1979. "The Athenian Pottery Trade: The Classical Period." *Expedition* 21, no. 4, pp. 33–39.

Bocquet, A., and J.-P. Couren. 1974. "Le four de potier de Sévrier, Haute-Savoie (Age du Bronze Final)." *Etudes Préhistoriques* 9:1–6.

Boessneck, J., A. von den Driesch, U. Meyer-Lemppenau, and E. Wechsler-von Ohlen. 1971. *Die Tierknochenfunde aus dem Oppidum von Manching*. Wiesbaden: Franz Steiner.

Bohn, O. 1925. "Amphorenschicksale." *Germania* 9:78–85.

Böhner, K. 1955–1956. "Frühmittelalterliche Töpferöfen in Walberberg und Pingsdorf." *Bonner Jahrbücher* 155–156:372–387.

———. 1958. *Die fränkischen Altertümer des Trierer Landes*. Berlin: Gebr. Mann.

———. 1970. "Die Franken." In K. Böhner, D. Ellmers, and K. Weidemann, eds., *Das frühe Mittelalter: Führer durch das Römisch-Germanische Zentralmuseum in Mainz*, pp. 75–125. Mainz: Philipp von Zabern.

———. 1975a. "Ausgrabungen von kaiserzeitlichen Siedlungen im freien Germanien." In *Ausgrabungen in Deutschland 1950–1975*, vol. 2, pp. 3–9. Mainz: Römisch-Germanisches Zentralmuseum.

———. 1975b. "Probleme der Kontinuität zwischen Römerzeit und Mittelalter in West- und Süddeutschland." In *Ausgrabungen in Deutschland 1950–1975*, vol. 2, pp. 53–63. Mainz: Römisch-Germanisches Zentralmuseum.

Bohnsack, D. 1976. "Bernstein und Bernsteinhandel." In J. Hoops, ed., *Reallexikon der germanischen Altertumskunde*, 2d ed., vol. 2, pp. 290–292. Berlin: Walter de Gruyter.

Boitani, F., M. Cataldi, and M. Pasquinucci. 1973. *Le città etrusche*. Florence: Mondadori.

Bökönyi, S. 1974. *History of Domestic Mammals in Central and Eastern Europe*. Budapest: Akadémiai Kaidó.

Bónis, É. B. 1971. "Beiträge zur Rolle der LT D-Siedlungen in Pannonien." *Archeologické rozhledy* 23:521–528.

Bonnamour, L. 1976. "Siedlungen der Spätbronzezeit (Bronze Final III) im Saône-Tal südlich von Chalon-sur-Saône." *Archäologisches Korrespondenzblatt* 6:123–130.

Bonnet, C. 1974. "Un nouvel aperçu sur la station d'altitude de Hohlandsberg, Wintzenheim (Haut-Rhin)." *Cahiers alsaciens d'archéologie, d'art et d'histoire* 18:33–50.

Bouzek, J., D. Koutecký, and E. Neustupný. 1966. *The Knovíz Settlement of North-West Bohemia*. Prague: National Museum.

Bradley, R. 1978. "Prehistoric Field Systems in Britain and North-West Europe." *World Archaeology* 9:265–280.

Bradley, R., S. Lobb, J. Richards, and M. Robinson. 1980. "Two Late

Bronze Age Settlements on the Kennet Gravels: Excavations at Aldermaston Wharf and Knight's Farm, Burghfield, Berkshire." *Proceedings of the Prehistoric Society* 46:217–295.

Braidwood, R. J., and G. R. Willey, eds. 1962. *Courses toward Urban Life.* Viking Fund Publications in Anthropology, no. 32. New York: Wenner-Gren.

Braudel, F. 1972. *The Mediterranean and the Mediterranean World in the Age of Philip II.* Trans. S. Reynolds. New York: Harper and Row.

———. 1981. *The Structures of Everyday Life.* Trans. S. Reynolds. New York: Harper and Row.

Břeň, J. 1966. *Třísov: A Celtic Oppidum in South Bohemia.* Prague: National Museum.

———. 1971. "Das keltische Oppidum in Třísov." *Archeologické rozhledy* 23:294–303.

Bretz-Mahler, D. 1971. *La civilisation de La Tène I en Champagne.* Paris: Centre National de la Recherche Scientifique.

Brisson, A., and J.-J. Hatt. 1967. "Fonds de cabanes de l'âge du Bronze final et du premier âge du Fer en Champagne." *Revue archéologique de l'Est et du Centre-Est* 18:7–51.

Brongers, J. A., and P. Woltering. 1973. "Prehistory in the Netherlands: An Economic-Technological Approach." *Berichten van de Rijksdienst voor het Oudheidkundig Bodermonderzoek* 23:7–47.

Brown, J. A. 1981. "The Search for Rank in Prehistoric Burials." In R. Chapman, I. Kinnes, and K. Randsborg, eds., *The Archaeology of Death*, pp. 25–37. Cambridge: Cambridge University Press.

Bruck, E. F. 1926. *Totenteil und Seelgerät im griechischen Recht.* Munich: Beck.

Bulleid, A., and H. St. G. Gray. 1911 and 1917. *The Glastonbury Lake Villages.* 2 vols. Glastonbury: Glastonbury Antiquarian Society.

Bulliot, J. G. 1899. *Fouilles de Mont Beuvray de 1865 à 1895.* Autun: Dejussieu.

Burford, A. 1972. *Craftsmen in Greek and Roman Society.* London: Thames and Hudson.

Burl, A. 1979. *Prehistoric Avebury.* New Haven: Yale University Press.

Capelle, T. 1968. *Der Metallschmuck aus Haithabu.* Neumünster: Karl Wachholtz.

Casson, L. 1971. *Ships and Seamanship in the Ancient World.* Princeton: Princeton University Press.

———. 1979. "Traders and Trading: Classical Athens." *Expedition* 21, no. 4, pp. 25–32.

Chapman, R., I. Kinnes, and K. Randsborg, eds. 1981. *The Archaeology of Death.* Cambridge: Cambridge University Press.

Chapotat, G. 1970. *Vienne Gauloise.* Lyon: Imprimerie Audin.

Charles-Edwards, T. M. 1976. "The Distinction between Land and Moveable Wealth in Anglo-Saxon England." In P. H. Sawyer, ed., *Medieval Settlement*, pp. 180–187. London: Edward Arnold.

Chevallier, R. 1962a. "L'Italie du nord au seuil de l'histoire: Villanoviens et Etrusques." *Latomus* 21:99–123.

———. 1962b. "La Celtique du Pô." *Latomus* 21:356–370.

Childe, V. G. 1930. *The Bronze Age*. New York: Macmillan.

———. 1950. "The Urban Revolution." *Town Planning Review* 21, no. 1, pp. 1–17.

———. 1951. *Social Evolution*. New York: Henry Schuman.

———. 1958. *The Prehistory of European Society*. Harmondsworth: Penguin.

Christ, K. 1957. "Ergebnisse und Probleme der keltischen Numismatik und Geldgeschichte." *Historia* (Wiesbaden) 6:215–253.

Christlein, R. 1963–1964. "Ein Bronzesiebfragment der Spätlatènezeit vom Zugmantel." *Saalburg-Jahrbuch* 21:16–19.

———. 1971. "Anzeichen von Fibelproduktion in der völkerwanderungszeitlichen Siedlung Runder Berg bei Urach." *Archäologisches Korrespondenzblatt* 1:47–49.

———. 1973. "Besitzabstufungen zur Merowingerzeit im Spiegel reicher Grabfunde aus West- und Südwestdeutschland." *Jahrbuch des Römisch-Germanischen Zentralmuseums* 20:147–180.

———. 1979. *Die Alamannen*. 2d ed. Stuttgart: Konrad Theiss.

Čižmář, M. 1972. "Společenská struktura moravských keltů podle výzkumu pohřebišť" (Die Gesellschaftsstruktur der Kelten in Mähren im Lichte der Erforschung von Gräberfeldern). *Časopis Moravského Musea* (Brno) 57:73–81.

Clark, J. G. D. 1952. *Prehistoric Europe: The Economic Basis*. London: Methuen.

Clark, J. G. D., and S. Piggott. 1965. *Prehistoric Societies*. London: Hutchinson.

Clarke, D. L. 1979. "The Economic Context of Trade and Industry in Barbarian Europe till Roman Times." In D. L. Clarke, *Analytical Archaeologist: Collected Papers*, pp. 263–331. London: Academic Press.

Clavel-Lévêque, M. 1974. "Das griechische Marseille: Entwicklungsstufen und Dynamik einer Handelsmacht." In E. C. Welskopf, ed., *Hellenische Poleis*, vol. 2, pp. 855–969. Berlin: Akademie-Verlag.

Coblenz, W. 1951. "Der Bronzegefässefund von Dresden-Dobritz." *Arbeits- und Forschungsberichte zur sächsischen Bodendenkmalpflege* 1:135–161.

———. 1967. "Zu den bronzezeitlichen Metallfunden von der Heidenschanze in Dresden-Coschütz und ihrer Rolle bei der zeitlichen und funktionellen Deutung der Burgen der Lausitzer Kultur." *Arbeits- und Forschungsberichte zur sächsischen Bodendenkmalpflege* 16–17; 179–211.

Coghlan, H. H. 1977. *Notes on Prehistoric and Early Iron in the Old World*. 2d ed. Oxford: Pitt Rivers Museum.

Coles, J. M. 1962. "European Bronze Age Shields." *Proceedings of the Prehistoric Society* 28:156–190.

———. 1973. *Archaeology by Experiment*. New York: Charles Scribner's Sons.

———. 1977. "Parade and Display: Experiments in Bronze Age Europe." In V. Markotic, ed., *Ancient Europe and the Mediterranean*, pp. 51–58. Warminster: Aris and Phillips.

———. 1979. *Experimental Archaeology*. London: Academic Press.

Coles, J. M., and A. Harding. 1979. *The Bronze Age in Europe*. New York: St. Martin's.

Coles, J. M., S. V. E. Heal, and B. Orme. 1978. "The Use and Character of Wood in Prehistoric Britain and Ireland." *Proceedings of the Prehistoric Society* 44:1–45.

Collis, J. 1975. *Defended Sites of the Late La Tène in Central and Western Europe*. British Archaeological Reports, Supplementary Series, vol. 2. Oxford: British Archaeological Reports.

———. 1976. "Town and Market in Iron Age Europe." In B. Cunliffe and T. Rowley, eds., *Oppida: The Beginnings of Urbanisation in Barbarian Europe*, pp. 3–23. British Archaeological Reports, Supplementary Series, vol. 11. Oxford: British Archaeological Reports.

———. 1979. "Urban Structure in the Pre-Roman Iron Age." In B. C. Burnham and J. Kingsley, eds., *Space, Hierarchy and Society*, pp. 129–136. British Archaeological Reports, International Series, vol. 59. Oxford: British Archaeological Reports.

———. 1980. "Aulnat and Urbanisation in France." *The Archaeological Journal* 137:40–49.

———. 1982. "Gradual Growth and Sudden Change: Urbanisation in Temperate Europe." In C. Renfrew and S. Shennan, eds., *Ranking, Resource and Exchange*, pp. 73–78. Cambridge: Cambridge University Press.

Contzen, L. 1861. *Die Wanderungen der Kelten*. Leipzig: Wilhelm Engelmann.

Courtain, J., J. Guilaine, and J.-P. Mohen. 1976. "Les débuts de l'agriculture en France: Les documents archéologiques." In J. Guilaine, ed., *La préhistoire française*, vol. 2, pp. 172–179. Paris: Centre National de la Recherche Scientifique.

Cowen, J. D. 1955. "Eine Einführung in die Geschichte der bronzenen Griffzungenschwerter in Süddeutschland und den angrenzenden Gebieten." *Berichte der Römisch-Germanischen Kommission* 36:52–155.

Crumley, C. L. 1974a. *Celtic Social Structures*. Ann Arbor: University of Michigan, Museum of Anthropology.

———. 1974b "The Paleoethnographic Recognition of Early States: A Celtic Example." *Arctic Anthropology* 11:254–260.

Cunliffe, B. 1976. "Danebury, Hampshire." *Antiquaries Journal* 56:198–216.

————. 1978. *Hengistbury Head*. London: Elek.

Dalton, G. 1977. "Aboriginal Economies in Stateless Societies." In T. K. Earle and J. E. Ericson, eds., *Exchange Systems in Prehistory*, pp. 191–212. New York: Academic Press.

Dämmer, H.-W. 1978. *Die bemalte Keramik der Heuneburg*. Mainz: Philipp von Zabern.

David, N. 1972. "On the Life Span of Pottery, Type Frequencies, and Archaeological Inference." *American Antiquity* 37:141–142.

David, N., and David-Hennig, H. 1971. "Zur Herstellung und Lebensdauer von Keramik." *Bayerische Vorgeschichtsblätter* 36:289–317.

Davies, O. 1935. *Roman Mines in Europe*. Oxford: Clarendon Press.

Déchelette, J. 1904. *Les fouilles de Mont Beuvray de 1897–1901*. Paris: A. Picard.

Deetz, J. 1977a. "Material Culture and Archaeology: What's the Difference?" In L. Ferguson, ed., *Historical Archaeology and the Importance of Material Things*, pp. 9–12. Special Publication no. 2. Washington: Society for Historical Archaeology.

————. 1977b. *In Small Things Forgotten: The Archaeology of Early American Life*. New York: Anchor Press.

Dehn, R. 1972. *Die Urnenfelderkultur in Nordwürttemberg*. Stuttgart: Müller and Gräff.

Dehn, W. 1951. "Die gallischen 'Oppida' bei Cäsar." *Saalburg-Jahrbuch* 10:36–49.

————. 1957. "Die Heuneburg beim Talhof unweit Riedlingen (Kr. Saulgau)." *Fundberichte aus Schwaben*, n.s. 14:78–99.

————. 1962–1963. "Frühe Drehscheibenkeramik nördlich der Alpen." *Alt-Thüringen* 6:372–382.

————. 1965. "'Mediolanum': Lagetypen spätkeltischer Oppida." *Beihefte der Bonner Jahrbücher*, vol. 10, pt. 2, pp. 117–128.

————. 1971. "Einige Bemerkungen zur Erforschung gallischer Oppida in Frankreich." *Archeologické rozhledy* 23:393–405.

————. 1979. "Einige Überlegungen zum Charakter keltischer Wanderungen." In P.-M. Duval and V. Kruta, eds., *Les mouvements celtiques du Vᵉ au Iᵉʳ siècle avant notre ère*, pp. 15–18. Paris: Centre National de la Recherche Scientifique.

Dehn, W., and O.-H. Frey, 1979. "Southern Imports and the Hallstatt and Early La Tène Chronology of Central Europe." In D. and F. R. Ridgway, eds., *Italy before the Romans*, pp. 489–511. London: Academic Press.

de Marinis, R. 1977. "The La Tène Culture of the Cisalpine Gauls." In M. Guštin, ed., *Keltske Študije*, pp. 23–50. Brežice: Posavski musej.

Demos, J. 1970. *A Little Commonwealth: Family Life in Plymouth Colony*. New York: Oxford University Press.

Denecke, D. 1973. "Der geographische Stadtbegriff und die räumlichfunktionale Betrachtungsweise bei Siedlungstypen mit zentraler Bedeutung in Anwendung auf historische Siedlungsepochen." In H. Jankuhn, W. Schlesinger, and H. Steuer, eds., *Vor- und Frühformen der europäischen Stadt im Mittelalter*, pt. 1, pp. 33–55. Göttingen: Vandenhoeck and Ruprecht.

Dethlefsen, E. S. 1981. "The Cemetery and Culture Change: Archaeological Focus and Ethnographic Perspective." In R. J. Gould and M. J. Schiffer, eds., *Modern Material Culture*, pp. 137–159. New York: Academic Press.

Dietz, K., U. Osterhaus, S. Rieckhoff-Pauli, and K. Spindler. 1979. *Regensburg zur Römerzeit*. Regensburg: Friedrich Pustet.

Dobiat, C. 1980. *Das hallstattzeitliche Gräberfeld von Kleinklein und seine Keramik*. Graz: Landesmuseum Joanneum.

Donat, P. 1968–1969. "Eine spätlatènezeitliche Siedlung am Fusse der Steinsburg bei Römhild." *Alt-Thüringen* 10:143–176.

———. 1977. "Stallgrösse und Viehbesitz nach Befunden germanischer Wohnstallhäuser." *Deutsche Akademie der Wissenschaften zu Berlin, Sektion für Vor- und Frühgeschichte, Schriften* 30:251–263.

———. 1978. "Haus, Hof und Dorf in Mitteleuropa vom 7.–12. Jahrhundert." *Ethnographisch-Archäologische Zeitschrift* 19:61–67.

Donat, P., and H. Ullrich. 1976. "Bevölkerungszahlen: Archäologie." In J. Hoops, ed., *Reallexikon der germanischen Altertumskunde*, vol. 2, pp. 349–353. Berlin: Walter de Gruyter.

Doppelfeld, O., and R. Pirling. 1966. *Fränkische Fürsten im Rheinland: Die Gräber aus dem Kölner Dom, von Krefeld-Gellep und Morken*. Düsseldorf: Rheinland-Verlag.

Drack, W. 1980. "Gold." In E. Lessing, ed., *Hallstatt: Bilder aus der Frühzeit Europas*, pp. 64–71. Vienna: Jugend und Volk.

Drack, W., ed. 1974. *Ur- und frühgeschichtliche Archäologie der Schweiz*, vol. 4, *Die Eisenzeit*. Basel: Schweizerische Gesellschaft für Ur- und Frühgeschichte.

Drescher, H. 1958. *Der Überfangguss*. Mainz: Römisch-Germanisches Zentralmuseum.

———. 1980. "Zur Technik der Hallstattzeit." In D. Straub, ed., *Die Hallstattkultur: Frühform europäischer Einheit*, pp. 54–66. Linz: Oberösterreichischer Landesverlag.

Driehaus, J. 1971. "Zum Grabfund von Waldalgesheim." *Hamburger Beiträge zur Archäologie* 1, no. 2, pp. 101–114.

Duby, G. 1968. *Rural Economy and Country Life in the Medieval West*. Trans. C. Postan. London: Edward Arnold.

———. 1974. *The Early Growth of the European Economy*. Trans. H. B. Clarke. Ithaca, N.Y.: Cornell University Press.

Dunbabin, T. J. 1948. *The Western Greeks*. Oxford: Clarendon Press.

REFERENCES CITED

Dušek, M. 1966. *Thrakisches Gräberfeld der Hallstattzeit in Chotín*. Bratislava: Vydavatel'stvo Slovenskej Akadémie Vied.

———. 1974a. "Die Thraker im Karpatenbecken." *Slovenská Archeologia* 22:361–434.

———. 1974b. "Der junghallstattzeitliche Fürstensitz auf dem Molpír bei Smolenice." In B. Chropovský, ed., *Symposium zu Problemen der jüngeren Hallstattzeit in Mitteleuropa*, pp. 137–150. Bratislava: Vydavatel'stvo Slovenskej Akadémie Vied.

———. 1980. "Slowakei." In E. Lessing, ed., *Hallstatt: Bilder aus der Frühzeit Europas*, pp. 100–104. Vienna: Jugend und Volk.

Dušek, S. 1977a. "Zur chronologischen und soziologischen Auswertung der hallstattzeitlichen Gräberfelder von Chotín." *Slovenská Archeologia* 25:13–44.

———. 1977b. "Zur sozialökonomischen Interpretation hallstattzeitlicher Fundkomplexe der Südwest-Slowakei." In J. Herrmann, ed., *Archäologie als Geschichtswissenschaft*, pp. 177–185. Berlin: Akademie-Verlag.

Dvořák, F. 1938. *Wagengräber der älteren Eisenzeit in Böhmen*. Prague: University of Prague.

Egg, M. 1978. "Das Grab eines unterkrainischen Kriegers in Hallstatt." *Archäologisches Korrespondenzblatt* 8:191–201.

Egger, R. 1961. *Die Stadt auf dem Magdalensberg*. Österreichische Akademie der Wissenschaften, Philosophisch-Historische Klasse, Denkschriften, vol. 79. Vienna: Böhlau.

Eggers, H. J. 1949–1950. "Lübsow: Ein germanischer Fürstensitz der älteren Kaiserzeit." *Praehistorische Zeitschrift* 34–35:58–111.

———. 1951. *Der römische Import im freien Germanien*. Hamburg: Museum für Völkerkunde und Vorgeschichte.

Eibner, C. 1974. *Das späturnenfelderzeitliche Gräberfeld von St. Andrä v. d. Hgt. P. B. Tulln, Nö.* Vienna: Franz Deuticke.

Eibner, C., L. Plank, and R. Pittioni. 1966. "Die Urnengräber vom Lebenberg bei Kitzbühel, Tirol." *Archaeologia Austriaca* 40:215–248.

Ennen, E. 1953. *Frühgeschichte der europäischen Stadt*. Bonn: L. Röhrscheid.

Eogan, G. 1981. "The Gold Vessels of the Bronze Age in Ireland and Beyond." *Proceedings of the Royal Irish Academy* 81, C, no. 14, pp. 345–382.

Fél, E., and T. Hofer. 1972. *Bäuerliche Denkweise in Wirtschaft und Haushalt*. Göttingen: Otto Schwarz.

Ferguson, L. 1977. "Historical Archaeology and the Importance of Material Things." In Ferguson, ed., *Historical Archaeology and the Importance of Material Things*, pp. 5–8. Special Publication no. 2. Washington: Society for Historical Archaeology.

Filip, J. 1962. *Celtic Civilization and Its Heritage*. Prague: New Horizons.

————. 1969. "Sichel." In J. Filip, ed., *Enzyklopädisches Handbuch zur Ur- und Frühgeschichte Europas*, vol. 2, pp. 1288–1290. Stuttgart: W. Kohlhammer.

————. 1971. "Die keltische Besiedlung Mittel- und Südosteuropas und das Problem der zugehörigen Oppida." *Archeologické rozhledy* 23:263–272.

————. 1978. Keltská Opevnění jako Ukazatel a Odraz Historického Vývoje a Struktury Keltské Společnosti" (Celtic Strongholds as an Indicator and a Reflection of the Evolution and the Structure of Celtic Society). *Archeologické rozhledy* 30:420–432.

Filtzinger, P., D. Planck, and B. Cämmerer, eds. 1976. *Die Römer in Baden-Württemberg*. Stuttgart: Konrad Theiss.

Finley, M. I. 1959. "Technology in the Ancient World." *Economic History Review*, 2d ser. 12:120–125.

————. 1965a. *The World of Odysseus*. New York: Viking Press.

————. 1965b. "Trade and Politics in the Ancient World: Classical Greece." In *Deuxième conférence internationale d'histoire économique*, pp. 11–35. Paris: Mouton.

————. 1973. *The Ancient Economy*. London: Chatto and Windus.

Firth, R. 1964. "Capital, Saving and Credit in Peasant Societies: A Viewpoint from Economic Anthropology." In R. Firth and B. S. Yamey, eds., *Capital, Saving and Credit in Peasant Societies*, pp. 15–34. Chicago: Aldine.

————. 1965. *Primitive Polynesian Economy*. 2d ed. London: Routledge and Kegan Paul.

Firth, R., and B. S. Yamey, eds. 1964. *Capital, Saving and Credit in Peasant Societies*. Chicago: Aldine.

Fischer, F. 1959. *Der spätlatènezeitliche Depot-Fund von Kappel (Kreis Saulgau)*. Stuttgart: Silberburg.

————. 1971. "Die keltische Oppida Südwestdeutschlands und ihre historische Situation." *Archeologické rozhledy* 23:417–431.

————. 1973. "ΚΕΙΜΗΛΙΑ: Bemerkungen zur kulturgeschichtlichen Interpretation des sogenannten Südimports in der späten Hallstatt- und frühen Latène-Kultur des westlichen Mitteleuropa." *Germania* 51:436–459.

————. 1976. "P. Silius Nerva: Zur Vorgeschichte des Alpenfeldzugs 15 v. Chr." *Germania* 54:147–155.

————. 1981. "Sinsheim-Dühren." In K. Bittel, W. Kimmig, and S. Schiek, eds., *Die Kelten in Baden-Württemberg*, pp. 471–472. Stuttgart: Konrad Theiss.

Flouest, J.-L., and I. M. Stead. 1977. "Une tombe de La Tène III à Hannogne (Ardennes)." *Mémoires de la société d'agriculture, commerce, sciences et arts du départment de la Marne* 92:55–72.

Foltiny, S. 1958. *Velemszentvid: Ein urzeitliches Kulturzentrum in Mitteleuropa.* Vienna: Österreichische Arbeitsgemeinschaft für Ur- und Frühgeschichte.

Forbes, R. J. 1964. "The Evolution of the Smith, His Social and Sacred Status." In R. J. Forbes, *Studies in Ancient Technology*, vol. 7, pp. 52–102. Leiden: Brill.

Frankenstein, S., and M. J. Rowlands. 1978. "The Internal Structure and Regional Context of Early Iron Age Society in South-Western Germany." *Institute of Archaeology Bulletin* 15:73–112.

Frey, O.-H. 1966. "Der Ostalpenraum und die antike Welt in der frühen Eisenzeit." *Germania* 44:48–66.

————. 1969. *Die Entstehung der Situlenkunst.* Berlin: Walter de Gruyter.

Frey, O.-H., and S. Gabrovec. 1971. "Zur Chronologie der Hallstattzeit im Ostalpenraum." In M. Garašanin, A. Benac, and N. Tasić, eds., *Actes du VIIIe congrès international des sciences préhistoriques et protohistoriques*, vol. 1, pp. 193–218. Belgrade: Union internationale des sciences préhistoriques et protohistoriques.

Gabrovec, S. 1960. "Grob z oklepom iz Novega mesta" (Panzergrab von Novo mesto). *Situla* 1:27–79.

————. 1966. "Zur Hallstattzeit in Slowenien." *Germania* 44:1–48.

————. 1973. "Začetek halštatskega obdobja v Sloveniji" (Der Beginn der Hallstattzeit in Slowenien). *Arheološki Vestnik* 24:367–373.

————. 1974. "Die Ausgrabungen in Stična und ihre Bedeutung für die südostalpine Hallstattkultur." In B. Chropovský, ed., *Symposium zu Problemen der jüngeren Hallstattzeit in Mitteleuropa*, pp. 163–187. Bratislava: Vydavatel'stvo Slovenskej Akadémie Vied.

————. 1976. "Zum Beginn der Hallstattzeit in Slowenien." In H. Mitscha-Märheim, H. Friesinger, and H. Kerchler, eds., *Festschrift R. Pittioni*, vol. 1, pp. 588–600. Vienna: Franz Deuticke.

————. 1980. "Der Beginn der Hallstattkultur und der Osten." In D. Straub, ed., *Die Hallstattkultur: Frühform europäischer Einheit*, pp. 30–53. Linz: Oberösterreichischer Landesverlag.

Gabrovec, S., O.-H. Frey, and S. Foltiny. 1970. "Erster Vorbericht über die Ausgrabungen im Ringwall von Stična (Slowenien)." *Germania* 48, 12–33.

I Galli e l'Italia. 1978. Rome: Soprintendenza Archeologica di Roma.

Gersbach, E. 1969. "Heuneburg-Aussensiedlung-jüngere Adelsnekropole." *Fundberichte aus Hessen*, suppl. 1, pp. 29–34.

————. 1975. "Das Modell der Heuneburg." In *Ausgrabungen in Deutschland 1950–1975*, vol. 3, pp. 317–319. Mainz: Römisch-Germanisches Zentralmuseum.

————. 1978. "Ergebnisse der letzten Ausgrabungen auf der Heuneburg bei Hundersingen (Donau)." *Archäologisches Korrespondenzblatt* 8:301–310.

———. 1981. "Neue Aspekte zur Geschichte des späthallstatt-frühlatène-zeitlichen Fürstensitzes auf der Heuneburg." In C. and A. Eibner, eds., *Die Hallstattkultur: Bericht über das Symposium in Steyr 1980 aus Anlass der Internationalen Ausstellung des Landes Oberösterreich*, pp. 357–374. Linz: Oberösterreichischer Landesverlag.

Gimbutas, M. 1965. *Bronze Age Cultures in Central and Eastern Europe.* The Hague: Mouton.

Glassie, H. 1977. "Archaeology and Folklore: Common Anxieties, Common Hopes." In L. Ferguson, ed., *Historical Archaeology and the Importance of Material Things*, pp. 23–35. Special Publication no. 2. Washington: Society for Historical Archaeology.

Glob, P. V. 1951. *Ard og plov in Nordens oldtid.* Aarhus: Universitetsforlaget.

———. 1954. "Plovbilleder i Val Camonica" (Plough Carvings in the Val Camonica). *Kuml* 7–17.

Goetze, A. 1900. "Depotfund von Eisengeräthen aus frührömischer Zeit von Körner (Sachsen-Coburg-Gotha)." *Zeitschrift für Ethnologie* 32:202–214.

Gray, H. St. G., and A. Bulleid. 1953. *The Meare Lake Village.* Vol. 2. Taunton: Taunton Castle.

Greenfield, S. M. 1979. "Entrepreneurship and Dynasty Building in the Portuguese Empire in the Seventeenth Century." In S. M. Greenfield, A. Strickon, and R. T. Aubey, eds., *Entrepreneurs in Cultural Context*, pp. 21–63. Albuquerque: University of New Mexico Press.

Greenfield, S. M., A. Strickon, and R. T. Aubey, eds. 1979. *Entrepreneurs in Cultural Context.* Albuquerque: University of New Mexico Press.

Grierson, P. 1959. "Commerce in the Dark Ages." *Transactions of the Royal Historical Society*, 5th ser. 9:123–140.

Grössler, H. 1907. "Das Fürstengrab im grossen Galgenhügel am Paulus-schachte bei Helmsdorf (im Mansfelder Seekreise)." *Jahresschrift für die Vorgeschichte der sächsisch-thüringischen Länder* 6:1–87.

Guilaine, J., ed. 1976. *La préhistoire française*, vol. 2, *Les civilisations néolithiques et protohistoriques de la France.* Paris: Centre National de la Recherche Scientifique.

Guštin, M., ed. 1977. *Keltske Študije.* Brežice: Posavski musej.

Guyan, W. U. 1977. "Neue archäologische Untersuchungen zur Eisen-verhüttung in der Schweiz." In A. Ohrenberger and K. Kaus, eds., *Archäologische Eisenforschung in Europa*, pp. 119–126. Eisenstadt: Burgenländisches Landesmuseum.

Haarnagel, W. 1975. "Die Wurtensiedlung Feddersen Wierde im Nordsee-

Küstengebiet." In *Ausgrabungen in Deutschland 1950–1975*, vol. 2, pp. 10–29. Mainz: Römisch-Germanisches Zentralmuseum.

———. 1977. "Das eisenzeitliche Dorf 'Feddersen Wierde.'" In H. Jankuhn, W. Schlesinger, and H. Steuer, eds., *Vor- und Frühformen der europäischen Stadt im Mittelalter*, pt. 1, pp. 253–284. Göttingen: Vandenhoeck and Ruprecht.

———. 1979. *Die Grabung Feddersen Wierde*. Wiesbaden: Franz Steiner.

Hachmann, R. 1956–1957. "Zur Gesellschaftsordnung der Germanen in der Zeit um Christi Geburt." *Archaeologia Geographica* 5–6:7–24.

Hachmann, R., G. Kossack, and H. Kuhn. 1962. *Völker zwischen Germanen und Kelten*. Neumünster: Karl Wachholtz.

Haevernick, T. E. 1978. "Urnenfelderzeitliche Glasperlen." *Zeitschrift für Schweizerische Archäologie und Kunstgeschichte* 35:145–157.

Haffner, A. 1969. "Das Treverer-Gräberfeld mit Wagenbestattungen von Hoppstädten-Weiersbach, Kreis Birkenfeld." *Trierer Zeitschrift* 32:71–127.

———. 1971a. "Ein hallstattzeitlicher Eisenschmelzofen von Hillesheim, Kr. Daun." *Trierer Zeitschrift* 34:21–29.

———. 1971b. *Das keltisch-römische Gräberfeld von Wederath-Belginum*, vol. 1, *Gräber 1–428, ausgegraben 1954–1955*. Mainz: Philipp von Zabern.

———. 1974a. "Zum Ende der Latènezeit im Mittelrhein." *Archäologisches Korrespondenzblatt* 4:59–72.

———. 1974b. *Das keltisch-römische Gräberfeld von Wederath-Belginum*, vol. 2, *Gräber 429–883, ausgegraben 1956–1957*. Mainz: Philipp von Zabern.

———. 1976. *Die westliche Hunsrück-Eifel-Kultur*. Berlin: Walter de Gruyter.

———. 1978. *Das keltisch-römische Gräberfeld von Wederath-Belginum*, vol. 3, *Gräber 885–1260, ausgegraben 1958–1960, 1971 und 1974*. Mainz: Philipp von Zabern.

Hald, M. 1950. *Olddanske Tekstiler*. Copenhagen: Nordisk Forlag.

Hampel, J. 1887. *Altertümer der Bronzezeit in Ungarn*. Budapest: Friedrich Kilian.

Hareven, T. K., and R. Langenbach. 1978. *Amoskeag: Life and Work in an American Factory-City*. New York: Pantheon.

Härke, H. G. H. 1979. *Settlement Types and Patterns in the West Hallstatt Province*. British Archaeological Reports, International Series vol. 57. Oxford: British Archaeological Reports.

Harris, W. V. 1980. "Towards a Study of the Roman Slave Trade." In J. H. D'Arms and E. C. Kopff, eds., *The Seaborne Commerce of Ancient Rome*, pp. 117–140. Rome: American Academy in Rome.

Harrison, R. J. 1980. *The Beaker Folk*. London: Thames and Hudson.

Hartley, D. 1979. *Lost Country Life*. New York: Pantheon.

Hartmann, A. 1970. *Prähistorische Goldfunde aus Europa.* Berlin: Gebr. Mann.

———. 1978. "Ergebnisse spektralanalytischer Untersuchung späthallstatt- und latènezeitlicher Goldfunde vom Dürrnberg, aus Süddeutschland, Frankreich und der Schweiz." In L. Pauli, ed., *Der Dürrnberg bei Hallein III*, pp. 601–617. Munich: Beck.

Hasebroek, J. 1933. *Trade and Politics in Ancient Greece.* Trans. L. M. Fraser and D. C. Macgregor. London: G. Bell and Sons.

Häusler, A. 1968. "Kritische Bemerkungen zum Versuch soziologischer Deutung ur- und frühgeschichtlicher Gräberfelder." *Ethnographisch-Archäologische Zeitschrift* 9:1–30.

Hawkes, C. F. C. 1940. *The Prehistoric Foundations of Europe to the Mycenaean Age.* London: Methuen.

Hedeager, L. 1979a. "Processes toward State Formation in Early Iron Age Denmark." In K. Kristiansen and C. Paludan-Müller, eds., *New Directions in Scandinavian Archaeology*, pp. 217–223. Copenhagen: National Museum of Denmark.

———. 1979b. "A Quantitative Analysis of Roman Imports in Europe North of the Limes (0–400 A.D.) and the Question of Roman-Germanic Exchange." In K. Kristiansen and C. Paludan-Müller, eds., *New Directions in Scandinavian Archaeology*, pp. 191–216. Copenhagen: National Museum of Denmark.

———. 1980. "Besiedlung, soziale Struktur und politische Organisation in der älteren und jüngeren römischen Kaiserzeit Ostdänemarks." *Praehistorische Zeitschrift* 55:38–109.

Hencken, H. 1971. *The Earliest European Helmets.* Cambridge, Mass.: Peabody Museum, Harvard University.

———. 1978. *The Iron Age Cemetery of Magdalenska gora in Slovenia.* Cambridge, Mass.: Peabody Museum, Harvard University.

Hensel, W. 1970. "Remarques sur les origines des villes en Europe centrale." In G. Mansuelli and R. Zangheri, eds., *Atti del convegno di studi sulla città etrusca e italica preromana*, vol. 1, pp. 323–328. Bologna: Istituto per la Storia di Bologna.

Herlihy, D. 1971. "The Economy of Traditional Europe." *Journal of Economic History* 31:153–164.

Herrmann, F.-R. 1966. *Die Funde der Urnenfelderkultur in Mittel- und Südhessen.* Berlin: Walter de Gruyter.

———. 1974–1975. "Die urnenfelderzeitliche Siedlung von Künzing." *Jahresbericht der bayerischen Bodendenkmalpflege* 15–16:58–106.

Herrmann, J. 1969. "Burgen und befestigte Siedlungen der jüngeren Bronze- und frühen Eisenzeit in Mitteleuropa." In K.-H. Otto and J.

Herrmann, eds., *Siedlung, Burg und Stadt*, pp. 56–94. Berlin: Akademie-Verlag.

Herskovits, M. J. 1940. *The Economic Life of Primitive Peoples.* New York: Knopf.

Hingst, H. 1978. "Vor- und frühgeschichtliche Eisenverhüttung in Schleswig-Holstein." In W. Kroker, ed., *Eisen und Archäologie: Eisenerzbergbau und -verhüttung vor 2000 Jahren in der VR Polen*, pp. 63–71. Bochum: Bergbau-Museum.

Hodder, I. 1982. *Symbols in Action: Ethnoarchaeological Studies of Material Culture.* Cambridge: Cambridge University Press.

Hodges, H. W. M. 1964. *Artifacts.* New York: Praeger.

Hodges, R. 1981. *The Hamwih Pottery.*, Research Report no. 37. London: Council for British Archaeology.

————. 1982. *Dark Age Economics: The Origins of Towns and Trade AD 60–1000.* London: Duckworth.

Hodges, R., and D. Whitehouse. 1983. *Mohammed, Charlemagne and the Origins of Europe.* Ithaca, N.Y.: Cornell University Press.

Hodson, F. R. 1964. "La Tène Chronology, Continental and British." *Institute of Archaeology Bulletin* 4:123–141.

————. 1968. *The La Tène Cemetery at Münsingen-Rain.* Bern: Stämpfli.

Holmqvist, W. 1976. "Die Ergebnisse der Grabungen auf Helgö (1954–1974)." *Praehistorische Zeitschrift* 51:127–177.

Homans, G. C. 1942. *English Villagers of the Thirteenth Century.* Cambridge, Mass.: Harvard University Press.

Hopkins, K. 1978. *Conquerors and Slaves.* Cambridge: Cambridge University Press.

Hrubý, V. 1965. *Staré Mesto.* Prague: Československé Akademie Ved.

Hundt, H.-J. 1958. *Katalog Straubing I.* Kallmünz/Opf.: Michael Lassleben.

————. 1970. "Gewebefunde aus Hallstatt: Webkunst und Tracht in der Hallstattzeit." In *Krieger und Salzherren: Hallstattkultur im Ostalpenraum*, pp. 53–71. Mainz: Römisch-Germanisches Zentralmuseum.

————. 1974. "Donauländische Einflüsse in der frühen Bronzezeit Norditaliens." *Preistoria Alpina* 10:143–178.

Hus, A. 1971. *Vulci étrusque et étrusco-romaine.* Paris, Éditions Klincksieck.

Hvass, S. 1975. "Das eisenzeitliche Dorf bei Hodde, Westjütland." *Acta Archaeologica* (Copenhagen) 46:142–158.

Ivanov, I. S. 1978. "Les fouilles archéologiques de la nécropole chalcolithique à Varna (1972–1975)." *Studia praehistorica* 1–2:13–26.

Jaanusson, H. 1971. "Bronsålderboplatsen vid Hallunda." *Fornvännen* 66:173–185.

Jackson, K. H. 1964. *The Oldest Irish Tradition: A Window on the Iron Age.* Cambridge: Cambridge University Press.

Jacobi, G. 1974. *Werkzeug und Gerät aus dem Oppidum von Manching.* Wiesbaden: Franz Steiner.

———. 1977. *Die Metallfunde vom Dünsberg.* Wiesbaden: Landesamt für Denkmalpflege Hessen.

Jacobstahal, P. 1944. *Early Celtic Art.* Oxford: Clarendon Press.

Jankuhn, H. 1969. *Vor- und Frühgeschichte vom Neolithikum bis zur Völkerwanderungszeit.* Stuttgart: Eugen Ulmer.

———. 1977. *Einführung in die Siedlungsarchäologie.* Berlin: Walter de Gruyter.

Jankuhn, H., R. Schützeichel, and F. Schwind, eds. 1977. *Das Dorf der Eisenzeit und des frühen Mittelalters.* Göttingen: Vanderhoeck and Ruprecht.

Jansová, L. 1965. *Hrazany.* Prague: Československé Akademie Věd.

———. 1971. "Keltisches Oppidum Závist." *Archeologické rozhledy* 23:273–281.

Janssen, W. 1976. "Some Major Aspects of Frankish and Medieval Settlement in the Rhineland." In P. H. Sawyer, ed., *Medieval Settlement,* pp. 41–60. London: Edward Arnold.

———. 1977. "Dorf und Dorfformen des 7. bis 12. Jahrhunderts im Lichte neuer Ausgrabungen in Mittel- und Nordeuropa." In H. Jankuhn, R. Schützeichel, and F. Schwind, eds., *Das Dorf der Eisenzeit und des frühen Mittelalters,* pp. 285–356. Göttingen: Vandenhoeck and Ruprecht.

Jehl, M., and C. Bonnet. 1968. "Un potier de l'époque champs d'urnes au sommet du Hohlandsberg." *Cahiers alsaciens d'archéologie, d'art et d'histoire* 12:5–30.

———. 1971. "La station d'altitude de Linsenbrunnen-Wintzenheim-Hohlandsberg." *Cahiers alsaciens d'archéologie, d'art et d'histoire* 15:23–48.

Joachim, H.-E. 1973. "Ein reich ausgestattetes Wagengrab der Spätlatènezeit aus Neuwied, Stadtteil Heimbach-Weis." *Bonner Jahrbücher* 173:1–44.

———. 1980. "Jüngerlatènezeitliche Siedlungen bei Eschweiler, Kr. Aachen." *Bonner Jahrbücher* 180:355–441.

Joachim, W., and J. Biel. 1977. "Untersuchung einer späthallstattfrühlatènezeitlicher Siedlung in Kornwestheim, Kreis Ludwigsburg." *Fundberichte aus Baden-Württemberg* 3:173–203.

Jockenhövel, A. 1973. "Urnenfelderzeitliche Barren als Grabbeigaben." *Archäologisches Korrespondenzblatt* 3:23–28.

———. 1974. "Zu befestigten Siedlungen der Urnenfelderzeit aus Süddeutschland." *Fundberichte aus Hessen* 14:19–62.

Joffroy, R. 1954. *Le trésor de Vix (Côte-d'Or).* Paris: Presses Universitaires de France.

————. 1962. *Le trésor de Vix: Histoire et portée d'une grande découverte*. Paris: Fayard.

Kahrstedt, U. 1938. "Eine historische Betrachtung zu einem prähistorischen Problem." *Praehistorische Zeitschrift* 28–29:401–405.

Kappel, I. 1969. *Die Graphittonkeramik von Manching*. Wiesbaden: Franz Steiner.

Kaus, K. 1977. "Zur Zeitstellung von ur- und frühgeschichtlichen Eisenverhüttungsanlagen Burgenlands auf Grund der Kleinfunde." In A. Ohrenberger and K. Kaus, eds., *Archäologische Eisenforschung in Europa*, pp. 63–70. Graz: Burgenländisches Landesmuseum.

————. 1981. "Herrschaftsbereiche der Kalenderbergkultur. In C. and A. Eibner, eds., *Die Hallstattkultur: Bericht über das Symposium in Steyr 1980 aus Anlass der Internationalen Ausstellung des Landes Oberösterreich*, pp. 149–158. Linz: Oberösterreichischer Landesverlag.

Kellner, H.-J. 1972. *Die Römer in Bayern*. 2d ed. Munich: Süddeutscher Verlag.

Kilian-Dirlmeier, I. 1970. "Bemerkungen zur jüngeren Hallstattzeit im Elsass." *Jahrbuch des Römisch-Germanischen Zentralmuseums* 17:84–93.

————. 1971. "Beobachtungen zur Struktur des Gräberfeldes von Hallstatt." *Mitteilungen der österreichischen Arbeitsgemeinschaft für Ur- und Frühgeschichte* 22:71–75.

————. 1974. "Zur späthallstattzeitlichen Nekropole von Mühlacker." *Germania* 52:141–146.

Kimmig, W. 1948–1950. "Neufunde der frühen Urnenfelderzeit aus Baden." *Badische Fundberichte* 18:80–95.

————. 1964. "Seevölkerbewegung und Urnenfelderkultur." In R. von Uslar and K. J. Narr, eds., *Stüdien aus Alteuropa*, vol. 1, pp. 220–283. Cologne: Böhlau.

————. 1968. *Die Heuneburg an der oberen Donau*. Stuttgart: Gesellschaft für Vor- und Frühgeschichte in Württemberg und Hohenzollern.

————. 1974. "Zum Fragment eines Este-Gefässes von der Heuneburg an der oberen Donau." *Hamburger Beiträge zur Archäologie* 4:33–102.

————. 1975a. "Die Heuneburg an der oberen Donau." In *Ausgrabungen in Deutschland 1950–1975*, vol. 1, pp. 192–211. Mainz: Römisch-Germanisches Zentralmuseum.

————. 1975b. "Early Celts on the Upper Danube: Excavations at the Heuneburg." In R. Bruce-Mitford, ed., *Recent Archaeological Excavations in Europe*, pp. 32–64. London: Routledge and Kegan Paul.

Kjaerum, P. 1954. "Striber på kryds og tvaers: Om plovfurer under en jysk stenalderhøj" (Criss-cross Furrows: Plough Furrows under a Stone Age Barrow in Jutland). *Kuml* 18–29.

Kleemann, O. 1954. "Eine neue Verbreitungskarte der Spangenbarren." *Archaeologia Austriaca* 14:68–77.

Knorringa, H. 1926. *Emporos: Data on Trade and Traders in Greek Literature from Homer to Aristotle.* Amsterdam: H. J. Paris.

Kooi, P. B. 1979. *Pre-Roman Urnfields in the North of the Netherlands.* Groningen: Wolters-Noordhoff.

Körber-Grohne, U. 1981. "Pflanzliche Abdrücke in eisenzeitlicher Keramik: Spiegelbild damaliger Nutzpflanzen?" *Fundberichte aus Baden-Württemberg* 6:165–211.

Kornemann, E. 1939. "Oppidum." In *Paulys Real-Encyclopädie der classischen Altertumswissenschaft,* vol. 35, cols. 708–725. Stuttgart: J. B. Metzler.

Kos, P. 1980. "Die Rolle der norischen Silbermünzen in der Geldwirtschaft des 1. Jahrhunderts v. Chr." *Situla* 20–21:389–396.

Kossack, G. 1954. "Pferdegeschirr aus Gräbern der älteren Hallstattzeit Bayerns." *Jahrbuch des Römisch-Germanischen Zentralmuseums* 1:111–178.

―――. 1959. *Südbayern während der Hallstattzeit.* Berlin: Walter de Gruyter.

―――. 1970. *Gräberfelder der Hallstattzeit an Main und Fränkischer Saale.* Kallmünz/Opf.: Michael Lassleben.

Koutecký, D. 1968. "Velké hroby, jejich konstrukce, pohřební ritus a sociální struktura obyvatelstva bylanská kultury" (Grossgräber: Ihre Konstruktion, Grabritus und soziale Struktur der Bevölkerung der Bylaner Kultur). *Památky Archeologické* 59:400–487.

Krämer, W. 1950. "Ein aussergewöhnlicher Latènefund aus dem Oppidum von Manching." In G. Behrens, ed., *Reinecke-Festschrift,* pp. 84–95. Mainz: Römisch-Germanisches Zentralmuseum.

―――. 1951–1952. "Siedlungen der mittleren und späten Latènezeit bei Steinebach am Wörthsee, Ldkr. Starnberg." *Bayerische Vorgeschichtsblätter* 18–19:190–194.

―――. 1952. "Das Ende der Mittellatènefriedhöfe und die Grabfunde der Spätlatènezeit in Südbayern." *Germania* 30:330–337.

―――. 1958. "Manching, ein vindelikisches Oppidum an der Donau." In W. Krämer, ed., *Neue Ausgrabungen in Deutschland,* pp. 175–202. Berlin: Gebr. Mann.

―――. 1960. "The *Oppidum* of Manching." *Antiquity* 34:191–200.

―――. 1964. *Das keltische Gräberfeld von Nebringen (Kreis Böblingen).* Stuttgart: Silberburg.

―――. 1975. "Zwanzig Jahre Ausgrabungen in Manching, 1955 bis 1974." In *Ausgrabungen in Deutschland 1950–1975,* vol. 1, pp. 287–297. Mainz: Römisch-Germanisches Zentralmuseum.

Krämer, W., and F. Schubert. 1970. *Die Ausgrabungen in Manching 1955–1961.* Wiesbaden: Franz Steiner.

[245]

REFERENCES CITED

Kromer, K. 1958. "Gedanken über den sozialen Aufbau der Bevölkerung auf dem Salzberg bei Hallstatt." *Archaeologia Austriaca* 24:39–58.

────. 1959. *Das Gräberfeld von Hallstatt.* Florence: Sansoni.

────. 1963. *Hallstatt: Die Salzhandelsmetropole des ersten Jahrtausends vor Christus in den Alpen.* Vienna: Naturhistorisches Museum.

Kruta, V. 1971. *Le trésor de Duchov dans les collections tchécoslovaques.* Ústí nad Labem.

Kubach, W. 1977. *Die Nadeln in Hessen und Rheinhessen.* Munich: Beck.

Kunow, J. 1980. *Negotiator et Vectura: Händler und Transport im freien Germanien.* Marburg: Vorgeschichtliches Seminar.

Kurtz, D. C., and J. Boardman. 1971. *Greek Burial Customs.* London: Thames and Hudson.

Kurz, S. 1982. "Ein hallstattzeitlicher Grabhügel und die Heuneburg-Aussensiedlung." In D. Planck, ed., *Archäologische Ausgrabungen in Baden-Württemberg 1981,* pp. 67–72. Stuttgart: Konrad Theiss.

Lamberg-Karlovsky, C. C., and J. A. Sabloff. 1979. *Ancient Civilizations: The Near East and Mesoamerica.* Menlo Park, Calif.: Cummings.

Landes, D. S. 1969. *The Unbound Prometheus: Technological Change and Industrial Development in Western Europe from 1750 to the Present.* Cambridge: Cambridge University Press.

Lang, A. 1974. *Die geriefte Drehscheibenkeramik der Heuneburg 1950–1970 und verwandte Gruppen.* Berlin: Walter de Gruyter.

────. 1976. "Neue geriefte Drehscheibenkeramik von der Heuneburg." *Germania* 54:43–62.

Laslett, P. 1973. *The World We Have Lost.* 2d ed. New York: Charles Scribner's Sons.

Lauffer, S. 1955–1956. *Die Bergwerkssklaven von Laureion.* Mainz: Akademie der Wissenschaften und der Literatur, Abhandlung der Geistes- und Sozialwissenschaftlichen Klasse.

Laur-Belart, R. 1955. "Lehrgrabung auf dem Kestenberg." *Ur-Schweiz* 19:1–28.

Leach, E. 1977. "A View from the Bridge." In M. Spriggs, ed., *Archaeology and Anthropology,* pp. 161–176. British Archaeological Reports, Supplementary Series, vol. 19. Oxford: British Archaeological Reports.

Leone, M. P. 1982. "Some Opinions about Recovering Mind." *American Antiquity* 47:742–760.

Liebschwager, C. 1972. "Zur Frühlatènekultur in Baden-Württemberg." *Archäologisches Korrespondenzblatt* 2:143–148.

Lindqvist, S. 1936. *Uppsala Högar och Ottarshögen.* Stockholm: Wahlström and Widstrand.

Lippert, A. 1972. *Das Gräberfeld von Welzelach (Osttirol).* Bonn: Habelt.

Lüdi, W. 1955. "Beiträge zur Kenntnis der Vegetationsverhältnisse im schweizerischen Alpenvorland während der Bronzezeit." In W. U. Guyan, ed., *Das Pfahlbauproblem*, pp. 89–109. Basel: Birkhäuser.

Ludikovský, K. 1968. "Ausgrabung des keltischen Siedlung in Mistřín (Bez. Hodonín)." *Přehled Výzkumů* 1967:57.

Macalister, R. A. S. 1931. *Tara*. New York: Scribners.

McEvedy, C., and R. Jones. 1978. *Atlas of World Population History*. Harmondsworth: Penguin.

MacKendrick, P. 1970. *Romans on the Rhine: Archaeology in Germany*. New York: Funk and Wagnalls.

Mahr, G. 1967. *Die jüngere Latènekulture des Trierer Landes*. Berlin: Bruno Hessling.

Maier, F. 1970. *Die bemalte Spätlatène-Keramik von Manching*. Wiesbaden: Franz Steiner.

———. 1973. "Keltische Altertümer in Griechenland." *Germania* 51:459–477.

———. 1974. "Gedanken zur Entstehung der industriellen Grosssiedlung der Hallstatt- und Latènezeit auf dem Dürrnberg bei Hallein." *Germania* 52:326–347.

Malmström, V. H. 1971. *Geography of Europe*. Englewood Cliffs, N.J.: Prentice-Hall.

Mansfeld, G. 1973. *Die Fibeln der Heuneburg 1950–1970*. Berlin: Walter de Gruyter.

Mansuelli, G. A., and R. Scarani. 1961. *L'Emilia prima dei Romani*. Milan: Il Saggiatore.

Martin-Kilcher, S. 1981. "Das keltische Gräberfeld von Vevey VD." *Jahrbuch der Schweizerischen Gesellschaft für Urgeschichte* 64:107–156.

Mauss, M. 1967. *The Gift*. Trans. I. Cunnison. New York: W. W. Norton.

Meduna, J. 1970. "Das keltische Oppidum Staré Hradisko in Mähren." *Germania* 48:34–59.

———. 1971. "Die keltische Oppida Mährens." *Archeologické rozhledy* 23:304–311.

———. 1980. *Die latènezeitlichen Siedlungen in Mähren*. Brno: Československá Akademie Věd.

———. 1982. Review of W. Stöckli, *Die Grob- und Importkeramik von Manching*. *Praehistorische Zeitschrift* 57:150–156.

Megaw, J. V. S. 1970. *Art of the European Iron Age*. New York: Harper and Row.

Megaw, J. V. S., and D. D. A. Simpson, eds. 1979. *Introduction to British Prehistory*. Leicester: Leicester University Press.

Menke, M. 1977. "Zur Struktur und Chronologie der spätkeltischen und frührömischen Siedlungen im Reichenhaller Becken." In B. Chropovský, ed., *Symposium: Ausklang der Latène-Zivilisation und Anfänge der germanischen Besiedlung im mittleren Donaugebiet*, pp. 223–238. Bratislava: Slowakische Akademie der Wissenschaften.

Milisauskas, S. 1978. *European Prehistory*. New York: Academic Press.

Millotte, J. P. 1963. *Le Jura et les plaines de Saône aux âges des métaux*. Paris: Société d'édition "Les Belles Lettres."

Minns, E. H. 1913. *Scythians and Greeks*. Cambridge: Cambridge University Press.

Mittauer, M. 1979. *Grundtypen alteuropäischer Sozialformen*. Stuttgart-Bad Cannstatt: Frommann-Holzboog.

Moberg, C.-A. 1977. "La Tène and Types of Society in Scandinavia." In V. Markotic, ed., *Ancient Europe and the Mediterranean*, pp. 115–120. Warminster: Aris and Phillips.

――――. 1981. "From Artifacts to Timetables to Maps (to Mankind?): Regional Traditions in Archaeological Research in Scandinavia." *World Archaeology* 13:209–221.

Moore, C. B., ed. 1974. *Reconstructing Complex Societies. American Schools of Oriental Research Bulletin*, suppl. no. 20.

Moosleitner, F. 1977. "Hallstattzeitliche Grabfunde aus Uttendorf im Pinzgau (Österreich)." *Archäologisches Korrespondenzblatt* 7:115–119.

――――. 1979. "Ein hallstattzeitlicher 'Fürstensitz' am Hellbrunnerberg bei Salzburg." *Germania* 57:53–74.

――――. 1980. "Scheibenförmiger Eisenbarren." In L. Pauli, ed., *Die Kelten in Mitteleuropa*, p. 300. Salzburg: Landesregierung.

Moosleitner, F., L. Pauli, and E. Penninger. 1974. *Der Dürrnberg bei Hallein II*. Munich: Beck.

Mordant, C., D. Mordant, and J.-Y. Prampart. 1976. *Le dépôt de bronze de Villethierry (Yonne)*. Paris: Centre National de la Recherche Scientifique.

Morton, F. 1954. *Hallstatt: Die letzten einhundertfünftig Jahre des Bergmannsortes*. Hallstatt: Musealverein.

――――. 1956. *Salzkammergut: Die Vorgeschichte einer berühmten Landschaft*. Hallstatt: Musealverein.

Mossler, G., and L. Pauli. 1980. "Ausstattung eines Frauengrabes in Niederösterreich." In L. Pauli, ed., *Die Kelten in Mitteleuropa*, pp. 235–236. Salzburg: Landesregierung.

Motyková, K., P. Drda, and A. Rybová. 1978. *Závist: Keltské hradiště ve středních Čechách (Závist: Ein keltischer Burgwall in Mittelböhmen)*. Prague: Československé Akademie Věd.

Motyková, K., A. Rybová, and P. Drda. 1981. "The Závist Stronghold and Its Importance for the Celtic Settlement of Bohemia." In J. Hrala, ed., *Archaeological News in the Czech Socialist Republic*, pp. 91–97. Prague: Czechoslovak Academy of Sciences.

Motyková-Šneidrová, K. 1960. "Osídlení z mladší doby laténské, z doby římské a stěhování národů v záluží u Čelákovic" (Die Siedlungen in Záluží bei Čelákovice aus der frühen La Tène-Periode, der römischen Kaiserzeit und aus der Zeit der Völkerwanderung). *Památky Archeologické* 51:161–183.

Muhly, J. D. 1973. *Copper and Tin.* New Haven: Connecticut Academy of Arts and Sciences.

Müller-Karpe, A. and M. 1977. "Neue latènezeitliche Funde aus dem Heidetränk-Oppidum im Taunus." *Germania* 55:33–63.

Müller-Karpe, H. 1952. *Das Urnenfeld von Kelheim.* Kallmünz/Opf.: Michael Lassleben.

———. 1955. "Das urnenfelderzeitliche Wagengrab von Hart a. d. Alz, Oberbayern." *Bayerische Vorgeschichtsblätter* 21:46–75.

———. 1957. *Münchener Urnenfelder.* Kallmünz/Opf.: Michael Lassleben.

———. 1959. *Beiträge zur Chronologie der Urnenfelderzeit nördlich und südlich der Alpen.* Berlin: Walter de Gruyter.

———. 1961. *Die Vollgriffschwerter der Urnenfelderzeit aus Bayern.* Munich: Beck.

———. 1969. "Das urnenfelderzeitliche Toreutengrab von Steinkirchen, Niederbayern." *Germania* 47:86–91.

Müller-Wille, M. 1977a. "Bäuerliche Siedlungen der Bronze- und Eisenzeit in den Nordseegebieten." In H. Jankuhn, R. Schützeichel, and F. Schwind, eds., *Das Dorf der Eisenzeit und des frühen Mittelalters,* pp. 153–218. Göttingen: Vandenhoeck and Ruprecht.

———. 1977b. "Der frühmittelalterliche Schmied im Spiegel skandinavischer Grabfunde." *Frühmittelalterliche Studien* 11:127–201.

———. 1979. "Siedlungs- und Flurformen als Zeugnisse frühgeschichtlicher Betriebsformen der Landwirtschaft." In H. Jankuhn and R. Wenskus, eds., *Geschichtswissenschaft und Archäologie,* pp. 355–372. Sigmaringen: Jan Thorbecke.

Müllner, A. 1908. *Geschichte des Eisens in Innerösterreich von der Urzeit bis zum Anfange des XIX. Jahrhunderts,* pt. 1, *Krain, Küstenland und Istrien.* Vienna: von Halm and Goldmann.

Multhauf, R. P. 1978. *Neptune's Gift: A History of Common Salt.* Baltimore: Johns Hopkins University Press.

Muncey, R. W. 1936. *Our Old English Fairs.* London: Sheldon Press.

Mutton, A. F. A. 1961. *Central Europe: A Regional and Human Geography.* London: Longmans.

Nash, D. 1976. "The Growth of Urban Society in France." In B. Cunliffe and T. Rowley, eds., *Oppida: The Beginnings of Urbanisation in Barbarian Europe,* pp. 95–133. British Archaeological Reports, Supplementary Series, vol. 11. Oxford: British Archaeological Reports.

———. 1978a. "Territory and State Formation in Central Gaul." In D.

Green, C. Haselgrove, and M. Spriggs, eds., *Social Organisation and Settlement*, pp. 455–475. British Archaeological Reports, Supplementary Series, vol. 47. Oxford: British Archaeological Reports.

————. 1978b. *Settlement and Coinage in Central Gaul c. 200–50 B.C.* British Archaeological Reports, Supplementary Series, vol. 39. Oxford: British Archaeological Reports.

————. 1981. "Coinage and State Development in Central Gaul." In B. Cunliffe, ed., *Coinage and Society in Britain and Gaul*, pp. 10–17. London: Council for British Archaeology.

Nebehay, S. 1971. "Das latènezeitliche Gräberfeld von der Flur Mühlbachäcker bei Au am Leithagebirge P. B. Bruck a. d. Leitha, NÖ." *Archaeologia Austriaca* 50:138–175.

————. 1973. *Das latènezeitliche Gräberfeld von der kleinen Hutweide bei Au am Leithagebirge, p. B. Bruck a. d. Leitha, NÖ*. Vienna: Franz Deuticke.

————. 1977. "La Tène in Eastern Austria." In M. Guštin, ed., *Keltske Študije*, pp. 51–58. Brežice: Posavski musej.

Nekvasil, J. 1980. "Die Býčí skála-Höhle." In E. Lessing, ed., *Hallstatt: Bilder aus der Frühzeit Europas*, pp. 94–99. Vienna: Jugend und Volk.

————. 1981. "Eine neue Betrachtung der Funde aus der Býčí Skála-Höhle." *Anthropologie* 19:107–110.

Nenquin, J. 1961. *Salt: A Study in Economic Prehistory*. Brugge: De Tempel.

Neubauer, H. 1956. "Uttenkofen." *Bayerische Vorgeschichtsblätter* 21:251.

Neuninger, H., R. Pittioni, and E. Preuschen. 1969. *Salzburgs Kupfererzlagerstätten und Bronzefunde aus dem Lande Salzburg. Archaeologia Austriaca*, suppl. vol. 9.

Neustupný, J. 1969. "Zu den urgeschichtlichen Vorformen des Städtewesens." In K.-H. Otto and J. Herrmann, eds., *Siedlung, Burg and Stadt*, pp. 26–41. Berlin: Akademie-Verlag.

————. 1970. "Essai d'explication de la fonction des stations préhistoriques fortifées en Europe centrale." In *Atti del convegno di studi sulla città etrusca e italica preromana*, vol. 1, pp. 339–343. Bologna: Istituto per la Storia di Bologna.

————. 1977. "The Time of the Hill-Forts." In V. Markotic, ed., *Ancient Europe and the Mediterranean*, pp. 135–139. Warminster: Aris and Phillips.

Nierhaus, R. 1954. "Kaiserzeitlicher Südweinimport nach dem freien Germanien?" *Acta Archaeologica* (Copenhagen) 25:252–260.

Niesiołowska-Wędzka, A. 1974. *Poczatki i rozwój grodów kultury Łużyckiej (Anfänge und Entwicklung der Burgen der Lausitzer Kultur)*. Wrocław: Wydawnictwo Polskiej Akademii Nauk.

Oberg, K. 1973. *The Social Economy of the Tlingit Indians*. Seattle: University of Washington Press.

Obermayr, A. 1971. *Kelten und Römer am Magdalensberg*. Vienna: Öster-reichischer Bundesverlag.

Oldenstein, J. 1975. "Die Zusammensetzung des römischen Imports in den sogenannten Lübsowgräbern als möglicher Hinweis auf die soziale Stellung der Bestatteten." *Archäologisches Korrespondenzblatt* 5:299–305.

O'Riordain, S. P. 1964. *Tara*. Dundalk: Dundalgan Press.

Orme, B. 1981. *Anthropology for Archaeologists*. Ithaca, N.Y.: Cornell University Press.

Otto, K.-H. 1955. *Die sozialökonomischen Verhältnisse bei den Stämmen der Leubinger Kultur in Mitteldeutschland*. Ethnographisch-Archäologische Forschungen, vol. 3, pt. 1. Berlin: Deutscher-Verlag der Wissenschaften.

———. 1978. "Die historische Bedeutung der mittleren und jüngeren Bronzezeit." In W. Coblenz and F. Horst, eds., *Mitteleuropäische Bronzezeit*, pp. 57–69. Berlin: Akademie-Verlag.

Otto, K.-H., and J. Herrmann, eds. 1969. *Siedlung, Burg und Stadt*. Berlin: Akademie-Verlag.

Overbeck, B. 1980. "Die Münzen." In L. Pauli, ed., *Die Kelten in Mitteleuropa*, pp. 101–110, 316–335. Salzburg: Landesregierung.

Pagès-Allary, J., J. Déchelette, and A. Lauby. 1903. "Le tumulus arverne de Celles." *L'Anthropologie* 14:385–416.

Pallottino, M. 1971. *Civiltà artistica etrusco-italica*. Florence: Sansoni.

Panciera, S. 1957. *Vita economica di Aquileia in età romana*. Aquileia: Associazione nazionale per Aquileia.

Papousek, D. A. 1981. *The Peasant-Potters of Los Pueblos*. Assen: Von Gorcum.

Párducz, M. 1952. "Le cimetière hallstattien de Szentes-Vekerzug." *Acta Archaeologica* (Budapest) 2:143–172.

———. 1954. "Le cimetière hallstattien de Szentes-Vekerzug II." *Acta Archaeologica* (Budapest) 4:25–91.

———. 1955. "Le cimetière hallstattien de Szentes-Vekerzug III." *Acta Archaeologica* (Budapest) 6:1–22.

———. 1966. "The Scythian Cemetery at Tápiószele." *Acta Archaeologica* (Budapest) 18:35–91.

Paret, O. 1942. "Der Goldreichtum im hallstättischen Südwestdeutschland." *IPEK* 15–16:76–85.

Patek, E. 1976. "A Hallstatt Kultúra Sopron Környéki Csoportja" (Die Gruppe der Hallstattkultur in der Umgebung von Sopron). *Archaeologiai Értesítö* 103:3–28.

———. 1981. "Die Anfänge der Siedlung und des Gräberfeldes von Sopron-Burgstall." In C. and A. Eibner, eds., *Die Hallstattkultur: Bericht über das Symposium in Steyr 1980 aus Anlass der Internationalen Ausstellung des Landes Oberösterreich,* pp. 93–104. Linz: Oberösterreichischer Landesverlag.

Pauli, L. 1972. *Untersuchungen zur Späthallstattkultur in Nordwürttemberg.* Hamburger Beiträge zur Archäologie, vol. 2, no. 1. Hamburg: Helmut Buske.

————. 1974. "Der goldene Steig: Wirtschaftsgeographisch-archäologische Untersuchungen im östlichen Mitteleuropa." In G. Kossack and G. Ulbert, eds., *Studien zur vor- und frühgeschichtlichen Archäologie,* vol. 1, pp. 115–139. Munich: Beck.

————. 1978. *Der Dürrnberg bei Hallein III.* Munich: Beck.

————. 1980a. *Die Alpen in Frühzeit und Mittelalter.* Munich: Beck.

————. 1980b. "Katalog." In L. Pauli ed., *Die Kelten in Mitteleuropa,* pp. 196–315. Salzburg: Landesregierung.

Peacock, D. P. S. 1971. "Roman Amphorae in Pre-Roman Britain." In D. Hill and M. Jesson, eds., *The Iron Age and Its Hillforts,* pp. 161–188. Southampton: University of Southampton Press.

Penninger, E., 1972. *Der Dürrnberg bei Hallien I.* Munich: Beck.

————. 1980. "Der Salzbergbau auf dem Dürrnberg." In L. Pauli, ed., *Die Kelten in Mitteleuropa,* pp. 182–188. Salzburg: Landesregierung.

Percival, J. 1980. *Living in the Past.* London: BBC.

Peroni, R. 1973. *Studi di cronologia hallstattiana.* Rome: de Luca.

————. 1979. "From Bronze Age to Iron Age." In D. and F. R. Ridgway, eds., *Italy before the Romans,* pp. 7–30. New York: Academic Press.

Pertlwieser, M. 1969. "Die hallstattzeitliche Höhensiedlung auf dem Waschenberg bei Bad Wimsbach/Neydharting, Politischer Bezirk Wels, Oberösterreich." *Jahrbuch des Oberösterreichischen Musealvereins* 114:29–48.

————. 1970. "Die hallstattzeitliche Höhensiedlung auf dem Waschenberg bei Bad Wimsbach/Neydharting, Politischer Bezirk Wels, Oberösterreich: Die Objekte." *Jahrbuch des Oberösterreichischen Musealvereins* 115:37–70.

————. 1971. "Die hallstattzeitliche Höhensiedlung auf dem Waschenberg bei Bad Wimsbach/Neydharting, Politischer Bezirk Wels, Oberösterreich: Die Funde." *Jahrbuch des Oberösterreichischen Musealvereins* 116:51–80.

Peschel, K. 1971a. "Zur Frage der Sklaverei bei den Kelten während der vorrömischen Eisenzeit." *Ethnographisch-Archäologische Zeitschrift* 12:527–539.

————. 1971b. "Höhensiedlungen der Spätlatènezeit in Mitteldeutschland." *Archeologické rozhledy* 23:470–485.

Pič, J. L. 1906. *Le Hradischt de Stradonitz en Bohême.* Trans. J. Déchelette. Leipzig: Karl W. Hiersemann.

Pichlerová, M. 1969. *Nové Košariská*. Bratislava: Slovenské Národné Múzeum.

Piggott, S. 1959. "A Late Bronze Age Wine Trade?" *Antiquity* 33:122–123.

———. 1965. *Ancient Europe*. Chicago: Aldine.

Piggott, S., ed. 1981. *The Agrarian History of England and Wales*, vol. 1, *Prehistory*. Cambridge: Cambridge University Press.

Pingel, V. 1971. *Die glatte Drehscheiben-Keramik von Manching*. Wiesbaden: Franz Steiner.

Pirenne, H. 1925. *Medieval Cities*. Trans. F. D. Halsey. Princeton: Princeton University Press.

———. 1936. *Economic and Social History of Medieval Europe*. Trans. I. E. Clegg. London: K. Paul, Trench, Truber.

Pirling, R. 1964. "Ein fränkisches Fürstengrab aus Krefeld-Gellep." *Germania* 42:188–216.

———. 1975. "Die Gräberfelder von Krefeld-Gellep." In *Ausgrabungen in Deutschland 1950–1975*, vol. 2, pp. 165–180. Mainz: Römisch-Germanisches Zentralmuseum.

———. 1980. *Die mittlere Bronzezeit auf der Schwäbischen Alb*. Munich: Beck.

Pittioni, R. 1951. "Prehistoric Copper-Mining in Austria." *Institute of Archaeology Annual Report* 7:16–43.

———. 1952. "Das Brandgrab vom Lebenberg bei Kitzbühel, Tirol." *Archaeologia Austriaca* 10:53–60.

———. 1976. "Bergbau: Kupfererz." In J. Hoops, ed., *Reallexikon der germanischen Altertumskunde*, 2d ed., vol. 2, pp. 251–256. Berlin: Walter de Gruyter.

Pleiner, R. 1962. *Staré evropské kovářstiví (Alteuropäisches Schmiedehandwerk)*. Prague: Československá Akademie Ved.

———. 1964. "Die Eisenverhüttung in der "Germania Magna" zur römischen Kaiserzeit." *Berichte der Römisch-Germanischen Kommission* 45:11–86.

———. 1976. "Bergbau: Eisenerz." In J. Hoops, ed., *Reallexikon der germanischen Altertumskunde*, 2d ed., vol. 2, pp. 258–261. Berlin: Walter de Gruyter.

———. 1977a. "Extensive Eisenverhüttungsgebiete im freien Germanien." In B. Chropovský, ed., *Symposium: Ausklang der Latène-Zivilisation und Anfänge der germanischen Besiedlung im mittleren Donaugebiet*, pp. 297–305. Bratislava: Vydavatel'stvo Slovenskej Akadémie Vied.

———. 1977b. "Neue Grabungen frühgeschichtlicher Eisenhüttenplätze in der Tschechoslowakei und die Bedeutung des Schachtofens für die Entwicklung des Schmelzvorganges." In A. Ohrenberger and K. Kaus, eds., *Archäologische Eisenforschung in Europa*, pp. 107–117. Graz: Burgenländisches Landesmuseum.

———. 1980. "Early Iron Metallurgy in Europe." In T. A. Wertime and J. D. Muhly, eds., *The Coming of the Age of Iron,* pp. 375–415. New Haven: Yale University Press.

———. 1981. "Metallography of La Tène Period Iron Implements from the Celtic Oppida." In *Archaeological News in the Czech Socialist Republic,* pp. 106–107. Prague: Czechoslovak Academy of Sciences.

Pleinerová, I. 1973. "Bronzové nádoby v bylanské kultuře" (Bronzegefässe in der Bylaner Kultur). *Památky Archeologické* 64:272–300.

Podborský, V. 1965. *Die Hallstattsiedlung in Těšetice.* Prague: National Museum.

Polanyi, K. 1944. *The Great Transformation.* New York: Rinehart.

———. 1959. "Anthropology and Economic Theory." In M. H. Fried, ed., *Readings in Anthropology,* vol. 2, pp. 161–184. New York: Thomas Y. Crowell.

Polenz, H. 1971. *Mittel- und spätlatènezeitliche Brandgräber aus Dietzenbach: Landkreis Offenbach am Main.* Offenbach: Stadt und Landkreis Offenbach.

Pounds, N. J. G. 1969. *Eastern Europe.* London: Longmans.

Powell, T. G. E. 1971. "The Introduction of Horse-Riding to Temperate Europe." *Proceedings of the Prehistoric Society* 27, pt. 2, pp. 1–14.

Pressmar, E. 1979. *Elchinger Kreuz, Ldkr. Neu-Ulm: Siedlungsgrabung mit urnenfelderzeitlichem Töpferofen.* Kallmünz/Opf.: Michael Lassleben.

Primas, M. 1977a. "Zur Informationsausbreitung im südlichen Mitteleuropa." *Jahresbericht des Instituts für Vorgeschichte der Universität Frankfurt am Main* 1977:164–184.

———. 1977b. "Beobachtungen zu den spätbronzezeitlichen Siedlungs- und Depotfunden der Schweiz." In K. Stüber and A. Zürcher, eds., *Festschrift Walter Drack,* pp. 44–55. Stäfa (Zurich): Gut and Co.

Primas, M., and U. Ruoff. 1981. "Die urnenfelderzeitliche Inselsiedlung 'Grosser Hafner' im Zürichsee (Schweiz)." *Germania* 59:31–50.

Rahtz, P. 1976. "Buildings and Rural Settlement." In D. M. Wilson, ed., *The Archaeology of Anglo-Saxon England,* pp. 49–98. London: Methuen.

Rajewski, Z. 1959. *Biskupin Polish Excavations.* Warsaw: Polonia.

———. 1974. "Was Wehrsiedlungen-Burgen sowie deren Überbauung an wirtschaftlich-gesellschaftlichem Wert bergen." In B. Chropovský, ed., *Symposium zu Problemen der jüngeren Hallstattzeit in Mitteleuropa,* pp. 427–433. Bratislava: Vydavateľstvo Slovenskej Akadémie Vied.

Randsborg, K. 1973. "Wealth and Social Structure as Reflected in Bronze Age Burials." In C. Renfrew, ed., *The Explanation of Culture Change,* pp. 565–570. Pittsburgh, Pa.: University of Pittsburgh Press.

———. 1974. "Social Stratification in Early Bronze Age Denmark." *Praehistorische Zeitschrift.* 49:38–61.

———. 1980. *The Viking Age in Denmark: The Formation of a State.* London: Duckworth.

Rathje, W. L. 1970. "Socio-Political Implications of Lowland Maya Burials." *World Archaeology* 1:359–374.

———. 1971. "The Origins and Development of Lowland Classic Maya Civilization." *American Antiquity* 36:275–287.

———. 1972. "Praise the Gods and Pass the Metates: An Hypothesis of the Development of Lowland Rainforest Civilizations in Mesoamerica." In M. P. Leone, ed., *Contemporary Archaeology*, pp. 365–392. Carbondale: Southern Illinois University Press.

Redman, C. L. 1978. *The Rise of Civilization.* San Francisco: Freeman.

Rees, S. E. 1979. *Agricultural Implements in Prehistoric and Roman Britain.* British Archaeological Reports, British Series, vol. 69. Oxford: British Archaeological Reports.

———. 1981. "Agricultural Tools: Function and Use." In R. Mercer, ed., *Farming Practice in British Prehistory*, pp. 66–84. Edinburgh: Edinburgh University Press.

Reim, H. 1981. "Handwerk und Technik." In K. Bittel, W. Kimmig, and S. Schiek, eds., *Die Kelten in Baden-Württemberg*, pp. 204–227. Stuttgart: Konrad Theiss.

Reinecke, P. 1934. "Der Bronzedepotfund von Hallstatt in Oberösterreich." *Wiener Prähistorsiche Zeitschrift* 21:1–11.

———. 1958. "Einfuhr- oder Beutegut?" *Bonner Jahrbücher* 158:246–252.

Reinerth, H. 1928. *Die Wasserburg Buchau.* Augsburg: Filser.

———. 1936. *Das Federseemoor.* Leipzig: Kabitzsch.

Reitinger, J. 1968. *Die ur- und frühgeschichtlichen Funde in Oberösterreich.* Linz: Oberösterreichischer Landesverlag.

———. 1971. "Die Latènezeit in Österreich." *Archeologické rozhledy* 23:452–469.

Renfrew, C. 1972. *The Emergence of Civilisation: The Cyclades and the Aegean in the Third Millennium B.C.* London: Methuen.

———. 1978. "Varna and the Social Context of Early Metallurgy." *Antiquity* 52:199–203.

Renfrew, C., and S. Shennan, eds. 1982. *Ranking, Resource and Exchange.* Cambridge: Cambridge University Press.

Renfrew, C., and M. Wagstaff, eds. 1982. *An Island Polity: The Archaeology of Exploitation in Melos.* Cambridge: Cambridge University Press.

Renfrew, J. 1973. *Palaeoethnobotany.* New York: Columbia University Press.

Reynolds, P. J. 1979. *Iron-Age Farm: The Butser Experiment.* London: British Museum.

Rieckhoff-Pauli, S. 1980. "Das Ende der keltischen Welt: Kelten—Römer—Germanen." In L. Pauli, ed., *Die Kelten in Mitteleuropa*, pp. 37–47. Salzburg: Landesregierung.

Riehm, K. 1954. "Vorgeschichtliche Salzgewinnung an Saale und Seille." *Jahresschrift für mitteldeutsche Vorgeschichte* 38:112–156.

REFERENCES CITED

Riek, G. 1962. *Der Hohmichele*. Berlin: Walter de Gruyter.

Rieth, A. 1942. *Die Eisentechnik der Hallstattzeit*. Leipzig: J. A. Barth.

Říhovský, J. 1972. "Dosavadní výsledky výzkumu velatického sídliště v Lovčičkách na Slavkovsku" (Die bisherigen Ergebnisse der Ausgrabung in der Velaticer Siedlung von Lovčičky bei Slavkov). *Archeologické rozhledy* 24:173–181.

―――. 1978. "Hrob bojovníka z počátku mladší doby bronzové z Ivančic" (Das frühe jungbronzezeitliche Kriegergrab aus Ivančice). *Památky Archeologické* 69:45–51.

Roebuck, C. 1959. *Ionian Trade and Colonization*. New York: Archaeological Institute of America.

Rogers, E. A., and F. F. Shoemaker. 1971. *The Communication of Innovations*. New York: Free Press.

Rolland, H. 1951. *Fouilles de Saint-Blaise (Bouches-du-Rhône)*. Paris: CNRS.

Rosenberg, G. 1937. *Hjortspringfundet*. Copenhagen: Nordisk Forlag.

Ross, A. 1967. *Pagan Celtic Britain*. London: Routledge and Kegan Paul.

Rowlands, M. J. 1972. "The Archaeological Interpretation of Prehistoric Metalworking." *World Archaeology* 3:210–223.

―――. 1973. "Modes of Exchange and the Incentives for Trade, with Reference to Later European Prehistory." In C. Renfrew, ed., *The Explanation of Culture Change*, pp. 589–600. Pittsburgh, Pa.: University of Pittsburgh Press.

Rowlett, R. M., H. L. Thomas, and E. S.-J. Rowlett. 1982. "Stratified Iron Age House Floors on the Titelberg, Luxembourg." *Journal of Field Archaeology* 9:301–312.

Russell, J. C. 1958. *Late Ancient and Medieval Populations*. Transactions of the American Philosophical Society, n.s. 48:3.

Rusu, M. 1969. "Das keltische Fürstengrab von Ciumeşti in Rumänien." *Berichte der Römisch-Germanischen Kommission* 50:267–300.

Rychner, V. 1979. *L'âge du bronze final à Auvernier*. Lausanne: Bibliothèque historique vaudoise.

Sage, W. 1969. *Die fränkische Siedlung bei Gladbach, Kreis Neuwied*. Bonn: Rheinisches Landesmuseum.

Sahlins, M. 1963. "Poor Man, Rich Man, Big Man, Chief: Political Types in Melanesia and Polynesia." *Comparative Studies in Society and History* 5:285–303.

―――. 1972. *Stone Age Economics*. Chicago: Aldino Atherton.

Šaldová, V. 1977. "Sociálně-ekonomické podmínky vzniku a funkce hradišť z pozdní doby bronzové v západních Čechách" (Die sozial-ökonomischen Bedingungen der Entstehung und Funktion der spätbronzezeitlichen Höhensiedlungen in Westböhmen). *Památky Archeologické* 68:117–163.

―――. 1981. "Rovinná sídliště pozdní doby bronzové z západních

Čechách" (Die Flachlandsiedlungen der Spätbronzezeit in West-böhmen). *Památky Archeologické* 72:93–152.

Sankot, P. 1978. "Struktur des latènezeitlichen Gräberfeldes." In J. Wald-hauser, ed., *Das keltische Gräberfeld bei Jenišův Újezd in Böhmen*, pp. 78–93. Teplice: Krajské Muzeum.

Šašel, J. 1977. "Strabo, Ocra and Archaeology." In V. Markotic, ed., *Ancient Europe and the Mediterranean*, pp. 157–160. Warminster: Aris and Phillips.

Sassatelli, G. 1978. "Bologna: Tomba Benacci 953." In *I Galli e l'Italia*, pp. 118–121. Rome: Soprintendenza Archeologica di Roma.

Sawyer, P. H. 1977. "Kings and Merchants." In P. H. Sawyer and I. N. Wood, eds., *Early Medieval Kingship*, pp. 139–158. Leeds: University of Leeds.

Schaaff, U. 1980. "Ein spätkeltisches Kriegergrab mit Eisenhelm aus Novo mesto." *Situla* 20–21:397–413.

Schaaff, U., and A. K. Taylor. 1975a. "Südimporte im Raum nördlich der Alpen (6.–4. Jahrhundert v. Chr.)." In *Ausgrabungen in Deutschland 1950–1975*, vol. 3, pp. 312–316. Mainz: Römisch-Germanisches Zentral-museum.

———. 1975b. "Spätkeltische Oppida im Raum nördlich der Alpen." In *Ausgrabungen in Deutschland 1950–1975*, vol. 3, pp. 322–327. Mainz: Römisch-Germanisches Zentralmuseum.

Schaeffer, C. F. A. 1930. *Les tertres funéraires préhistoriques dans la Fôret de Hagenau II: Les tumulus de l'âge du Fer*. Hagenau: Imprimerie de la Ville.

Schauberger, O. 1960. *Ein Rekonstruktionsversuch der prähistorischen Gruben-baue im Hallstätter Salzberg*. Vienna: Anthropologische Gesellschaft.

———. 1976. "Neue Aufschlüsse im 'Heidengebirge' von Hallstatt und Dürrnberg/Hallein." *Mitteilungen der Anthropologischen Gesellschaft in Wien* 106:154–160.

Schauer, P. 1971. *Die Schwerter in Süddeutschland, Österreich und der Schweiz I*. Munich: Beck.

Scheers, S. 1981. "The Origins and Evolution of Coinage in Belgic Gaul." In B. Cunliffe, ed., *Coinage and Society in Britain and Gaul*, pp. 18–23. London: Council for British Archaeology.

Schiek, S. 1959. "Vorbericht über die Ausgrabung des vierten Fürsten-grabhügels bei der Heuneburg." *Germania* 37:117–131.

Schietzel, K. 1975. "Haithabu." In *Ausgrabungen in Deutschland 1950–1975*, vol. 3, pp. 57–71. Mainz: Römisch-Germanisches Zentralmuseum.

———. 1981. *Stand der siedlungsarchäologischen Forschungen in Haithabu*. Neumünster: Karl Wachholtz.

Schindler, R. 1971. "Ein Kriegergrab mit Bronzehelm der Spätlatènezeit aus Trier-Olewig." *Trierer Zeitschrift* 34:43–82.

Schlesinger, W. 1973. "Der Markt als Frühform der deutschen Stadt." In H. Jankuhn, W. Schlesinger, and H. Steuer, eds., *Vor- und Frühformen der europäischen Stadt im Mittelalter*, pt. 1, pp. 262–293. Göttingen: Vandenhoeck and Ruprecht.

Schmid, W. 1933. "Die Fürstengräber von Klein Glein in Steiermark." *Praehistorische Zeitschrift* 24:219–282.

Schönberger, H. 1952. "Die Spätlatènezeit in der Wetterau." *Saalburg-Jahrbuch* 11:21–130.

Schönberger, M. 1926. "Die Bevölkerungsstatistik eines Gebirgstales: 1621–1920." *Mitteilungen der Anthropologischen Gesellschaft in Wien* 56:271–281.

Schröter, P. 1975. "Zur Besiedlung des Goldberges im Nördlinger Ries." In *Ausgrabungen in Deutschland 1950–1975*, vol. 1, pp. 98–114. Mainz: Römisch-Germanisches Zentralmuseum.

Schubert, F. 1972. "Manching IV: Vorbericht über die Ausgrabungen in den Jahren 1965 bis 1967." *Germania* 50:110–121.

Schwartz, D. W. 1979. Foreword. In S. M. Greenfield, A. Strickon, and R. T. Aubey, eds., *Entrepreneurs in Cultural Context*, pp. vii–viii. Albuquerque: University of New Mexico Press.

Schweingruber, F. H. 1976. *Prähistorisches Holz*. Bern: Paul Haupt.

Scudder, T., and E. F. Colson. 1972. "The Kariba Dam Project: Resettlement and Local Initiative." In H. R. Bernard and P. J. Pelto, eds., *Technology and Social Change*, pp. 39–69. New York: Macmillan.

Scullard, H. H. 1967. *The Etruscan Cities and Rome*. Ithaca, N.Y.: Cornell University Press.

Seltman, C. T. 1957. *Wine in the Ancient World*. London: Routledge.

Semple, E. C. 1931. *The Geography of the Mediterranean Region: Its Relation to Ancient History*. New York: Henry Holt.

Service, E. R. 1962. *Primitive Social Organization*. New York: Random House.

Shennan, S. 1975. "The Social Organisation at Brač." *Antiquity* 49:279–288.

Sherratt, A. 1981. "Plough and Pastoralism: Aspects of the Secondary Products Revolution." In I. Hodder, G. Isaac, and N. Hammond, eds., *Pattern of the Past*, pp. 261–305. Cambridge: Cambridge University Press.

Speck, J. 1955. "Die Ausgrabungen in der spätbronzezeitlichen Ufersiedlung Zug- 'Sumpf.' " In W. U. Guyan, ed., *Das Pfahlbauproblem*, pp. 275–334. Basel: Birkhäuser.

Spehr, E. 1968. "Zwei Gräberfelder der jüngeren Latène- und frühesten römischen Kaiserzeit von Naumburg (Saale)." *Jahresschrift für mitteldeutsche Vorgeschichte* 52:233–290.

Spehr, R. 1966. "Ein spätkaiserzeitlich-völkerwanderungszeitlicher Hortfund mit Eisengeräten von Radeberg-Lotzdorf, Kreis Dresden: Die Funde." *Arbeits- und Forschungsberichte zur sächsischen Bodendenkmalpflege* 14–15:169–219.

_____. 1971. "Die Rolle der Eisenverarbeitung in der Wirtschaftsstruktur des Steinsburg-Oppidums." *Archeologické rozhledy* 23:486–503.

Sperber, L. 1980. "Grabungen in den hallstattzeitlichen Fürstengrabhügeln und in der Heuneburg-Aussensiedlung." In D. Planck, ed., *Archäologische Ausgrabungen 1979*, pp. 39–44. Stuttgart: Gesellschaft für Vor- und Frühgeschichte in Württemberg und Hohenzollern.

_____. 1981. "Fürstengrabhügel und Heuneburg-Aussensiedlung auf dem 'Giessübel' bei Hundersingen, Gemeinde Herbertingen, Kreis Sigmaringen." In D. Planck, ed., *Archäologische Ausgrabungen 1980*, pp. 43–49. Stuttgart: Gesellschaft für Vor- und Frühgeschichte in Württemberg und Hohenzollern.

Spicer, E. H., ed. 1952. *Human Problems in Technological Change.* New York: Russell Sage Foundation.

Spindler, K. 1971–1977. *Magdalenenberg.* 5 vols. Villingen: Neckar-Verlag.

_____. 1975. "Zum Beginn der hallstattzeitlichen Besiedlung auf der Heuneburg." *Archäologisches Korrespondenzblatt* 5:41–45.

Sprockhoff, E. 1930. *Zur Handelsgeschichte der germanischen Bronzezeit.* Berlin: Walter de Gruyter.

Šramko, B. A. 1974. "Zur Frage über die Technik und die Bearbeitungszentren von Bundmetallen in der Früheisenzeit." In B. Chropovský, ed., *Symposium zu Problemen der jüngeren Hallstattzeit in Mitteleuropa*, pp. 469–485. Bratislava: Vydavatel'stvo Slovenskej Akadémie Vied.

_____. 1981. "Die ältesten Eisenfundstücke in Osteuropa." In R. Pleiner, ed., *Frühes Eisen in Europa*, pp. 109–114. Schaffhausen: Verlag Peter Meili.

Stadelmann, J. 1980. "Der Runde Berg bei Urach, ein bronze- und urnenfelderzeitliche Höhensiedlung." *Archäologisches Korrespondenzblatt* 10:33–38.

Staehelin, F. 1948. *Die Schweiz in römischer Zeit.* 3d ed. Basel: Benno Schwabe.

Stary, P. F. 1980. "Das spätbronzezeitliche Häuptlingsgrab von Hagenau, Kr. Regensburg." In K. Spindler, ed., *Vorzeit zwischen Main und Donau*, pp. 46–97. Erlangen: Universitätsbund Erlangen-Nürnberg.

Stead, I. M. 1967. "A La Tène III Burial at Welwyn Garden City." *Archaeologia* 101:1–62.

Steensberg, A. 1936. "North West European Plough-Types of Prehistoric Times and the Middle Ages." *Acta Archaeologica* (Copenhagen) 7:244–280.

———. 1943. *Ancient Harvesting Implements.* Copenhagen: Nordisk Forlag.

Steuer, H. 1979. "Frühgeschichtliche Sozialstrukturen in Mitteleuropa." In H. Jankuhn and R. Wenskus, eds., *Geschichtswissenschaft und Archäologie,* pp. 595–633. Sigmaringen: Jan Thorbecke.

Stjernquist, B. 1972. "Archaeological Analysis of Prehistoric Society." *Norwegian Archaeological Review* 2:2–26.

———. 1981. *Gårdlösa: An Iron Age Community in Its Natural and Social Setting.* Lund: CWK Gleerup.

Stöckli, W. E. 1979a. *Die Grob- und Importkeramik von Manching.* Wiesbaden: Franz Steiner.

———. 1979b. "Die Keltensiedlung von Altendorf (Landkreis Bamberg)." *Bayerische Vorgeschichtsblätter* 44:27–43.

Strickon, A. 1979. "Ethnicity and Entrepreneurship in Rural Wisconsin." In S. M. Greenfield, A. Strickon, and R. T. Aubey, eds., *Entrepreneurs in Cultural Context,* pp. 159–189. Albuquerque: University of New Mexico Press.

Süss, L. 1973. "Zur latènezeitlichen Salzgewinnung in Bad Nauheim." *Fundberichte aus Hessen* 13:167–180.

Szabó, M. 1971. *Auf den Spuren der Kelten in Ungarn.* Trans. S. Baksa-Soós. Budapest: Corvina Verlag.

Szombathy, J. 1903. "Das Grabfeld zu Idria bei Baca." *Mitteilungen der Prähistorischen Kommission* 1:291–363.

Taus, M. 1963. "Ein spätlatènezeitliches Schmied-Grab aus St. Georgen am Steinfeld, p. B. St. Pölten, NÖ." *Archaeologia Austriaca* 34:13–16.

Tax, S. 1953. *Penny Capitalism.* Washington: Smithsonian Institution.

Terenožkin, A. I. 1980. "Die Kimmerier und ihre Kultur." In *Die Hallstattkultur: Frühform europäischer Einheit,* pp. 20–29. Linz: Oberösterreichischer Landesverlag.

Thill, G. 1967a. "Die Keramik aus vier spätlatènezeitlichen Brandgräbern bei Goeblingen-Nospelt." *Hémecht* 19:199–213.

———. 1967b. "Die Metallgegenstände aus vier spätlatènezeitlichen Brandgräbern bei Goeblingen-Nospelt." *Hémecht* 19:87–98.

Tierney, J. J. 1960. *The Celtic Ethnography of Posidonius.* Dublin: Royal Irish Academy.

Tischler, F. 1952. "Zur Datierung der frühmittelalterlichen Tonwaren von Badorf." *Germania* 30:194–200.

Todd, M. 1975. *The Northern Barbarians 100 B.C.–A.D. 300.* London: Hutchinson.

Todorović, J. 1968. *Kelti u jugoistočnoj Evropi (Die Kelten in Süd-ost Europa).* Belgrade: Muzej Grada.

Torbrügge, W. 1970–1971. "Vor- und frühgeschichtliche Flussfunde." *Berichte der Römisch-Germanischen Kommission* 51–52:1–145.

Tourtellot, G., and J. A. Sabloff. 1972. "Exchange Systems among the Ancient Maya." *American Antiquity* 37:126–135.

Toynbee, A. J. 1965. *Hannibal's Legacy: The Hannibalic War's Effects on Roman Life*. London: Oxford University Press.

Ucko, P. 1969. "Ethnography and Archaeological Interpretation of Funerary Remains." *World Archaeology* 1:262–280.

Unz, C. 1973. *Die spätbronzezeitliche Keramik in Südwestdeutschland, in der Schweiz, und in Ostfrankreich*. Berlin: Walter de Guyter.

van Es, W. A. 1965. *Wijster: A Native Village beyond the Imperial Frontier 150–425 A.D.* Groningen: J. B. Wolters.

———. 1973. "Die neuen Dorestad-Grabungen 1967–1972." In H. Jankuhn, W. Schlesinger, and H. Steuer, eds., *Vor- und Frühformen der europäischen Stadt im Mittelalter*, pt. 1, pp. 202–217. Göttingen: Vandenhoeck and Ruprecht.

van Regteren Altena, H. H., and H. A. Heidinga. 1977. "The North Sea Region in the Early Medieval Period." In B. L. van Beels, R. W. Brandt, and W. Groenman-van Waatringe, eds., *Ex Horreo IPP 1951–1976*, pp. 47–67. Amsterdam: University of Amsterdam.

Vermeule, E. 1964. *Greece in the Bronze Age*. Chicago: University of Chicago Press.

Villard, F. 1960. *La céramique grecque de Marseille*. Paris: de Boccard.

Vladár, J. 1973. *Pohrebiská zo staršej doby bronzovej v Branči*. Bratislava: Vydavateľstvo Slovenskej Akadémie Vied.

Vogt, E. 1949–1950. "Der Beginn der Hallstattzeit in der Schweiz." *Jahrbuch der Schweizerischen Gesellschaft für Urgeschichte* 40:209–231.

von Brunn, W. A. 1968. *Mitteldeutsche Hortfunde der jüngeren Bronzezeit*. Berlin: Walter de Gruyter.

von Föhr, J. 1892. *Hügelgräber auf der schwäbischen Alb*. Stuttgart: W. Kohlhammer.

von Hase. F.-W. 1973. "Unbekannte frühetruskische Edelmetallfunde mit Maskenköpfen: Mögliche Vorbilder keltischer Maskendarstellungen." *Hamburger Beiträge zur Archäologie* 3, no. 1, pp. 51–64.

von Merhart, G. 1952. "Studien über einige Gattungen von Bronzegefässen." In H. Klumbach, ed., *Festschrift des Römisch-Germanischen Zentralmuseums*, vol. 2, pp. 1–71. Mainz.

von Miske, K. 1929. "Bergbau, Verhüttung und Metallbearbeitungswerkzeuge aus Velem St. Veit (Westungarn)." *Wiener Prähistorische Zeitschrift* 16:81–94.

Vouga, P. 1923. *La Tène*. Leipzig: Karl W. Hiersmann.

Wackernagel, H. G. 1930. "Massalia." In *Paulys Real-Encylopädie der classischen Altertumswissenschaft*, vol. 28, cols. 2130–2152. Stuttgart: J. B. Metzler.

Wahle, E. 1964. *Tradition und Auftrag prähistorischer Forschung.* Ed. H. Kirchner. Berlin: Duncker and Homblot.

Wailes, B. 1970. "The Origins of Settled Farming in Temperate Europe." In G. Cardona, H. M. Hoenigswald, and A. Senn, eds., *Indo-European and Indo-Europeans,* pp. 279–305. Philadelphia: University of Pennsylvania Press.

———. 1972. "Plow and Population in Temperate Europe." In B. Spooner, ed., *Population Growth: Anthropological Implications,* pp. 154–179. Cambridge, Mass.: MIT Press.

———. 1981. "Early Medieval Ireland: An Ethnohistorical Perspective for Europe?" Paper presented at American Anthropological Association annual meeting, Los Angeles.

Wainwright, G. J. 1979. *Gussage All Saints.* London: Her Majesty's Stationery Office.

Waldhauser, J. 1977. "Keltské sídliště u Radovesic v severozápadních Čechách" (Die keltische Siedlung bei Radovesice, Bez. Teplice in Nordwest-Böhmen). *Archeologické rozhledy* 29:144–177.

———. 1979. "Beitrag zum Studium der keltischen Siedlungen, Oppida und Gräberfelder in Böhmen." In P.-M. Duval and V. Kruta, eds., *Les mouvements celtiques du Vᵉ au Iᵉʳ siècle avant notre ère,* pp. 117–156. Paris: Centre National de la Recherche Scientifique.

———. 1981. "Strategie der gemeinsamen anthropologischen und archäologischen Forschung der Latènezeit in Böhmen." *Anthropologie* 19:115–120.

Waldhauser, J., ed. 1978. *Das keltische Gräberfeld bei Jenišův Újezd in Böhmen.* Teplice: Krajské Muzeum.

Walford, C. 1883. *Fairs, Past and Present.* London: Elliot Stock.

Waterbolk, H. T. 1964. "The Bronze Age Settlement of Elp." *Helinium* 4:97–131.

Wells, C. M. 1972. *The German Policy of Augustus.* Oxford: Clarendon Press.

Wells, P. S. 1978. "Twenty-Six Graves from Hallstatt Excavated by the Duchess of Mecklenburg." *Germania* 56:66–88.

———. 1980a. "The Early Iron Age Settlement of Hascherkeller in Bavaria: Preliminary Report on the 1979 Excavations." *Journal of Field Archaeology* 7:313–328.

———. 1980b. *Culture Contact and Culture Change: Early Iron Age Central Europe and the Mediterranean World.* Cambridge: Cambridge University Press.

———. 1981. *The Emergence of an Iron Age Economy: The Mecklenburg Grave Groups from Hallstatt and Stična.* Cambridge, Mass.: Peabody Museum, Harvard University.

———. 1983. *Rural Economy in the Early Iron Age: Excavations at Hascherkeller 1978–1981.* Cambridge, Mass.: Peabody Museum, Harvard University.

Wells, P. S., and L. Bonfante. 1979. "West-Central Europe and the Mediterranean: The Decline in Trade in the Fifth Century B.C." *Expedition* 21:18–24.

Werner, J. 1939. "Die Bedeutung des Städtewesens für die Kulturentwicklung des frühen Keltentums." *Die Welt als Geschichte* 4:380–390.

———. 1954. "Die Bronzekanne von Kelheim." *Bayerische Vorgeschichtsblätter* 20:43–73.

———. 1961. "Bemerkungen zu norischen Trachtzubehör und zu Fernhandelsbeziehungen der Spätlatènezeit im Salzburger Land." *Mitteilungen der Gesellschaft für Salzburger Landeskunde* 101:143–160.

———. 1964. "Frankish Royal Tombs in the Cathedrals of Cologne and Saint-Denis." *Antiquity* 38:201–216.

———. 1970. "Zur Verbreitung frühgeschichtlicher Metallarbeiten." *Antikvariskt Archiv* 38:65–81.

———. 1978. "Zur Bronzekanne von Kelheim." *Bayerische Vorgeschichtsblätter* 43:1–18.

Wheeler, R. E. M. 1943. *Maiden Castle, Dorset*. London: Society of Antiquaries.

Wightman, E. M. 1970. *Roman Trier and the Treveri*. New York: Praeger.

Will, E. 1958. "Archéologie et histoire économique." *Études d'archéologie classique* 1:149–166.

Wilson, D. M., ed. 1976. *The Archaeology of Anglo-Saxon England*. London: Methuen.

Winkelmann, W. 1958. "Die Ausgrabungen in der frühmittelalterlichen Siedlung bei Warendorf (Westfalen)." In W. Krämer, ed., *Neue Ausgrabungen in Deutschland*, pp. 492–517. Berlin: Gebr. Mann.

Winner, I. 1971. *A Slovenian Village*. Providence: Brown University Press.

Winters, H. D. 1968. "Value Systems and Trade Cycles of the Late Archaic in the Midwest." In S. R. and L. R. Binford, eds., *New Perspectives in Archeology*, pp. 175–222. Chicago: Aldine.

Wittvogel, K. A. 1957. *Oriental Despotism*. New Haven: Yale University Press.

Wyss, R. 1954. "Das Schwert des Korisios." *Jahrbuch des Bernischen Historischen Museums* 34:201–222.

———. 1956. "The Sword of Korisios." *Antiquity* 30:27–28.

———. 1967. *Bronzezeitliche Gusstechnik*. Bern: Paul Haupt.

———. 1969. "Wirtschaft und Technik." In W. Drack, ed., *Ur- und frühgeschichtliche Archäologie der Schweiz*, vol. 2, *Die Jüngere Steinzeit*, pp. 117–138. Basel: Schweizerische Gesellschaft für Ur- und Frühgeschichte.

———. 1971a. "Siedlungswesen und Verkehrswege." In W. Drack, ed., *Ur- und frühgeschichtliche Archäologie der Schweiz*, vol. 3, *Die Bronzezeit*, pp. 103–122. Basel: Schweizerische Gesellschaft für Ur- und Frühgeschichte.

―――. 1971b. "Technik, Wirtschaft und Handel." In W. Drack, ed., *Ur- und frühgeschichtliche Archäologie der Schweiz*, vol. 3, *Die Bronzezeit*, pp. 123–144. Basel: Schweizerische Gesellschaft für Ur- und Frühgeschichte.

―――. 1974a. "Grabritus, Opferplätze und weitere Belege zur geistigen Kultur der Latènezeit." In W. Drack, ed., *Ur- und frühgeschichtliche Archäologie der Schweiz*, vol. 4, *Die Eisenzeit*, pp. 167–196. Basel: Schweizerische Gesellschaft für Ur- und Frühgeschichte.

―――. 1974b. "Technik, Wirtschaft, Handel und Kriegswesen der Eisenzeit." In W. Drack, ed., *Ur- und frühgeschichtliche Archäologie der Schweiz*, vol. 4, *Die Eisenzeit*, pp. 105–138. Basel: Schweizerische Gesellschaft für Ur- und Frügeschichte.

Zahlhaas, G. 1971. "Der Bronzeeimer von Waldalgesheim." *Hamburger Beiträge zur Archäologie* 1, no. 2, pp. 115–130.

Zannoni, A. 1876–1884. *Gli scavi della Certosa di Bologna*. Bologna: Regia Tipografia.

Zeller, K. W. 1980. "Die modernen Grabungen auf dem Dürrnberg." In L. Pauli, ed., *Die Kelten in Mitteleuropa*, pp. 159–181. Salzburg: Landesregierung.

Zimmermann, W. H. 1978. "Economy of the Roman Iron Age Settlement at Flögeln, Kr. Cuxhaven, Lower Saxony." In B. Cunliffe and T. Rowley, eds., *Lowland Iron Age Communities in Europe*, pp. 147–165. British Archaeological Reports, International Series, vol. 48. Oxford: British Archaeological Reports.

Zirra, V. 1979. "A propos de la présence des éléments laténiens sur la rive occidentale de la mer Noire." In P.-M. Duval and V. Kruta, eds., *Les mouvements celtiques du Ve au Ier siècle avant notre ère*, pp. 189–193. Paris: Centre National de la Recherche Scientifique.

Zürn, H. 1957. *Katalog Zainingen*. Stuttgart: Silberberg.

―――. 1970. *Hallstattforschungen in Nordwürttemberg*. Stuttgart: Staatliches Amt für Denkmalpflege.

Sources of Illustrations

H. T. Waterbolk, Biological-Archaeological Institute, University of Groningen, The Netherlands:
Figure 4, from H. T. Waterbolk, "The Bronze Age Settlement of Elp," *Helinium* 4 (1964), p. 117, fig. 11

Verlag C. H. Beck, Munich:
Figure 5, from H. Dannheimer, "Siedlungsgeschichtliche Beobachtungen im Osten der Münchener Schotterebene," *Bayerische Vorgeschichtsblätter* 41 (1976), p. 112, fig. 3
Figure 12, from P. Schauer, *Die Schwerter in Süddeutschland, Österreich und der Schweiz, I,* 1971, pl. 123A
Figure 13, from Schauer 1971, pl. 62, 422 and pl. 70, 477
Figure 50, from J. Werner, "Zur Bronzekanne von Kelheim," *Bayerische Vorgeschichtsblätter* 43 (1978), p. 3, fig. 1(1)
Figure 51, from Werner 1978, p. 7, fig. 3

Jysk Arkaeologisk Selskab, Moesgard:
Figure 6, from P. V. Glob, *Ard og plov i Nordens oldtid,* 1951, p. 26, fig. 23
Figure 56, from Glob 1951, p. 37, fig. 37

Walter de Gruyter & Co., Berlin:
Figure 7, from H. Müller-Karpe, *Beiträge zur Chronologie der Urnenfelderzeit nördlich und südlich der Alpen,* 1959, pl. 149
Figure 8, from Müller-Karpe 1959, pl. 177C
Figure 9, from Müller-Karpe 1959, pls. 164 and 165A
Figure 11, from Müller-Karpe 1959, pl. 128A

Journal of Field Archaeology, Boston:
Figure 10, from P. S. Wells, "The Early Iron Age Settlement of Hascher-

keller in Bavaria: Preliminary Report on the 1979 Excavations," *Journal of Field Archaeology* 7 (1980), p. 320, fig. 12. Photograph by Hillel Burger.

Wilhelm Angeli, Naturhistorisches Museum, Prähistorische Abteilung, Vienna:
Figure 18

Römisch-Germanisches Zentralmuseum, Mainz:
Figure 19, from P. S. Wells, "Eine bronzene Rinderfigur aus Hallstatt," *Archäologisches Korrespondenzblatt* 8 (1978), p. 108, fig. 1
Figure 35, from K. Spindler, "Grabfunde der Hallstattzeit vom Magdalenenberg bei Villingen im Schwarzwald," in *Ausgrabungen in Deutschland 1950–1975*, Monographs of the Römisch-Germanisches Zentralmuseum No. 1, vol. 1, (1975), p. 232, fig. 36
Figure 63, from W. Haarnagel, "Die Wurtensiedlung Feddersen Wierde im Nordsee-Küstengebiet," in *Ausgrabungen in Deutschland 1950–1975*, Monographs of the Römisch-Germanisches Zentralmuseum No. 1, vol. 2, (1975) p. 23, fig. 14
Figure 65, from K. Schietzel, "Haithabu," in *Ausgrabungen in Deutschland 1950–1975*, Monographs of the Römisch-Germanisches Zentralmuseum No. 1, vol. 3, (1975) p. 61, fig. 4

Peabody Museum, Harvard University, Cambridge, Massachusetts:
Figure 22, from H. Hencken, *The Iron Age Cemetery of Magdalenska gora in Slovenia*, 1978, p. 108, fig. 39
Figure 23, from P. S. Wells, *The Emergence of an Iron Age Economy: The Mecklenburg Grave Groups from Hallstatt and Stična*, 1981, p. 46, text fig. 23
Figure 24, from Wells 1981, p. 214, fig. 162a
Figure 25, from Wells 1981, p. 206, fig. 147c; p. 195, fig. 126a, b; p. 153, fig. 37a
Figure 40, from Hencken 1978, p. 153, fig. 125

Wolfgang Kimmig, Institut für Vor- und Frühgeschichte, Universität Tübingen:
Figure 28

René Joffroy, Musée des Antiquités Nationales, Saint-Germain-en-Laye:
Figure 29

Hilmar Schickler, Württembergisches Landesmuseum, Stuttgart:
Figures 30, 36, 44

[266]

Egon Gersbach, Institut für Vor- und Frühgeschichte, Universität Tübingen and Amt der Oberösterreichischer Landesregierung, Kulturabteilung, Linz:

Figure 31, from E. Gersbach, "Neue Aspekte zur Geschichte des späthallstatt-frühlatènezeitlichen Fürstensitzes auf der Heuneburg," in *Die Hallstattkultur: Symposium 1980*, 1981, p. 360, fig. 4

Figure 32, from Gersbach 1981, p. 363, fig. 7

Figure 33, from Gersbach 1981, p. 361, fig. 5(2)

Wilhelm Angeli, Naturhistorisches Museum, Prähistorische Abteilung, Vienna, and Römisch-Germanisches Zentralmuseum, Mainz:

Figure 43, from *Krieger und Salzherren: Hallstattkultur im Ostalpenraum*, Römisch-Germanisches Zentralmuseum, Exhibition Catalogue No. 4, 1970, pl. 78, left. Drawing by M. Kliesch.

Franz Steiner Verlag GmbH, Wiesbaden:

Figure 47, from G. Jacobi, *Werkzeug und Gerät aus dem Oppidum von Manching*, 1974, pl. 1

Figure 48, from Jacobi 1974, p. 251, fig. 57

Figure 49, from W. E. Stöckli, *Die Grob- und Importkeramik von Manching*, 1979, pl. 72, 943

Figure 54, from Jacobi 1974, pl. 27

Figure 57, from Jacobi, 1974, p. 79, fig. 23

Verlag Philipp von Zabern, Mainz:

Figure 59, from A. Haffner, "Zum Ende der Latènezeit im Mittelrheingebiet unter besonderer Berücksichtigung des Trierer Landes," *Archäologisches Korrespondenzblatt* 4 (1974), p. 63, fig. 3

Römisch-Germanische Kommission des Deutschen Archäologischen Instituts Frankfurt:

Figure 53, from W. Krämer, "Manching II: Zu den Ausgrabungen in den Jahren 1957 bis 1961," *Germania* 40 (1962), insert 2

Gebr. Mann Verlag GmbH, Berlin:

Figure 64, from W. Winkelmann, "Die Ausgrabungen in der frühmittelalterlichen Siedlung bei Warendorf (Westfalen)," *Neue Ausgrabungen in Deutschland*, 1958, insert 2

Index

Library of Congress Cataloging in Publication Data

Wells, Peter S.
  Farms, villages, and cities.

  Bibliography: p.
  Includes index.
  1. Iron age—Europe. 2. Commerce, Prehistoric—Eu-
rope. 3. Urbanization—Europe. 4. Europe—Antiquities. I. Title.
GN780.2.A1W45 1984   936   84–45142
ISBN 0–8014–1554–3 (alk. paper)